R. Romano (signature)

FOUNDATIONS OF MODERN ECONOMICS SERIES

Otto Eckstein, *Editor*

PUBLISHED

American Industry: Structure, Conduct, Performance, *Richard Caves*
Prices and Markets, *Robert Dorfman*
The Price System, *Robert Dorfman*
Money and Credit: Impact and Control, *James S. Duesenberry*
Public Finance, *Otto Eckstein*
Managerial Economics, *Farrar and Meyer*
Economic Development: Past and Present, *Richard T. Gill*
Evolution of Modern Economics, *Richard T. Gill*
Economic Systems, *Gregory Grossman*
Student Guide, *Hartman and Gustafson*
International Economics, *Kenen and Lubitz*
National Income Analysis, *Charles L. Schultze*

IN PRESS

Labor Economics, *Richard B. Freeman*

FOUNDATIONS OF MODERN ECONOMICS SERIES

ROBERT DORFMAN   *Harvard University*

Prices and Markets

SECOND EDITION

PRENTICE-HALL, INC.   *Englewood Cliffs, New Jersey*

ISBN: 0-13-699603-5

Library of Congress Catalog Number 70-170036

PRENTICE-HALL FOUNDATIONS
OF MODERN ECONOMICS SERIES

Otto Eckstein, *Editor*

10   9   8   7   6   5   4   3   2   1

PRENTICE-HALL INTERNATIONAL INC., *London*
PRENTICE-HALL OF AUSTRALIA, PTY., LTD., *Sydney*
PRENTICE-HALL OF CANADA, LTD., *Toronto*
PRENTICE-HALL OF INDIA PVT. LIMITED, *New Delhi*
PRENTICE-HALL OF JAPAN, INC., *Tokyo*

Contents

v

Foundations
of Modern Economics Series

Economics has grown so rapidly in recent years, it has increased so much in scope and depth, and the new dominance of the empirical approach has so transformed its character, that no one book can do it justice today. To fill this need, the Foundations of Modern Economics Series was conceived. The Series, brief books written by leading specialists, reflects the structure, content, and key scientific and policy issues of each field. Used in combination, the Series provides the material for the basic one-year college course. The analytical core of economics is presented in *Prices and Markets* and *National Income Analysis*, which are basic to the various fields of application. Two books in the Series, *The Evolution of Modern Economics* and *Economic Development: Past and Present*, can be read without prerequisite and can serve as an introduction to the subject.

The Foundations approach enables an instructor to devise his own course curriculum rather than to follow the format of the traditional textbook. Once analytical principles have been mastered, many sequences of topics can be arranged and specific areas can be explored at length. An instructor not interested in a complete survey course can omit some books and concentrate on a detailed study of a few fields. One-semester courses stressing either macro- or micro-economics can be readily devised. The Instructors Guide to the Series indicates the variety of ways the books in the Series can be used.

The books in the Series are also being used as supplements to the basic textbooks, to permit a fuller curriculum on some topics. Intermediate level courses are using volumes in the Series as the core text and are combining these with various readings.

This Series is an experiment in teaching. The positive response to the first two editions has encouraged us to continue to develop and improve the approach. New books are being added and the previous books revised and updated. The thoughtful reactions of many teachers who have used the books in the past have been of immense help in preparing the third edition.

The books do not offer settled conclusions. They introduce the central problems of each field and indicate how economic analysis enables the reader to think more intelligently about them, to make him a more thoughtful citizen, and to encourage him to pursue the subject further.

Otto Eckstein, *Editor*

The Task of Economics

Ours is a privately controlled economy. Most economic decisions are made by private individuals in pursuit of their private interests. They are made by consumers who decide what to buy with their incomes, by workers who decide what jobs to take, by businessmen who decide what to produce and how to produce it. This book is concerned with those decisions: how they are made, and how the billions of them that are made every day combine to determine the workings of the whole economy. For the operation of our economy is controlled by just such decisions, large and small, mostly taken without any thought of remote consequences.

The surprising thing about allowing the operation of an economy to be controlled by billions of independent and irresponsible decisions is that it works at all. You could never run a railroad on such permissive principles. No one is in a position to decide how many shoes or ships or sticks of sealing wax should be produced, and yet definite quantities are produced. Are they the right quantities? That's a very hard question, but at least they are not disastrously far off. The economy functions, and for most participants in it it functions well in terms of meeting their personal needs. Most of our attention will be devoted to perceiving how this comes about.

But, we shall also see, this system of economic organization has some inherent limitations. There are legitimate questions to be raised, such as: Does it make the rich too rich and the poor too numerous? Does it generate material plenty at the expense of the quality of life? Does it lay waste our natural inheritance in order to produce too many freeways and too many gadgets? Those questions, we shall find, are

1

too searching to admit definitive answers. Even to pose them properly and to weigh pros and cons we shall have to know a great deal about the way an economy operates and about the social and moral standards that it can be expected to meet.

Our main task, in short, is to understand how an economy based on private decision making functions. This accomplishment will enable us to observe it intelligently, to know what to expect of it and what not, and to contribute to forming public policies designed to improve its operation.

A FEW BIG QUESTIONS

How much should we spend on missile defense? How much on job training for unemployed youths? How much on developing a supersonic transport plane? How much on medical research? How much on secondary and higher education? These are more hard questions that no one can answer conclusively. They are the stuff of congressional debates and political campaigns.

How much should we spend on shoes? How much on television programs? How much on automobiles, houses, cigarettes, and oil wells? These are important questions, too, but we don't debate them so much. By and large we leave these questions to be resolved by millions of individual consumers who decide how they want to spend their incomes and by thousands of individual businesses who try to find the most profitable things to produce and sell. This is decentralized decision making. It is the easiest way to arrive at such decisions, and we tend to prefer it when the results are reasonably satisfactory and even when they are modestly objectionable.

How much wheat shall we grow? How much shall we spend on medical care for the aged? How much on newspapers and magazines? How much on renovating our cities? These decisions are made by a combination of means. The details are left to millions of private individuals; however, the government tries to influence their decisions by taxes, subsidies, and other means.

All of these decisions concern economic problems or have strong economic aspects. That is, they are concerned with which things our society should produce, how it should produce them, and who should consume them. They have to do with the everyday work of producing and distributing useful (or, at least, desirable) things. But they have consequences that extend far beyond the creation of material objects and useful services. They determine the whole flavor of our society and even the kind of people we are. Karl Marx, in his materialist conception of history, insisted that the methods of production used in a society determined its class structure and the main lines of its history. Thorstein Veblen pointed out that life in an industrial society inculcates standards and values entirely different from those of life in a rural environment. Numerous anthropologists have indicated that a business-dominated, competitive economy breeds aggressive, competitive individuals. Kenneth Galbraith and many others have

2

emphasized that a highly industrialized economy, through its advertising and marketing efforts, consciously molds our tastes. All these contentions are live issues, and of deep significance.

On a less-profound level, consider the automobile, which has become our predominant mode of local transportation as a result of millions of individual decisions—some 10,000,000 a year—without anyone's having given much thought to the consequences. But the consequences extend far beyond permitting millions of people to drive when and where they want (if they can find reasonably uncongested highways). The automobile has changed the character of our cities by making it easy for the wealthy and middle class to move out to pleasant suburbs, leaving the social problems of the poor behind. It has created intractable problems of air pollution, let alone 50,000 road casualties a year. All this through the quiet, almost invisible working of the economy.

And consider cigarettes. Should we leave it to businessmen, in their search for profits, to determine how many should be produced and smoked? Should we continue to subsidize tobacco advertisements in magazines and to franchise them on television? Here again the economy impinges on aspects of life that superficially seem far removed from the day-to-day work of farm and factory.

We have raised above many questions of economic policy—some major, some minor—and have noted some of their implications. Such questions have to be answered every day and we have seen that they are answered in various ways: some are left to private decisions, some are decided politically, some are resolved by a mixture of public and private decisions. Even when we leave decisions in private hands, we often impose restrictions politically, as when we require safety features on automobiles or control of the use of land by zoning ordinances. The fundamental social issue that arises is which of these decisions should be left to which of these processes.

All modern economies use both centralized (that is, political) and decentralized (that is, private) decisions. The areas allotted to each type vary, but the role of private decision making is always large; otherwise the governmental machinery would be swamped by the details. The results of governmental decisions therefore depend very heavily on how private decision makers respond to them. Thus the issue of who should make particular decisions, and under what restrictions, requires us to understand how private decisions are made and how they influence the operation of the entire economy. We should also, of course, understand the characteristics of political decision making. When we have attained this understanding we shall be in a position to appraise the proper roles of the two major forms of decision making in economics.

The primary task of this book is to explain private decision making in the economic sphere and to see the results that it is likely to lead to. Some attention will be paid to political decision making in the same sphere, especially in Chapter 8, but this treatment will have to be only partial.

Thus this book will be concerned most explicitly with the way in which certain important social decisions are reached in a particular institutional context.

3

But just under the surface another deeper and more pervasive insight will be at work. It is far from true that the best things in life are free, nice as that would be. On the contrary, everything costs something, and the crucial, excruciating decisions of both personal and public life often concern what to take and what to forgo. This is such a universal and evident truth that it shouldn't be worth mentioning, except that it is sometimes forgotten.

Economists have wrestled with this unpleasant fact of life for many years and more self-consciously than anyone else. They have cultivated the habit of asking of any desirable proposal, "What will it cost?" When they ask that question they do not mean what it will cost in terms of dollars and cents (though mere money is often a convenient measure of cost), but, rather, what it will cost in terms of other desirable proposals that it precludes or interferes with. And they have developed with some subtlety the art of answering that question. That question and the art of answering it will be in the background throughout this book, and sometimes in the foreground.

In its most fundamental interpretation, in short, economics is the theory of making rational choices. The economic point of view can be applied beneficially to many problems that are not business or money problems at all. It applies whenever an objective is to be striven for at the cost of other objectives.

THE BASIC ELEMENTS OF AN ECONOMY

To understand how an economy operates we begin with its ultimate constituents: the firms, households, and governments that comprise it. *Firms* are organizations that hire and buy labor, land, and other raw materials and resources, and use them to produce the wide variety of things wanted by other firms and by households. The things that firms use are called sometimes resources, sometimes raw materials, sometimes inputs. The things they produce are called outputs or *commodities*. Commodities are classified into *goods* if they are tangible (examples: books, printing presses) and *services* if they are not (examples: medical treatments, television repairs, college instruction).[1] Each firm decides which commodities to produce, which resources to use, and in which way to perform its various operations. The motives that guide the firm in making these decisions are not altogether simple, as we shall see, but they all revolve around the sale of its outputs so as to earn gross revenues that exceed their cost of production. In Chapters 3, 4, and 6 particularly we shall discuss the behavior of firms in some detail.

Households participate in the economy by providing labor and other resources to firms, and using the income so earned to buy desired commodities and to save. As distinct from firms, households do not devote themselves pri-

4

[1] This is one of the least-important distinctions in economics. The borderline is neither very clear nor worth worrying about.

marily to securing an excess of receipts over disbursements, though that is often an important consideration in their decisions. Their primary interest, rather, is in the kind of life that they achieve as a result of their work and their purchases. In Chapter 5 we shall discuss the aspects of household behavior that are of principal importance for the operation of the economy. Households are sometimes called *consumers*. The main social purpose of the economy and everything that goes on in it is to provide consumers with the things they want.

In addition to firms and households, every economy contains a government. A government affects its economy in two ways. In the first place, it is a very large participant in the economy, one of its very biggest businesses, so to speak. In the United States about a fifth of the workers are employed by the various levels of government—federal, state, and local. These governmental units produce some of the most important commodities, including national defense, all levels of education, administration of justice, sewage disposal, and much more.

In addition, the government is concerned with regulating and fostering all aspects of the economy. It sets limits on virtually all the private decisions. For example, it specifies certain safety features that have to be included in automobiles and houses, it sets minimum wages and regulates other conditions of work, it supervises all public utilities and transportation companies very closely and reviews their major decisions, it specifies the qualifications of doctors, lawyers, real estate agents, and numerous other professional groups, it supervises the safety and sanitariness of drugs, foods, and restaurants. All these functions have been assumed, of course, because the unregulated decisions of firms and households in these areas have been found to be unsatisfactory for one reason or another.

Moreover, governments actively promote the health and vigor of their economies. They influence the growth and prosperity of different industries by a wide variety of taxes, tariffs, and subsidies. They undertake research on behalf of different industries and disseminate information. Governments are particularly active in the regulation of their economies' banking and monetary systems. This is partly done to assure the safety and reliability of the systems; however, the main reason for a government's concern with money and banking is the fact that the money supply and credit conditions have profound influence on the performance of the entire economy. Though our economy is primarily private, the government plays an important role in it.

All these regulatory, supervisory, and promotional activities constitute a government's economic policy. The primary practical application of economics is to the formulation of economic policy. If you will review the different kinds of control that the government exerts, both those listed above and those that you can think of for yourself, you will see that their effects depend upon the way in which firms and households respond to the different incentives and discouragements that the government can put forth. Economic policy must therefore be formulated with a view to the probable reactions of private firms and households. For this reason we concentrate our attention, in economics, on firms and households. If we know how they behave and respond, then we shall be able to predict the probable results of different policy measures open to the government.

Finally, an economy normally contains a few organizations that cannot be classified as firms, households, or governmental units. The most important of these are nonprofit organizations such as foundations, churches, and educational institutions. Altogether they do not account for a significant proportion of economic effort or output (about 3 percent of employment in the United States), and they will be neglected in this book.

A FIRST OVERVIEW

Imagine the economy as a vast enterprise for which we all work and from which we make all our purchases. Its purpose is to produce all the things the populace needs and wants in quantities as ample as possible, in return for the work devoted to it and the raw materials of various sorts that it uses up. We have called the useful things that an economy produces *commodities*. The performance of an economy can be described and measured to a large extent by the quantities it produces of all the different commodities that its population desires.

We have already noticed that no one decides on the quantities of different commodities to be produced by an economy such as ours. It is, so to speak, self-planned. This fact has been noticed by control engineers, men whose job it is to design self-regulating devices such as thermostats, autopilots, and voltage regulators, and they have pointed out that an economy is a gigantic self-regulator. This was a shrewd perception. Economists have made good use of it, and so shall we.

The principle of an automatic control system is simple, though the implementation can be impressively intricate. A control system consists of a machine that does something (say a house furnace), a sensing device that keeps track of the machine's output (say a thermometer) and that compares it with the desired output, and a control or switch that changes the operation of the machine when the output diverges from the desired one. Figure 1–1 is a schematic diagram of an ordinary house-heating thermostat. The furnace at the bottom produces hot water or steam that heats the radiator and eventually the thermometer. If the house is cooler than the temperature for which the thermostat is set, the movable arrow attached to the thermometer points to the "on" range and the furnace operates. As the house warms up, the movable arrow moves up until it reaches the "off" range. Then the control turns the furnace off, the house cools, the arrow rotates down until it reaches the "on" range, and the cycle begins again. That's all there is, and all control systems are built on this simple building block.

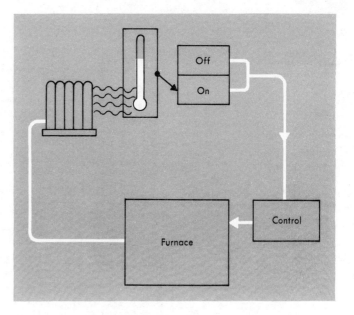

FIG. 1–1 Schematic diagram of a home thermostat. This simple device illustrates the basic mechanism of all self-regulating systems—even economies.

Now consider our vast economic system from this point of view. The heating system produced only one output, namely heat, so it needed only one control. An economy produces thousands of outputs or commodities, so it needs thousands of controls. Conceivably it could operate with one control for each commodity, but actually we use many more than that. We can, however, schematize the control system for a single commodity very simply as in Fig. 1–2. The factories at the bottom produce a flow of the commodity, which is sent, more or less directly, to some stores. Instead of a thermometer, there is a scale of prices. If the flow of the commodity is lower than desired, the price tends to rise. This makes it more profitable to produce that commodity. Instead of an automatic switch, there are businessmen who notice the increase in profitability and respond to it by increasing the flow of the commodity from the factories. Then the price ceases to rise. It may even fall if the businessmen increase the flow more than their customers desire. In that case, the price will begin to fall and the businessmen will be induced to reduce the flow of that commodity. It is important to notice the role of prices in this economic control system. They are the sensing device that reflects any divergences between actual and desired output of the commodity.

The next three chapters will be devoted to the determination of the output and price of a single commodity, the economic control mechanism that we have just sketched schematically. In technical terms this is the study of a single market in isolation, by *market* meaning all the people and business firms who produce, buy, and sell a single commodity.[2] In the next chapter we shall look,

[2] We shall use this word often, and the definition should be remembered.

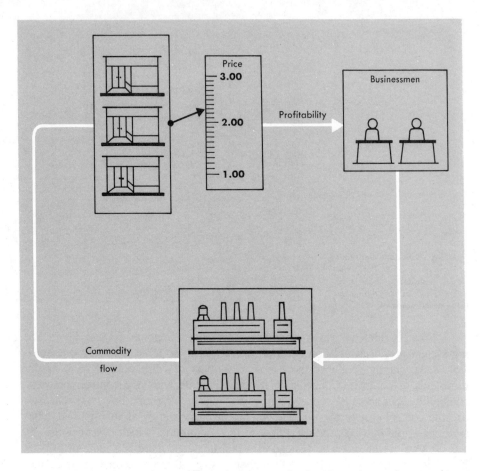

FIG. 1–2 Schematic diagram of control of a commodity flow. Economic controls are analogous to thermostats but much more subtle.

in a general way, at the interaction between the quantity of a commodity that is produced and its price. The following two chapters will consider more closely how businessmen react to changes in prices. In Chapter 5 we shall take up consumers' reactions to price and other circumstances, but there we shall have to step beyond the confines of a single commodity in isolation.

The analogy with an automatic control mechanism is illuminating but, like all analogies, it can be taken too literally. There are important differences between an economy and a self-regulating machine. One of them has to do with setting the controls. In a house someone sets the thermostat to the desired temperature, and the machine then takes over and controls the actual temperature. In an aircraft the pilot sets the desired course, and the autopilot then flies it. But in an economy there is usually no one who determines the desired output of a commodity. The economic system determines this for itself. In this respect it is a superautomatic control mechanism. As it happens, the desired quantity of any commodity depends largely on the amounts of other commodities that are being produced and on their prices. Thus, this feature of an economic system cannot be understood by looking at a single market in isolation. We shall have to consider all markets together, and how they interact. This is the business of Chapters 7 and 8.

Before we move on from the automatic-control analogy, we should notice a couple of other aspects. One is the nature of the "switch" that controls the physical operation. In most self-regulating mechanisms the switch is a piece of electrical or mechanical apparatus, designed to do its job in the way intended. But in an economy the "switches" are the businessmen who make the decisions for the individual firms, and businessmen are far more intricate and unpredictable than even the most temperamental piece of electromechanical apparatus. An economy is a control system with human intervention.

One of the complicating characteristics of businessmen is that they do not look only at prices, as our simplified scheme presumed, but take many other things into account, including the behavior of other businessmen. By doing so they change the behavior of the whole system. Some consequences of this complication will be dealt with in Chapter 6.

Another complicating side of businessmen is that, unlike pieces of machinery, they have to be motivated. A businessman responds to a price or other stimulus in the way that seems advantageous to him. This is why the "profit motive" is such an important part of the economic system. It determines how businessmen respond to different circumstances, and thereby how the whole system operates. We shall refer to it repeatedly in the chapters to come.

Finally we should notice that control systems do not always perform very well. One failing to which they are subject is variously called "hunting," or "oscillating," or "overshooting." A simple example will make this phenomenon clear. A man in a shower forms a simple control system with human intervention. If the water is too cold he turns up the hot water. For a while nothing happens. He may get impatient and turn up the "hot" further. Presently, and quite swiftly, the water becomes warmer. Pretty soon it's too hot, and he turns back the hot faucet. For a while nothing happens, but then the shower cools off almost abruptly. You know that this can go on for a long time without his ever attaining a comfortable temperature. That's "hunting," and a very bad thing in a control system. It can happen in any control system, and the more responsive a system is, the more likely it is to hunt. It happens in economic systems also; in fact, hunting is a large part of the explanation of the business cycle and of some other economic misbehavior that we shall encounter below. Largely for this reason the control-system analogy is helpful not only as a conceptual analogy but as a theoretical model of the way in which an economy operates.

9

SOME FUNDAMENTAL CONCEPTS

Let us focus on the market for a single commodity. We have seen that we can conceive of it as an automatic control system in which the quantity produced influences the price and the price induces properly motivated businessmen to adjust the quantity produced. It may happen that the system will hunt, that the price and the quantity will jostle each other around indefinitely. Such a market is said to be *unstable*. But there can't be very many unstable markets in an economy, for then the economy could not operate. So we shall suppose that in this market the price and the quantity tend to settle down, relatively quickly, to certain definite values. At those values the price will elicit the quantities that keep the price unchanging. That price and the corresponding quantity are the *equilibrium* values for the market (I am not yet ready to propose a formal definition). If no external event happens to upset the market, the equilibrium values will persist and nothing will happen except a steady flow of output and purchase of the commodity.

For many purposes the equilibrium values are the most important characteristic of the market. To see this, think of the market for fresh lobsters, which operates rather differently from most markets, and much more simply. Suppose that the catch is bad this year. At the prices inherited from last season, consumers will want to buy more lobsters than are arriving at the wharves. The price will rise. There is nothing much that the lobstermen can do about this. They may try a bit harder, but there is no way they can persuade many more lobsters to crawl into their pots. So the market will adjust, perforce, in another way. When lobsters are expensive, people will eat something else, and the price will move to the level at which consumers will want to buy the number of lobsters that lobstermen are able to catch. The price will find its way to an equilibrium level, higher than last year's.

The significant thing about all this, from everyone's point of view, is what the new equilibrium level will be. The lobstermen's incomes and the pinch on the housewives' budgets both depend on that. The exact process by which the equilibrium is attained and the length of time it takes, as long as it is reasonably short, are strictly secondary matters.

Much the same is true of all markets, including those far more important to an economy than that for fresh lobsters. The important characteristics are the price and quantity toward which the market tends under the impetus of its inherent adjustment mechanism, the equilibrium price and quantity. In a mechanical control system, we know, the output will tend toward the desired level (or else that system would not have been installed in the first place). But in an economic market there isn't any consciously set desired output. Where any market tends to go depends on circumstances outside that market. Most of our attention in this book will be devoted to understanding how the equilibrium levels are determined in various markets of importance. We shall be much less interested in how the market attains those equilibrium levels, though we shall not neglect that question entirely.

This brings us to the distinction between dynamics and statics in economic analysis. *Dynamics* consists of those parts of economic analysis that deal with the process by which markets attain their equilibrium values, or whether they do, and how long it takes, and what paths through time the prices and quantities follow in the interim. *Statics* consists of those parts of economic analysis that deal with the determination of a market's equilibrium values and their change in accordance with changing circumstances external to the market.

Statics is much more important than dynamics, partly because it's the ultimate destination that counts in most human affairs, and partly because the ultimate equilibrium strongly influences the time paths that are taken to reach it, whereas the reverse influence is much weaker. Statics is also much easier than dynamics and much more highly developed. For the most part, as I said, we shall stick to it.

Now we must define equilibrium for a market and for an entire economy. In a market, buyers are continually making up their minds how much to purchase in the light of the current price and other considerations. Sellers are simultaneously making up their minds how much to produce in the light of the price and still other considerations. Suppose it should happen that buyers in the aggregate decide to purchase just the amount that sellers in the aggregate decide to produce and sell.[3] Then everybody in the market will be able to do what he would like to do, and this is the only circumstance in which that will be possible. We seize on this pleasant property as the defining characteristic of *equilibrium*: A market is in equilibrium when every participant in it can carry out the decision that he considers most advantageous in the given circumstances. An economy is in equilibrium when all the markets that comprise it are in equilibrium.

In other words, a market is in equilibrium when it "clears," that is when every prospective seller of the commodity can find a buyer and vice versa. A more technical way of expressing this is to say that a market is in equilibrium when *supply* equals *demand*. In this terminology, supply means the amount of the commodity that sellers wish to sell and demand the amount that purchasers wish to buy. Many circumstances influence the quantities supplied and demanded but, as we have already seen, the price of the commodity is the principal control and we shall pay most attention to it.

The price at which the market clears, other circumstances being given, is the equilibrium price. When the equilibrium price obtains on the market it will persist, at least until some other conditions change that alter the quantity supplied or demanded at that price. You may not be sure, at first glance, that the equilibrium price and quantity defined in this way are the values to which the market adjustment process will tend. If so, your skepticism is justifiable. The

---

[3] Of course, this "decision" may be a forced option, as in the case of the lobstermen.

assertion requires substantiation, but it can be provided easily. For suppose the market adjustment process tended toward any price at which the amount that consumers wished to buy did not match the amount that producers wished to sell. Suppose, to be concrete, that it tended to a price at which consumers wished to buy less than producers wished to sell. Then some producers with unsold goods on their hands would shade the price in order to get rid of them and some consumers, seeing plentiful supplies of the commodity, would shop for bargains. The price would tend to fall. The only price that can maintain itself is the one at which both consumers and producers can carry out the transactions that they wish. This is the price that satisfies our definition.

SUMMARY

This chapter has sketched the major problems that will be dealt with in this book. It also has introduced a large number of concepts, which constitute the fundamental vocabulary of economic analysis. Many of the later chapters will end with reviews of the principal concepts introduced, but this first chapter was devoted so heavily to introduction and definition that a summary of concepts would be unduly repetitious.

Supply and Demand

CHAPTER TWO

In Chapter 1 we saw that an economy is a vast interrelated system which no one controls. Yet it doesn't behave like an uncontrolled system: day after day it turns out the commodities that people desire in about the amounts that they want to buy. One of the main tasks of economics, and the central task of this book, is to understand how this comes about.

The basic unit in our economy is the business enterprise, or company, or firm. There are about 10 million business enterprises of all kinds in the American economy. About a third of them are farms, mostly very small. At the other extreme are some 10,000 large corporations with 500 or more employees each. Every firm, large or small, farm or foundry or finance company, is in the business of producing some commodities in order to sell them at a profit.

All these firms are grouped into industries in accordance with the commodities that they produce. The grouping is necessarily arbitrary; for example, are the firms that produce carbon paper an industry, or are they part of the paper and pulp industry? Consider also the large auto makers; should they be included in the transportation industry or in some other? Despite this problem of classification, however, it pays to think of an economy like ours as comprising some 10,000 or more industries each specializing in some commodity or a limited range of commodities. The behavior of individual industries will be our main concern in this and the next few chapters, since the production of every commodity is determined by what happens in its own industry.

VARIETIES OF MARKETS

Each industry, we have seen, consists of a number of firms that produce some commodity or a group of closely allied commodities. These firms together with the firms and people to whom they sell their product constitute the *market* for their commodity. Note that when a businessman says "market" he means the people and firms who buy his product, but when an economist uses that word he includes the sellers as well as the buyers.

A few markets have compact physical embodiments, for example, the Chicago Board of Trade for wheat or the wholesale produce market in any city. But it is more typical for a market to be highly dispersed. In short, the market for a commodity exists wherever that commodity is bought and sold and comprises all the firms and people who buy, sell, or otherwise deal in it.

The physical form of the market is not of much importance for economic analysis, but the way in which it is organized and the way in which business is conducted in it are important because these arrangements influence the decisions of the participants. Some of the characteristics of markets are so familiar that we take them as a matter of course and hardly notice them. For example, in the vast majority of markets the sellers announce a price and stand prepared to make as many sales at that price as the customers call for, within reason. The customers simply accept the price and buy as much as they choose. In short, the sellers decide the price and the buyers decide the quantity sold. The main issue that arises about such markets is to understand how these twin decisions are made.

But before tackling that, we should notice that this arrangement is by no means universal. In one very important kind of market just the opposite custom prevails: in labor markets the buyer (employer) announces the price and the seller (employee) takes it, leaves it, or bargains about it. Some markets, such as the organized commodity exchanges, are conducted like auctions. In some markets the price is firmly set, in others bargaining is prevalent. These various arrangements do affect the behavior and decisions of everyone concerned, and yet their importance is smaller than appears on the surface and we shall pay scant attention to them. The true determinants of market behavior lie deeper.

One important set of determinants of behavior lies at the level of anticipations: every decision in a market is influenced by expectations about how other people will react to it. The simplest expectations are those of the typical small purchaser. He expects that when he makes an offer to buy something the seller will provide it and will then forget the matter. Large purchasers often have more complicated expectations. When they place orders, they have to allow for the possibility that their orders may be large enough to induce sellers to change the price.

Sellers, in deciding on their prices, typically have to worry about the reactions of both buyers and competitors. With respect to the buyers, the seller has to make a guess about how much they are likely to want at the proposed price. Most of the time this guess is a fairly offhand extrapolation from recent experience, but sometimes it is based on elaborate market research. Buyers' reactions are always an important consideration to the seller, and we shall inquire into them in Chapter 5.

Sellers' anticipations of competitors' reactions are one of the most important, and difficult, determinants of market behavior. In fact, they are the basis of the most significant classification of market types. Chapter 6 will be devoted to exploring some of the possibilities and intricacies; here we can merely outline the main possibilities, of which there are three.

1. *Competitive Industries.* The simplest possibility is that the managers of each firm may be confident that their competitors—the other firms in the industry—pay no attention to what they do, and in particular, to the price that they charge. This will be the case when the industry consists of a large number of fairly small firms, none of which accounts for an appreciable proportion of the sales of the commodity. Farming is the most important competitive industry.

There are two main types of competitive industry. In one type, exemplified by farming, the firms produce virtually indistinguishable products and the buyers, accordingly, have no strong preference about whom they buy from. An important consequence of this lack of preference, as we shall see, is that all firms are compelled to charge the same price for the commodity. This type of market is called *undifferentiated* competition.

In the other type of competition each firm's product has some characteristics or selling points that distinguish it from the products offered by competitors, perhaps only a brand name with a reputation or a convenient store location. The firms in such an industry may charge somewhat different prices, but each firm's volume of sales will be very sensitive to the relation between its price and the prices of competing firms and brands. This type of market is called *monopolistic* competition because each firm monopolizes its own brand or variant of the product.

The competitive market, and particularly undifferentiated competition, is the most important type for purposes of economic analysis. This is so partly because the behavior of competitive markets is comparatively simple and can be analyzed fully. But also, as we shall see later, competitive markets possess some significant social properties not shared by other markets. The analysis of competitive markets therefore serves as the point of departure for the analysis of all markets, and we shall concentrate on them in this chapter.

2. *Monopolies.* An industry that consists of only a single firm is called a monopoly. The most familiar monopolies are railroads and public utility companies. Aside from these cases, all of which are closely regulated by the government, monopoly is virtually illegal in this country. Notice that a monopoly tends to be large and, if it produces an important commodity, to wield great economic

15

power over its customers. Like a competitive firm, a monopolist pays no attention to the reactions of other firms in his industry, but for the very different reason that there are none. The analysis of monopoly is comparatively simple, too, and will be treated in Chapter 6.

3. *Oligopolies.* An oligopoly is an industry in which each firm feels that its competitors pay attention to its price and other decisions and are likely to react to any changes it may make. By the same token each firm in an oligopolistic industry is alert to the reactions of its competitors and is prepared to respond to them. This pattern of action and conjectured reaction introduces a complicated strategic ingredient into the decisions of firms in oligopolistic industries. The economist has at least as much trouble in predicting the behavior of such firms as their competitors do.

Oligopoly is far and away the most prevalent market type in American industry. Virtually every well-known branded commodity you can think of is produced in an oligopolistic industry. We shall have more to say about this market type in Chapter 6.

As mentioned above, economic analysis uses the behavior of competitive markets as its point of departure and standard of comparison. These markets are comparatively simple to analyze, and the concepts developed in order to study them are applicable to the analysis of other types of market as well. We turn now to the behavior of a competitive market.

SUPPLY IN A COMPETITIVE INDUSTRY

There are two distinguishing marks of a competitive industry, as economists use that term. One is that the customers do not have strong preferences about which seller they buy from, but tend to seek out the firm that is charging the lowest prices at the moment. The other is that the manager of the typical firm does not expect that his competitors will respond or retaliate to any change in price or other decision that he might make. To have these characteristics, an industry must contain a substantial number of firms of similar size (enough so that none of them feels conspicuous), and the products made by all the firms must be very similar if not entirely standardized. The most familiar competitive industries are the various branches of agriculture and the parts of the clothing industries in which branding has not become prevalent. But competition—in this technical sense—thrives best in industries whose customers are themselves businessmen who are not easily impressed by advertising or fancy packaging and who don't care much from whom they buy as long as they get a favorable price. Industries such as light machine shops and printing plants are typical of competitive industries that serve other businesses.

The most important decision open to a businessman in a competitive industry is the price he charges. But in making this decision he is so hemmed in by competitive pressures that he often feels that he has no real room for choice, that he is at the mercy of the market. Consider the situation from the business-man's point of view. At the moment he is charging a certain price, and so are his competitors. He is entitled to raise his price, but if he does so his customers will desert him rapidly for his competitors. This is such an unappealing prospect that the businessman does not regard it as a real option at all unless he already has more customers than he can handle or he has reason to believe that his competitors are about to raise their prices also.

On the other hand, he might lower his price. The consequences of this choice are slightly more complicated. One result would be that he would attract customers rapidly from the other firms in the industry. But the gain from making these additional sales would be offset by the fact that his profit on each sale would be smaller than he could make without the price reduction. These two conse-quences have to be weighed against each other. For example, suppose that a firm is selling 1,000 units a month at $10 each, that production costs are $6 a unit, and that the firm can make as many as 1,500 units a month at that cost. The businessman might estimate that he could sell his full capacity output if he reduced his price to $9. If he did that he would lose $1,000 a month on his current sales, but also he would be selling 500 additional units a month at a profit of $3 on each. In those circumstances he would be very likely to reduce his price.

At the same time his competitors, who, after all, are very similarly situated, would be reducing their prices for the very same reasons. As a result, in a competitive industry the price tends to gravitate to a level that is so low that further reductions are not worthwhile because firms are already making about as many sales as are profitable at that price. Altogether, then, leaving transitory episodes aside, a firm in a competitive industry sees no genuine opportunity for either raising or lowering its price. It merely charges the going market price, which appears to be established by competitive conditions beyond its control.

The economist's concern is to understand what determines the going market price to which individual firms conform. This determination follows from two sets of data. One of them specifies how consumers of the product re-spond to different possible market prices. The other, and our immediate interest, describes how the businessmen in the industry react to different prices.

We have already seen that the businessmen's reactions depend in large part on the potential profits from making additional sales. These, in turn, depend on a comparison between the price and the costs of the additional output. In our little example above, however, we made the cost side of the comparison unduly simple, and now we have to take some complications into account. Our crucial oversimplification lay in pretending that the firm had some rigid capacity output which it could attain without affecting its costs of production. This is almost never the case. The normal situation is that whatever may be the cur-rent rate of production, a firm can always squeeze out some additional output if it is worthwhile to do so. It can operate overtime or open an additional shift,

17

it can purchase subassemblies, it can cram more work and workers into its plant, it can offer bonuses or other incentives for additional production. All of these expedients are expensive, but the point is that they are available and will be used if the price is high enough to justify them. Thus it was overly simplistic to imagine that our firm had a rigid capacity of 1,500 units a month irrespective of the price it was charging. At a price of $9 a unit it would be prepared to make and offer that amount. At a somewhat higher price it would take on additional workers, at some expense, to speed up its rate of production. At a still higher price, the firm would find it worthwhile to operate overtime. And at a lower price it would try to trim expenses, even though this meant a reduction in the rate of output.

So we must recognize that the quantity a competitive firm is prepared to make and sell of its commodity depends upon the price (which, remember, it selects). If the current price is so high that the firm could profitably produce a great many more units than it is currently selling, the firm is under a strong inducement to cut its price in order to attract sales. On the other hand, if the price is so low that the firm has more customers than it can handle profitably, the firm will be strongly tempted to raise its price and forgo some sales, particularly if it perceives that competing firms are similarly overloaded, so that the decline in sales will be limited. Finally the firm will be content with its current price when it is selling about the quantity it regards as most profitable at that price.

We have now identified the most important factor that determines the behavior of a firm in a competitive industry. This is the relationship between the price of the product and the quantity that the firm could most profitably produce. This relationship is known as the *supply curve* or *supply schedule* for the firm. Specifically, the supply curve tells, for each possible price, the quantity that the firm would prefer to sell at that price. Its shape depends primarily on the costs of producing different quantities of output, and we shall study it more carefully in the next chapter.

The supply curve is one of the fundamental tools of economic analysis, so it is well to become thoroughly familiar with it at the outset. It is a reasonable approximation to assume that the quantity a firm will find most profitable increases gradually when the price increases. Such a supply curve is shown in Table 2–1 and Fig. 2–1. Study the figure carefully. Possible prices are shown on the vertical axis; monthly output is graphed horizontally. The firm whose supply curve is depicted will not find it profitable to produce at all at prices of $4 a unit or less. As we look at prices above $4, the profitable rate of output rises, at first rapidly, but later, as evermore severe impediments to increasing production are encountered, slowly. At a price of $5, the firm would want to produce nearly 600 units a month. At $9, the firm would find an output of 1,500 a month most profitable. At $20, the profitable output is about 2,070 and is increasing slowly, presumably because the firm is approaching something close to its absolute maximum.

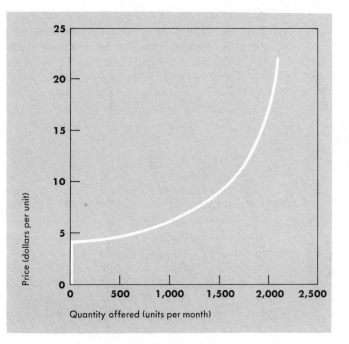

FIG. 2–1 A firm's supply curve. The curve shows the quantity (per month) that a competitive firm would want to sell at each market price.

In actuality, a firm's supply curve is likely to be a good deal less smooth than the one in the figure because costs tend to change rather abruptly as different expedients for increasing output are put into operation. But the irregularities are much less important than the basic trend here depicted.

Now, each firm in the industry has a supply curve resembling the one just described, though the exact figures are likely to be somewhat different for each of the firms. At each price, there will be a quantity that each firm will find most profitable, and if we add these quantities up we shall find the quantity that

Table 2–1 SUPPLY CURVE FOR A COMPETITIVE FIRM. A COMPETITIVE FIRM WILL OFFER A LARGER QUANTITY OF ITS PRODUCT AT HIGHER PRICES.

Price ($ per unit)	Quantity Offered (Units per month)
$ 4	0
5	580
7	1180
9	1500
11	1700
13	1825
15	1920
17	2000
19	2040

the industry as a whole will regard as appropriate at that price. For example, at a price of $9 one firm in the industry might want to sell 1,500 units a month, a second might want to sell 2,000 units, a third 1,100 units, and so on.

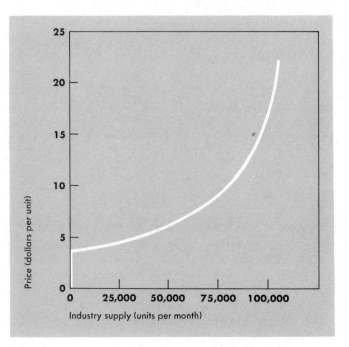

FIG. 2–2 Supply curve of a competitive industry. The amount supplied at each price is the sum of the amounts offered by the individual firms at that price.

By adding up all these desired supplies we might find that the industry as a whole would want to supply 75,000 units a month when the price is $9. This sum is the industry's supply at a price of $9. The industry supply can be defined similarly for any price. The curve that shows the industry supply for various prices is the *industry's supply curve*. This is another key concept. The supply curve for a competitive industry shows the quantity of output that the firms in the industry, all together, would want to sell at every possible price. The supply curve for the industry we are talking about is shown in Fig. 2–2. It is drawn on the assumption that the typical firm we have been considering offers about one-fiftieth of the total industry output. This curve is interpreted in much the same way as the firm's supply curve. It shows, for example, that at a price of $9 all the firms taken together would want to sell about 75,000 units a month. If more than 75,000 units a month were sold, some of the firms would have to be selling units that cost them more than $9 to produce; they would lose money on those sales. If less were sold, some of the firms would find it advantageous to cut their prices.

There is better justification for assuming that the industry supply grows smoothly as price increases than for making the similar assumption for individual firms, because abrupt changes in production costs occur at different levels of output for different firms and get smoothed out when the firms' supply curves are added together.

The industry supply curve is one of the two basic data that determine the behavior of a competitive industry. The other basic datum specifies the reactions of purchasers of the product. We turn to it now.

CONSUMERS' REACTIONS: DEMAND CURVES

The behavior of consumers in a competitive market is more straightforward than that of producers. That is because producers have to set the price they will charge without being able to control the amount of the commodity they sell, whereas purchasers merely accept the price and buy the amount that they wish at that price. We shall discuss consumers' reactions to price changes at some length in Chapter 5. For the present we can proceed on the basis of what everyone knows: that people tend to buy and use more of any commodity when it is cheap than when it is dear. It is just as true of business firms as of private consumers that when a commodity is expensive it is used sparingly and cheaper commodities are used in its place if they are almost as satisfactory. In short, the higher the price of a commodity, the less of it consumers will want to buy.

This notion is expressed quantitatively by the *demand curve,* which is analogous to the supply curve that we have just studied. An individual's demand curve for a commodity tells the amount that he would want to buy at every price that might be charged. By adding up the amounts that all the individuals would want to buy at a given price we can obtain the total market demand for

Table 2–2 DEMAND CURVE. SHOWS THE QUANTITY OF A COMMODITY THAT CAN BE SOLD AT DIFFERENT PRICES.

Price ($ per unit)	Quantity Demanded (Units per month)
$ 3	330,000
5	175,000
7	110,000
9	75,000
11	52,000
13	36,000
15	24,000
17	15,000
19	8,000
21	2,500
22	0

the commodity at that price. By performing the same operation for different prices we can obtain the market demand at those prices. A table or graph of the market demand at different prices shows the amount of the commodity that the industry as a whole can sell at those prices. This is the market demand curve.

The general appearance of a market demand curve is shown in Table 2–2 and Fig. 2–3. According to these data, there is a maximum price at which any of the commodity can be sold at all, namely $22. The farther the price is

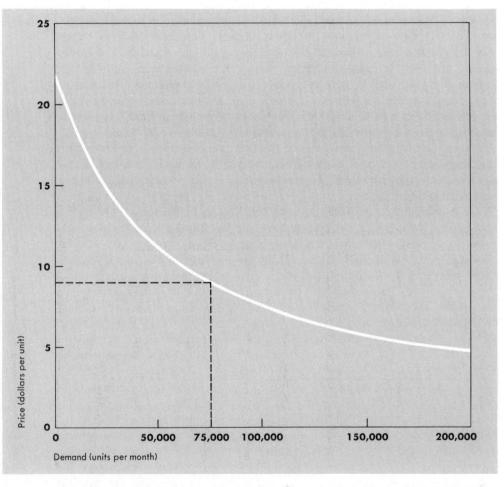

FIG. 2–3 A demand curve. The curve shows the amount that consumers would wish to purchase at every possible price.

below the limit, the more people will want to buy. When the price is $9 a unit, demand (that is, the amount consumers want to buy) is 75,000 units a month. At still lower prices still more is demanded, until at very low prices the quantity demanded is too great to fit on the graph.

The demand curve is the second main determinant of the behavior of a competitive market. Together with the supply curve it determines the amount of the commodity that will be produced and sold, and the price that it will command.

INTERACTION OF SUPPLY AND DEMAND

The supply and demand curves contain all the data that determine the price of the commodity and the quantity that will be produced and consumed. They express both the wishes of consumers (how much they are willing to buy at different prices) and the capabilities of producers (how much they can produce profitably at different selling prices). These data are brought together in the market—that is, in the dealings of the people who buy and sell the commodity; the supply and demand curves show just how this happens. And if we plot the supply and demand curves on a single graph we can easily compare the amounts supplied and demanded at every price. This is done in Fig. 2–4.

The two curves in Fig. 2–4 are the ones we are already familiar with. The point where they cross is the most important point in the graph. It shows that if the price is $9 and if we add up the amounts that producers find it most profitable to sell at that price, we shall arrive at a total of 75,000 units a month. Simultaneously it shows that customers will want to buy 75,000 units a month when the price is $9. From everybody's point of view this is a most agreeable price. It is, indeed, the equilibrium price as we defined it in the first chapter, the price at which the amount people want to buy is equal to the amount that people want to sell.

Furthermore, the equilibrium price is the one to which a competitive market will naturally gravitate. For suppose that for some reason the current price should be higher, say $13. At that price producers in the aggregate will find it profitable to sell about 90,000 units a month, but consumers will want to buy only about 36,000 units. Inevitably some of the producers will be selling a great deal less than they would like to at that price. Our typical producer of Fig. 2–1, for example, might be selling 700 units a month in comparison with 1,825 units he could produce profitably at a price of $13. If he reduced his price to, say, $12 he would forgo $1 profit on each of his current sales, for a total reduction of $700. But he could expect a great increase in sales, perhaps an increase to 1,200 or more units, since in a competitive market the purchasers are easily attracted to the firm that is offering lower prices than the others. But we know, from Table 2–1, that it would be profitable for this firm to sell 1,200 units if the price were as low as $7. Evidently it would be making

23

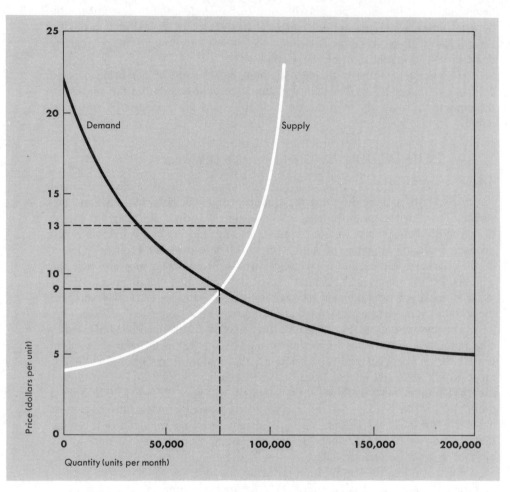

FIG. 2–4 Demand and supply curves for a competitive market. Together these curves determine the quantity that will be sold and the price.

a profit of at least $5 on each unit sold for $12, and the 500 or more additional sales attracted by the price reduction would add at least $2,500 to monthly profits, or about four times as much as the reduction in profit on current sales. Faced with such an inducement, this firm and the others similarly situated would reduce their prices, first to $12, perhaps, and then still further, for the same reasons, until the equilibrium price of $9 was reached.

Similar pressures drive the price up if the current price is below the equilibrium. Suppose the current price is $7. At this low price producers find it worthwhile to turn out only about 60,000 units a month, whereas consumers want to buy 110,000. The typical firm finds that its customers are ordering more than it can produce profitably. It knows that if it raises its price its customers will not be able to get deliveries from its competitors for they are just as busy as it is. By raising its price it could increase its profit on every sale without incurring a significant loss in sales. Each firm is therefore under strong inducement to raise its price, and this inducement remains until the equilibrium is attained.

Thus the equilibrium price and the corresponding quantity of production and sales are the unique values toward which a competitive market tends to move. This equilibrium is determined entirely by the industry's supply and demand curves, which is why they are so important. Of course, on the day you read this passage, or on any other day, many competitive markets will not be in equilibrium because some disturbance will have affected the supply or demand curves so recently that the buyers and sellers will not have had time to react to it. Sometimes the reactions may be very slow. For example, when natural gas becomes available in a city (causing an abrupt change in the supply curve for household gas) it may take years before householders convert their furnaces from the use of other fuels. But, whatever the speed of response, both buyers and sellers react in ways that drive the price and quantity toward the values at which the supply and demand curves cross.

CHANGES IN SUPPLY CONDITIONS

In practice the principal use for supply and demand curves is to estimate the effects of changes in economic conditions on the prices of commodities and the quantities bought and sold. Typical instances are the problems of foreseeing the effects of changes in excise taxes (as on liquor or tobacco), or of tariff changes, or of wage rates.

Any such change in circumstances will influence the market for the commodity affected by changing either the supply or the demand curve, that is, by changing the amounts that producers want to sell or that consumers want to buy at different prices. We shall first consider the effect of a change in the supply curve.

Suppose, to be concrete, that the cost of producing some commodity should increase. This might happen because of an increase in wage rates or in the price of some raw material used in producing the commodity. The result would be that at any market price the typical producer would want to sell less of the commodity than previously because some of the relatively high-cost output that had been barely worth producing before the cost increase would no longer be profitable at the given price.

In terms of the market diagram, the supply curve would be shifted upward. This is shown in Fig. 2–5. The normal downward sloping demand curve

25

is shown in black. The supply curve, as it was before the cost increase, is drawn as a dashed upward sloping curve. They cross at the previously existing equilibrium of 400 million tons a year selling at $4.50 a ton. The new supply curve is shown as the solid upward sloping line. It is drawn on the assumption that the cost increase amounts to 25 cents a ton, the same at all levels of output.

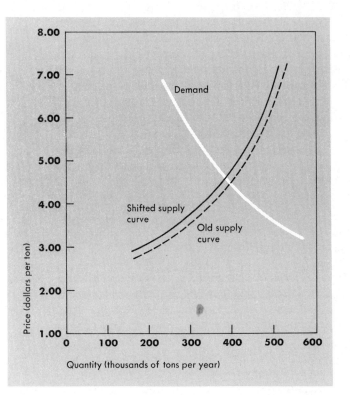

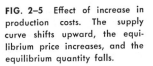

FIG. 2–5 Effect of increase in production costs. The supply curve shifts upward, the equilibrium price increases, and the equilibrium quantity falls.

It is easy to see the effects of the cost increase. Tons that were barely worth producing at a price of $4.50 before the cost increase are too expensive to produce after the cost increase, whereas if the price were to rise correspondingly to $4.75 a ton, they would remain worth producing. Thus, the amount that producers will want to sell after the cost increase at $4.75 a ton is the same as the amount they wanted to sell at $4.50 a ton before the increase. The same reasoning applies to every other price. The new supply curve can be derived simply from the old one because the price required to evoke any given supply after the cost increase is just 25 cents higher than the price that would elicit the same supply before. Graphically, this amounts to moving every point on the supply curve upward by 25 cents, and that is how the after-change supply curve was drawn.[1]

The shift in the supply curve has shifted the equilibrium point in the market diagram. The new supply curve intersects the demand curve at a quantity of 390 million tons and a price of $4.60. Note, especially, that the equilibrium price has not increased by the full amount of the cost increase or anything like it.

Newspaper discussions of prospective increases in wages or the prices of raw materials generally presume that the increases in production costs will be reflected fully in price rises. The market diagram, however, suggests that this will not be so. Therefore we should consider how the more modest price increase predicted by the supply–demand diagram is likely to come about. Perhaps the initial response of producers to a 25 cent increase in production costs will be to increase their prices by 25 cents. At the new price the producers will continue to offer 400 million tons a year, but the demand curve tells us that at a price of $4.75 purchasers will want only 375 million tons. The producers then find that they cannot sell all the output that would be profitable at a price of $4.75 or even of $4.70. Under this incentive they begin to cut prices. As the price falls, the amount that consumers are willing to purchase increases in accordance with the demand curve. Simultaneously the amount that producers can supply profitably declines in accordance with the new supply curve. When these two amounts become equal—at a price of about $4.60 a ton—the pressure on prices abates and equilibrium is restored.

The movement from an old equilibrium to a new one is never instantaneous. Markets are perpetually being disturbed by occurrences that shift the supply curve or the demand curve or both, and then adjust themselves to the equilibrium that corresponds to the new conditions by processes such as the one just sketched, in which sellers experiment with different prices and revise them in the light of experience until the new equilibrium price emerges.

It is not hard to see why the increase in the equilibrium price is smaller than the increase in production costs. The initial effect is to make the units of output that are produced under the most expensive conditions (least-efficient factories, poorest veins of ore, and so on) cost more to produce than purchasers are willing to pay for them. The ultimate effect is to discourage the production of those units of output, and to establish a price that corresponds to the cost of producing under somewhat more favorable conditions. The net result is to increase the price by the amount of the cost increase minus the saving from curtailing the production of the most costly units of output.

The producers and the consumers, therefore, end up by sharing the impact

---

[1] The effect on a supply curve of an increase in production costs can be specified more generally as follows. If production costs increase by $x a unit, then the amount that will be offered at any price, say $p, is the same as the amount that was offered previously at a price of $(p–x) or, alternatively, the price required to elicit any given supply after the increase is $x greater than before.

of the increase in costs. In our illustration these shares were 40 per cent for the consumers, 60 per cent for the producers. In other cases these shares would generally be different. They depend upon the shapes of the supply and demand curves and particularly upon the willingness of consumers to accept a price increase. This willingness is reflected in the steepness of the demand curve. Consider, for instance, the situation shown in Fig. 2–6. This diagram shows the same before-and-after supply curves as before, but a much steeper demand curve. Notice that the change in quantity demanded that corresponds to any given change in price is much smaller in the light of this demand curve than in the previous case. We can describe this by saying that Fig. 2–6 shows a market in which demand is less responsive than in Fig. 2–5.[2]

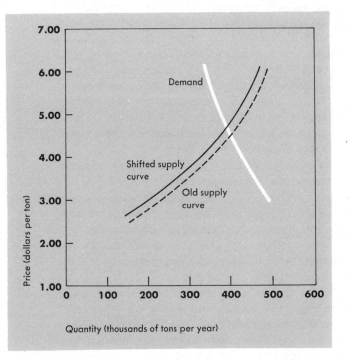

FIG. 2–6 Effect of increase in production costs with unresponsive demand curve. A greater proportion of the cost increase is shifted to consumers when demand is unresponsive to price changes.

The initial equilibrium position in Fig. 2–6 is the same as before but, because the demand curve is less responsive, it intersects the new supply curve at a point that indicates a higher equilibrium price ($4.65) and larger equilibrium quantity (393 million tons) than the previous diagram. It is clear that the less responsive the demand for a commodity is, the larger will be the proportion of any cost increase that will be reflected in the price. Indeed, if demand were

[2] Many economists would say that demand is less "elastic" in Fig. 2–6 than in Fig. 2–5, but we shall see later that the elasticity of a supply or demand curve is a technical concept with a somewhat different meaning.

totally unresponsive (in which case the demand curve would be a vertical line showing the same amount demanded at all prices) the increase in price would be as great as the increase in unit production costs, but only in that case.[3]

In summary, when production costs of any commodity change, its supply curve shifts and the impact of the change is shared by the producers and the consumers of the commodity in proportions that depend largely on the responsiveness of the demand curve. The producers, of course, do not normally intend to share the burden of a cost increase or the benefit of a cost reduction with their customers, but the forces of competition compel them to do so.

CHANGES IN DEMAND CONDITIONS

A market equilibrium can be upset by occurrences that affect demand as well as by events that shift the supply curve. The most important occurrences that are likely to affect demand are changes in consumers' tastes and preferences (because of changes in fashion or for any other reason), changes in the prices of competing products, technological changes, and improvement either in the product itself or in competing products. An instance of a change in fashion is the concern about lung cancer, which affected the demand for cigarettes (though disappointingly little). An example of the effect of changes in the price of competing products is the influence of the price of household gas on the demand for heating oil. When natural gas is introduced into a community, thus reducing the price of gas, the amount of fuel oil demanded at every price declines. Technical change is illustrated by the development of wash-and-wear fabrics, which reduced the demand for laundry services. Such changes are occurring all the time.

But for purposes of economic decisions and policy the most important changes that affect demand are changes in the taxes and tariffs levied on various commodities. For example, the federal government taxes tobacco products, liquors, gasoline, automobiles, air transportation, and so on. Until recently a number of other "luxuries" were subject to federal tax. How do these taxes affect the prices and consumption of the commodities taxed? The analysis of the effect of abolishing the 10 per cent excise tax on luggage is typical.

We can see the effect of removing the 10 per cent excise tax on luggage by referring to Fig. 2–7. This figure contains the familiar supply curve and two demand curves, one showing demand with the tax and one without. When the tax was in force, there were two prices, one received by the seller and one, 10 per cent greater, paid by the buyer. In the figure we have plotted the price received by the sellers.

The lower, dashed, demand curve shows the number of luggage cases of a

[3] Visualize the opposite extreme, of infinite responsiveness. Would a change in production costs have any effect on price then? Note the generalization: the larger the effect on price, the smaller the effect on quantity, and vice versa.

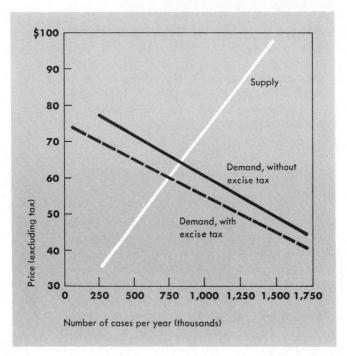

$100

90

80

Supply

70

60

Demand, without
excise tax

Price (excluding tax)

50

Demand, with
excise tax

40

30

0   250   500   750   1,000 1,250 1,500 1,750

Number of cases per year (thousands)

FIG. 2–7 Effect of rescinding an excise tax. The demand curve moves up, carrying along the equilibrium price and quantity sold.

particular sort that could be sold at each price while the tax applied. For example, at a price of $60 (total cost to buyers of $66) purchasers were willing to buy 750,000 cases a year. Since the supply curve crosses the demand curve at that point, this was the equilibrium price and quantity while the tax applied.

The higher demand curve shows the quantity that would be purchased at each price after the tax was revoked. The easiest way to derive it from the old demand curve is to notice that a 10 per cent increase in price would just offset the removal of the tax from the buyer's point of view. For example, if the price were increased to $66 simultaneously with the removal of the tax, the cost to buyers would remain the same and they would continue to buy the same quantity as before. In general the price that will induce buyers to purchase any quantity after the repeal of the tax is 10 per cent higher than the price that evoked the same rate of sales with the tax in effect. In terms of the graph, repealing the tax raised the demand curve by 10 per cent. Note that this does *not* mean that sales will be 10 per cent higher at any price but, rather, that the price corresponding to any level of sales is increased by 10 per cent.

The without-tax demand curve intersects the supply curve at a price of $64.30 and an annual volume of 830,000 cases. This, accordingly, is the new equilibrium of the market. The removal of the tax reduces the cost to a buyer of a case by $1.70 and increases the receipts of a seller by $4.30. It increases the volume of sales by 80,000 cases a year.

The new equilibrium will be established by a process of trial and error. In such a situation, the sellers are likely not to increase prices initially. But if they maintain the price at $60, over a million cases a year will be demanded, whereas the supply curve shows that the profitable quantity to produce is only 750,000. To keep abreast of demand, manufacturers will be forced to a higher-cost rate of production than the price justifies and they will raise their prices. This will relax the pressure on their facilities by abating demand and simultaneously cover some of the increase in production costs. When prices have risen enough to bring the amounts demanded and supplied into balance, the new equilibrium will be found.

At the new equilibrium, the cost to buyers will be about 3 per cent lower than before; most of the benefit of the tax cut will have gone to the producers. This is because the demand curve was quite responsive; a substantial increase in the price received by sellers was required to bring demand back down to the supply curve after the tax was removed. It would be instructive to work out this same problem with a steeper, less responsive, demand curve and compare the results.

A warning is in order about the analysis of tax changes. The method just discussed is appropriate when the tax change applies to a single commodity or a small group of commodities. It is not applicable to a change in a general sales tax or to widespread tax changes. The reason is that the analysis presumes that the prices of commodities other than the one being studied remain fixed. If other prices change, the demand curve is likely to shift for that reason, and the analysis would become more complicated.

Other events that change the demand curve can be analyzed in a similar manner.

ESTIMATION OF SUPPLY AND DEMAND CURVES

The principles discussed in the last few sections apply whether the demand and supply curves are known or not. But, of course, quantitative estimates of the consequences of changes in circumstances cannot be made unless estimates of the curves are at hand. One of the tasks of economic statisticians and marketing analysts is to prepare such estimates. It is, in practice, a surprisingly difficult task.

Demand curves are estimated by reviewing the responses of consumers to different prices. For example, a study of the use of water by households in 21 communities where different prices were charged yielded the demand curve shown in Fig. 2–8.[4] The solid line in the diagram is the estimated demand curve. Naturally, the actual data from the 21 communities did not lie along such a nice, straight line. The two dashed lines parallel to the solid line indicate

[4] C. W. Howe and F. P. Linaweaver, "The Impact of Price on Residential Water Demand and Its Relation to System Design and Price Structure," Water Resources Research, 3 (First quarter, 1967), 13–32.

the range of variation in the data. Virtually all the observations (95 per cent of them) lay within the range shown. The curve shows, for example, that if the water rate in a community is 80 cents per thousand gallons, the best estimate of use by a typical family is 175 gallons a day and that it is almost certain that a typical family will use between 95 and 205 gallons a day. Average use increases by 25 gallons a day when the price is reduced by 20 cents per thousand gallons.

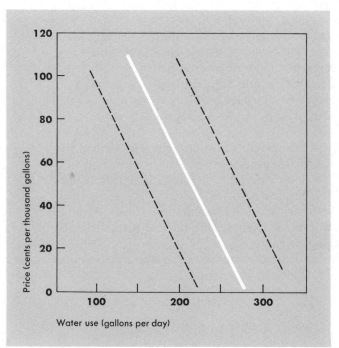

FIG. 2–8 An empirical demand curve. Households use less water in communities where the price is higher.

A few moment's consideration will suggest some of the difficulties that arise in either estimating or using such a demand curve. There are many obvious factors other than the price of water that affect the amount of it used by households: climate, size of house, family size and composition, income, and so on. These complicating influences have to be averaged out properly when the demand curve is being estimated, and then allowed for when the curve is applied in any specific instance.

Even with such complications, the demand curve for water is comparatively easy to estimate. This is so because water is peculiarly expensive to transport away from its natural lines of flow. In consequence there are many isolated markets for water, with considerable differences in price, so that the effect of price variation can be observed. For most commodities the market is virtually national and the spread of prices among localities is very small. The effect of price on the quantity demanded can then be observed only by following changes in prices and amounts sold for considerable periods of time. But many things that affect demand change in the course of time. The basic problem of estimating a demand curve is to eliminate the effects of these other changes so that the effects of price changes on demand will stand out in isolation. It is a difficult task at best, and not always possible.

Supply curves are estimated by the same methods as those used for demand curves or, alternatively, are deduced from a careful study of the costs of production at different levels of output. The first method is by far the more prevalent.

TIMING AND DYNAMICS: THE COBWEB

The market adjustments that we have been discussing are the result of numerous specific actions taken by buyers and sellers. A change in conditions or price will lead a purchaser to buy more or less than before. A seller's options are more numerous. He may change his price, change his rate of production by hiring or laying off a few workers, build a large, new plant, introduce a new product, or do many other things. These different actions have, naturally, differing consequences. To analyze them it is convenient to divide the possible responses to changes in market conditions into two broad classes, called short-run adjustments and long-run adjustments. This distinction is more important for producers' responses than for purchasers', and we shall concentrate on them.

Short-run adjustments include all market responses that can be reversed quickly and easily. Illustrations are hiring a few more hourly employees or working overtime. They are normally responses to changes that are deemed to be temporary or are preliminary responses to permanent changes in conditions. *Long-run* responses are those that cannot be reversed easily, such as acquiring a new plant.

We can see the force of this distinction by recalling our discussion of supply curves. There we defined a firm's supply at any price as the quantity that the firm would want to produce and sell at that market price. We took it for granted that the firm's preferences among different rates of output were determined by the costs of producing different rates of output in the firm's current plant. We were, in effect, thinking only of short-run options, and the curve so determined was really a short-run supply curve. But if a firm's facilities have been overloaded for some time, it will begin to think about expanding its plant. Then somewhat different questions become appropriate. We can ask with respect to any market price, what size and type of plant would the firm acquire if it expected that price to persist for a long time. And then we can ask how much the firm would produce at that same price if it had the desired plant. The answer to the second question is a point on the firm's long-run supply curve.

33

Notice that the long-run supply curve is not determined by costs of production in the plant currently available, but that it is determined by the costs of acquiring and operating new facilities.

We have now distinguished two supply curves for a firm:

The firm's *short-run supply curve* tells for each market price the quantity that the firm would want to produce or otherwise supply, using the plant that it now has.

The firm's *long-run supply curve* tells for each market price the quantity that the firm would want to produce in the plant that it would acquire if that price persisted for a long time.

There are correspondingly short-run and long-run supply curves for the entire market or industry. The market's short-run supply at any price is already familiar. It is the amount that all the firms in the industry would want to supply at that price using their current plants, or the sum of the individual firms' short-run supply curves. The market's long-run supply curve is similarly the sum of individual firms' long-run supply curves, but now allowance has to be made for new firms that might enter the market at any price that persisted for a long time. Conceptually, long-run supply at any price is the total amount of the commodity that all firms would want to offer at that price when they had had time enough to adapt their plants to that price and even to enter and leave the industry.

Clearly the long-run supply curve is a fairly iffy and complicated concept, and we shall have to discuss it more carefully in the next chapter. Its importance, however, is evident. When a short-run equilibrium is attained (that is, the intersection of the demand curve with the short-run supply curve) the price is likely to be one that motivates businessmen to expand or contract their facilities. As soon as they do that they have new short-run supply curves and the market is no longer in equilibrium. Thus the market will be continually disturbed until the price reaches a value that leaves businessmen content with their current plants. That price can be called the long-run equilibrium price, and it is the intersection of the demand curve with the long-run supply curve.

We have then a picture of a market evolving through a sequence of short-run equilibria to its long-run equilibrium (if the demand curve stays put for a long enough time). This is not easy to visualize, and we shall explain it in two steps.

The first step is to notice that this evolution of a market toward its long-run equilibrium is very similar in principle to a simpler phenomenon, the behavior of markets for farm produce. The peculiarity of those markets is that a farmer must decide on the amount he is going to produce long before he knows the market price.[5] He does know the price that the previous year's harvest brought and uses it as the basis for deciding on this year's planting. Thus, if

[5] Notice the relevance to the long-run supply curve: every businessman must decide on changes in the size and design of his plant long before he knows what the market prices will be when the altered plant comes into operation.

last year's price was high, this year's crop is likely to be large, and similarly if last year's price was low, this year's crop is likely to be small. This gives rise to a dynamic kind of behavior known as the cobweb theorem, which can be illustrated easily.

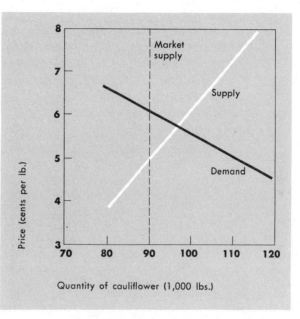

FIG. 2–9 Temporary and long-run data for a market crop. Available supply determines temporary equilibrium price, which influences next season's supply in accordance with the supply curve.

The behavior of a market for an annual agricultural product can be explained by using a diagram such as Fig. 2–9. That diagram shows supply and demand curves for, say, fresh cauliflower in a local produce market. The demand curve has the conventional interpretation. It shows, for example, that at a price of 5 cents a pound, about 108,000 pounds will be purchased. The supply curve, however, is defined somewhat differently from before. Remember that a farmer cannot decide on the amount to produce by observing the current price; his decision has to be based on the price at which the previous harvest sold. Accordingly, on this supply curve we plot opposite each price the quantity that that price will induce farmers to plant. For example, the supply curve asserts that if the price in one year was 5 cents a pound, the harvest in the following year will be 90,000 pounds.

Such a market generates a predictable sequence of prices and quantities. For, suppose that in some year (year 1) the price was 5 cents a pound. Then, according to the supply curve, the next year (year 2) the farmers would plant and harvest 90,000 pounds. What will the price be in year 2? The forces of demand and supply will be at work, but the supply curve will not be effective

35

because it represents reactions that cannot take effect until year 3. In year 2 the supply is 90,000 pounds, neither more nor less (abstracting from the possibilities of import and export), and the price must be such that consumers will wish to buy that amount. The effective supply curve, therefore, is the vertical line labeled "market supply" in the figure. The price in year 2 is established where the market supply line cuts the demand curve, which is at 6 cents a pound.

At this point the supply curve becomes effective. A price of 6 cents a pound induces a planting of 99,000 pounds to be harvested in year 3. This determines the price in year 3, which must be the price at which 99,000 pounds will be purchased, or 5.5 cents a pound. And we can continue this reasoning for as many years as we please.

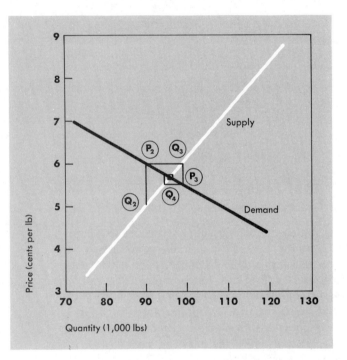

FIG. 2–10 Cobweb behavior in a market. Each year's price is determined by the available quantity, and determines the following year's quantity.

This sequence of events is depicted in Fig. 2–10. The initial price of 5 cents a pound elicits a quantity of 90,000 pounds in year 2, as shown by the point designated Q_2. Vertically above Q_2 on the demand curve is the price at which that quantity can be sold, indicated by point P_2. Directly to the right, on the supply curve, is the quantity that year 2's price will elicit for year 3. This is shown by point Q_3. The resulting price in year 3 is P_3 on the demand curve. And so it goes. The sequence traces out a kind of cobweb, and the points move ever closer to the intersection of the supply and demand curves at a price of 5.7 cents a pound and a quantity of 96,000 pounds. This intersection is the equilibrium price and quantity for the market. Once it is attained neither the price nor the quantity will change until either the demand or the supply curve is disturbed.

This convergence to the equilibrium is not inevitable, though. If the demand curve had been much steeper (that is, if consumers had been less responsive to price changes), a crop below the equilibrium would cause such a high price in that year that the next crop would be farther above the equilibrium than the first crop was below. Then prices and quantities would gyrate wildly without ever attaining equilibrium. (You should draw this diagram yourself and observe the ever expanding cobweb that it generates.) This possibility illustrates a market with an unstable equilibrium.

It is remarkable, but true, that in a number of instances farmers have been found to behave in accordance with the simple cobweb scheme. Our interest in the cobweb, however, is that it illustrates that there are several levels of equilibrium in a market and that they interact. Each year the market attains a temporary equilibrium price at which purchasers are willing to take the amount available. This price then influences the amount that becomes available in the following year and the temporary equilibrium in that year. If the market is stable, which is the usual case, the sequence of temporary equilibria leads eventually to a supply for which the price induces the very same supply the following year. Then the permanent, or long-run, equilibrium has been attained.

Now we apply the same approach to other commodities not produced on an annual schedule. This is the second step in the explanation of long-run equilibrium.

THE DYNAMICS OF LONG-RUN SUPPLY

There are several differences between the market for a nonagricultural commodity and the simple agricultural market just considered. One is that in the agricultural market the supply available is predetermined by last year's price and unresponsive to this year's, whereas for most commodities the available supply responds to price, and interacts with it, in accordance with a short-run supply curve. Such a supply curve is shown in Fig. 2–11 as "short-run supply no. 1." Everything we said earlier about the behavior of competitive markets with supply and demand curves applies to it. In particular, the intersection of short-run supply no. 1 with the demand curve determines a temporary equilibrium price, p_1, and quantity, q_1.

But now we recognize that this is not the end of the story. The figure includes a long-run supply curve that shows that if businessmen expect the price to remain at p_1 for some time, they will enlarge their facilities and then offer

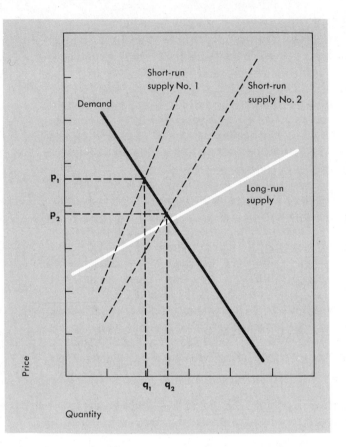

Short-run
supply No. 1

Short-run
supply No. 2

Demand

Long-run
supply

p_1

p_2

Price

q_1 q_2

Quantity

FIG. 2–11 Short-run and long-run curves for a manufactured commodity. Each short-run equilibrium induces investments that shift the short-run supply curve.

an amount considerably greater than q_1 at that price. Herein lies the second main difference from the agricultural case. Nonagricultural plants do not ripen on an annual schedule the way agricultural plants do. Some time is required before businessmen become convinced that the high price is here to stay, and more time must elapse before new facilities can be installed and completed. But under such a stimulus, after some time new facilities *will* enter the market. Then businessmen, in the aggregate, will want to sell a larger quantity than before at price p_1 and at other prices. That is, a new short-run supply curve comes into existence. This is shown in the diagram by "short-run supply no. 2," which portrays the conditions in the market after some new capacity has been installed. The enhanced supplies will drive the temporary equilibrium price down to p_2 and will increase the quantity purchased correspondingly. As the figure is drawn, this second temporary equilibrium is also above the long-run supply curve and the process will continue.

For the sake of clarity, only two short-run supply curves are shown in the figure. In reality, the short-run supply curve will not jump abruptly from one position to a quite different one but, rather, will drift gradually to the right, moving almost imperceptibly every time one of the firms completes a small addition. Eventually it will reach a position in which it goes through the inter- section of the demand curve and the long-run supply curve.[6] When this occurs (not shown in the figure), the temporary equilibrium will be right on the long- run supply curve. Firms will be offering from their current plants the same amount that they would offer if they had the opportunity to revise their plants. This indicates that they are under no incentive to invest further because their current plants are adequate to satisfy current demand at the current price. The long-run equilibrium has then been attained.

Of course, this long-run adjustment process takes a great deal of time. Its time scale has to be measured in years rather than in weeks or months. The temporary, short-run equilibria encountered along the way are of interest be- cause they embody the immediate effects of changes in economic circumstances; they indicate the prices and outputs that will be observed in the months immediately after some economic change. The ultimate, long-run equilibrium is significant, too. It expresses basic, underlying economic conditions, such as the cost of producing the commodity after the effects of temporary shortages and disturbances have run their courses. Apart from times of abrupt and vio- lent change, the short-run equilibria will not be very far from the long-run one.

SUMMARY

The quantity of any commodity that is produced and exchanged, and the price at which it sells, are determined primarily by conditions in its market. Structurally, markets are of many different kinds, the three most im- portant for analysis being competitive markets, monopolies, and oligopolies. Oligopolies are the most prevalent market type in the United States, but com- petitive markets are also numerous and have such important social and analytic implications that most analyses concentrate on them. Monopolies are rare and generally are closely regulated by the government.

In a competitive market, the principal data that determine the price charged and the quantity produced and sold are contained in the supply curve and the demand curve. If these two curves are drawn on the same chart, their intersection shows the equilibrium values of the amount produced and also the price.

Any change in the cost of producing a commodity will shift its supply curve. The new intersection will determine the new market equilibrium. Typ-

[6] Since plant additions take time, some investments that were initiated before this eventuality may not be completed until after it. Then the short-run supply curve would move somewhat beyond the crossing of the demand curve and the long-run supply curve. In such a case, some plants, presumably older ones, would have to be retired before a long-run equilibrium was established. But "overshooting" of this sort is not as prominent a feature of a gradual adjustment process as it is of the agricultural cobweb.

ically, the increase or decrease in production costs will be shared by producers and purchasers in proportions that depend on the slope, or responsiveness, of the demand curve. Similarly, changes in demand conditions are reflected by changes in the position, and perhaps shape, of the demand curve. The analysis of the effects of those changes is similar to the analysis of changes in production costs or other supply conditions.

The practical estimation of supply and demand curves is difficult and technical, but important for many governmental and business decisions. An example showed that the demand curve for even so basic a commodity as household water supply displays a considerable responsiveness to price changes.

Markets normally respond quite quickly to changes in their short-run supply and demand curves. Responses to changes in the long-run curves are, as the name suggests, slow and complicated. Yet the long-run curves strongly influence the positions of the short-run curves at any instant.

MAIN CONCEPTS INTRODUCED

MARKET. The market for any commodity is all the people and business firms who buy, sell, and produce it.

COMPETITIVE MARKET. A competitive market is a market in which the firms that produce the commodity are sufficiently numerous and their products are sufficiently similar so that consumers do not care which firm they buy from and no firm has an appreciable effect on the prices charged by other firms.

MONOPOLY. A monopoly is a market with only one producer.

OLIGOPOLY. An oligopoly is a market in which producing firms respond consciously to each other's price changes. The products of the different firms may be distinguishable, and purchasers may have strong preferences among them.

SUPPLY CURVE FOR A FIRM. A supply curve for a firm is a table, chart, or mathematical formula that shows how much of its commodity the firm would want to produce and sell at every possible price.

SUPPLY CURVE FOR A COMMODITY. A supply curve for a commodity is a table, chart, or mathematical formula which shows the amount of that commodity that the firms producing it would want to produce and sell in toto at every possible price. It is (approximately) the sum of the supply curves for the firms that produce that commodity.

DEMAND CURVE FOR A CONSUMER. A consumer's demand curve for any commodity is a table, chart, or mathematical formula which shows the amount of that commodity that the consumer would purchase at every possible price. The consumer in question may be a household, a business firm, a government agency, etc.

DEMAND CURVE FOR A COMMODITY. The demand curve for any commodity is a table, chart, or mathematical formula that shows the total amount of the commodity that purchasers would buy at every possible price. It is the sum of the demand curves for individual purchasers of that commodity.

SHORT-RUN SUPPLY CURVE. The short-run supply curve for a firm shows the amount of its commodity that the firm would want to produce and sell by the use of its currently available plant and facilities at every possible price. The short-run supply curve for a commodity shows the total amount that all the producers of that commodity would want to produce and sell at every possible price, by use of their currently available plant and facilities.

Long-Run Supply Curve. The long-run supply curve for a firm shows the amount of its commodity that the firm would want to produce and sell at every possible price, on the assumptions that that price would remain in effect a long time and the firm could modify, expand, and contract its facilities accordingly. The long-run supply curve for a commodity shows the total amount of the commodity that all the firms that produce it would want to produce and sell at every possible price, on the assumption that that price would remain in effect long enough to justify modifications, expansions, and contractions of their plants. It allows for the possibility that a particular price may induce new firms to enter the industry or old firms to withdraw.

Behind the Supply Curves

CHAPTER THREE

In Chapter 2 we learned that the supply curve is one of the two factors that determine the price of a commodity and the quantity traded. It follows that to understand what determines prices and quantities in an industry we must understand what determines the industry's supply curve.

Recall the concept of the supply curve for a commodity: it specifies the amount of the commodity that the firms in the industry would want to produce and sell at any given price. It is derived by adding up the supply curves of the individual firms in the industry. The supply curve of each individual firm specifies the most profitable amount for that firm to produce and sell at any given price. So the whole concept rests on the profitability to the individual firms of different amounts of output, price being given.

The factors that affect the profitability of any level of production and sales can be grasped most easily by looking at the consequences of any choice from the businessman's point of view. Tables 3–1 and 3–2, adapted from an authoritative accounting text,[1] illustrate how a businessman perceives the results of producing and selling a particular volume. The tables summarize the accounts of a small and simple company that has produced 100,000 units of its product and sold 105,500 at a price of $3.00. Though the accounts may look formidable at first glance, they are self-explanatory when read line by line.[2]

[1] H. A. Finney and H. E. Miller, *Principles of Accounting, Introductory*, 6th ed. (Englewood Cliffs, N.J.: Prentice-Hall, Inc., 1963), pp. 250, 251.

[2] It should be mentioned, however, that the clarity of accounting statements, including this one, is a bit deceptive. A good deal of subtlety lurks under the surface. For example,

Table 3–1

THE *A B C* COMPANY
Statement of Cost of Goods Manufactured
For the Year Ended December 31, 1964

Materials:

Inventory, December 31, 1963			$ 12,000
Purchases		$87,400	
Purchase returns and allowances	$ 500		
Purchase discounts	1,200	1,700	
Net purchases		$85,700	
Transportation in		875	
Total			86,575
Total inventory and purchases			$ 98,575
Inventory, December 31, 1964			9,000
Cost of materials used			$ 89,575
Direct labor			66,255
Manufacturing overhead:			
Indirect labor		$15,325	
Heat, light, and power		3,000	
Machinery repairs and maintenance		6,795	
Depreciation:			
Building		3,200	
Machinery and equipment		6,000	
Insurance expense		850	
Property taxes		1,200	
Factory supplies used		4,200	
Miscellaneous factory expense		3,600	
Total manufacturing overhead			44,170
Total cost of manufacturing			$200,000
Add goods in process, December 31, 1963			21,525
Total			$221,525
Deduct goods in process, December 31, 1964			12,000
Cost of goods manufactured			$209,525

Source: H. A. Finney and H. E. Miller, *Principles of Accounting, Introductory,* 6th ed., p. 250.

Such an accounting statement is a record of history, and the most important record that a business firm possesses. Our concern, however, and often the businessman's, is with how this record would have been changed if the firm had manufactured and sold some other amount, for decisions depend on estimates of the effects of alternative decisions. It is easy to see the effect of a change in output on gross and net sales, for these figures change very nearly in proportion to the physical volume of output. If output had been x units instead of 100,000, net sales would have been just about $3x$. In general, if a firm sells x units at a price of p, its sales will be very close to px.

The effect of different volumes of output on the various categories of cost shown in the accounts, and on their aggregate, is far more complicated. Some of the categories, such as direct labor, purchased materials and supplies, and

the estimation of such entries as "depreciation" and "goods in process" is difficult and often fairly arbitrary. The accounts of more complicated firms than this one will include even more questionable estimates. The difficulties of estimating costs will be discussed later in the chapter.

Table 3–2

THE *A B C* COMPANY
Income Statement
For the Year Ended December 31, 1964

Gross sales			$316,500
Sales returns and allowances		$ 2,000	
Sales discounts		2,500	4,500
Net sales			$312,000
Cost of goods sold:			
Finished goods inventory, December 31, 1963		$ 20,000	
Cost of goods manufactured—per Table 3–1		209,525	
Total		$229,525	
Finished goods inventory, December 31, 1964		17,000	212,525
Gross profit on sales			$ 99,475
Operating expenses:			
Selling expenses:			
Salesmen's salaries	$20,360		
Advertising	9,000		
Salesmen's traveling expenses	8,000		
Heat and light	150		
Depreciation:			
Building	100		
Furniture and fixtures	200		
Insurance expense	40		
Property taxes	75		
Miscellaneous selling expenses	1,085	$ 39,010	
Administrative expenses:			
Officers' salaries	$18,000		
Office salaries	4,040		
Office supplies used	700		
Heat and light	350		
Depreciation:			
Building	300		
Furniture and fixtures	550		
Insurance expense	100		
Property taxes	200		
Bad debts expense	800		
Miscellaneous administrative expenses	900	25,940	64,950
Net income before federal income tax			$ 34,525
Federal income tax			10,500
Net income			$ 24,025

Source: H A. Finney and H. E. Miller, *Principles of Accounting, Introductory,* 6th ed., p. 251.

salesmen's salaries may vary in direct proportion to the volume produced and sold. But they may not. If increased volume requires overtime wages or tighter work schedules resulting in more spoilage, then direct labor and materials purchases may increase more than in proportion to the number of units produced. On the other hand, if the larger output permits organizing the work in larger and more efficient production lots, then labor costs will go up less than in proportion to the volume produced.

44   Other categories of cost increase when output does, but not even approximately in the same proportion. Examples are machinery repair and mainten-

ance, indirect labor, miscellaneous administrative expenses (for example, salaries of bookkeepers, purchasing agents, and the like). Still other kinds of cost are not influenced at all, or only negligibly, by changes in the rate of output. Officers' salaries, property taxes, depreciation, insurance of the plant and offices are of this type.

So, in short, most kinds of cost tend to rise when output does, but the relationship is not simple. Because it is so important, we shall analyze this relationship at length in this chapter and the next. For the present let us simply denote the total cost of producing a specific level of output, say x units a year, by $TC(x)$. Then, remembering that net sales will be very close to px, we can write that

$$\text{Net income} = \text{net sales} - \text{total costs}$$
$$= px - TC(x)$$

This is the figure that, ultimately, the businessman keeps his eye on.

The most profitable output, x, is the volume that makes net income as just defined as large as possible. To ascertain this volume we use a method called *marginal analysis*. This method consists in contemplating any possible quantity of output and asking whether net income could be increased by producing one more unit. We also ask whether net income could be increased by producing one less unit. The assumed level of output is the one that maximizes net income only if the answers to both these questions are negative.

Consider the first question. If output were increased by one unit, sales would increase by the amount of the price, p. Costs would increase by the cost of the additional unit, called the *marginal cost*. Analysis of the behavior of the various cost categories would tell us how much this amounts to. We denote this increase in cost by $MC(x)$ (read: marginal cost at output level x),[3] and notice the formal definitional relationship

$$MC(x) = TC(x + 1) - TC(x).$$

Using these concepts, the effect on net income of increasing output by one unit is to increase it by the increase in sales, p, offsets by the increase in costs, $MC(x)$. If $MC(x) < p$, this will be a positive number, that is, net income would be increased by a unit increase in output and sales, and the proposed level of output is too small to maximize net income. The indication is that the proposed level of output should be increased until the marginal cost is no longer less than the price, if that ever happens. Our subsequent analysis will show that marginal costs must increase when output does, so that an income-maximizing output will be determined by this process. The analysis of the sec-

---

[3] The formal definition of marginal cost varies slightly among different texts, but all definitions in use convey precisely the same idea. The definitional problem arises from the arbitrariness of the choice of a unit of output: should output be measured in single units, dozens, or grosses, or perhaps in ounces, pounds, or tons? For many purposes it is most satisfactory to regard output as a continuous variable and to define $MC(x) = \dfrac{d}{dx} TC(x)$.

ond question is exactly the same, and uses the same concepts, except that successive reductions in output are considered.

From this pair of analyses we conclude that the income-maximizing level of output will satisfy two inequalities.[4] From considering successive increases it must satisfy $MC(x + 1) \not< p;$ and from considering decreases it must satisfy $MC(x) \not> p$. These two determine the income-maximizing level of output, give or take one unit. No one but a mathematician thinks in terms of pairs of opposing inequalities, so it is best to summarize by the very good approximation: the income-maximizing level of output is the one that satisfies

$$MC(x) \cong p.$$

To apply this: The ABC Company should analyze its cost data and strive to produce and sell the level of output for which the marginal cost is as close as possible to $3.00 per unit. The accounting forms illustrated in Tables 3–1 and 3–2 are not very convenient for this purpose, but various subsidiary documents, such as cost-accounting reports, are.

In general, the formula $MC(x) \cong p$ gives the point on the supply curve of any company that corresponds to a prescribed price of p.[5] If the market circumstances are such that customers are demanding more output than the formula calls for, the company will be making some sales that cost it more than they contribute to its receipts. It will be dissatisfied with the current price, with the consequences discussed in the preceding chapter. The firm will also be restive, for other reasons, if marginal costs are significantly smaller than the going price. So the formula does convey the crucial comparison by which a firm determines whether a given level of output is satisfactory at a given price, which is the essence of its supply curve and of its price–output decisions.

This whole analysis rested heavily on the behavior of costs. We must now look further into them.

FIXED COSTS AND VARIABLE COSTS

To pursue the analysis of costs it is useful to divide the accountants' categories of cost into two broad classes: fixed costs and variable costs.

Fixed costs include all kinds of expense whose magnitude depends on the fixed plant and permanent organization of the firm but does not vary appreciably with changes in the output from a given plant. Several categories of fixed costs were encountered above. In general, the most important fixed costs in a firm are those entailed by the ownership and maintenance of its plant and equipment. These include the interest on the capital tied up or borrowed, the rental value of the land occupied, the gradual wearing out or depreciation of its buildings and machinery, insurance, real-estate taxes, and the like. These ex-

[4] Which reduce to one equality if output is a continuous variable.
[5] An important qualification of this statement will be mentioned below.

penses are incurred month after month whatever the level of operation of the firm's plant or plants, and even if they are closed down.

The second important category of fixed costs comprises the general expenses of management. The executive staff and other key personnel, and the accounting department, the purchasing department, the personnel department, and the other central functions of the firm must all be paid for, and their costs do not vary much whether the firm is running full tilt or on short shifts. Fixed costs are determined by the long-run adjustments discussed in the previous chapter.

Variable costs include all kinds of expense whose level depends significantly on the current rate of output. The wages of production employees paid by the hour or piece are an important component of variable costs. Salesmen's commissions, the costs of raw materials, purchased parts, power, shipping, and storage and insurance of inventories are all of this general type because their levels are very sensitive to the rate of output and sales. Variable costs change in response to short-run adjustments.

HOW COSTS VARY WITH OUTPUT

When a firm changes its rate of output, its variable costs change in response. But we have already seen that these costs do not change in any simple way. Their behavior depends on all the factors that affect the firm's efficiency at different levels of output. Generally speaking, firms tend to be inefficient both at very low and at very high rates of production. The best way to understand this phenomenon and to see how it affects cost is to trace through a schematic example.

Table 3–3 shows how costs might vary with output in a hypothetical manufacturing firm. The first column shows the possible levels of output per month,

Table 3–3   HOW COSTS VARY WITH OUTPUT IN A HYPOTHETICAL FIRM

Monthly Production (Units)	Fixed Cost ($ per month)	Variable Cost ($ per month)	Total Cost ($ per month)	Average Cost ($ per unit)	Marginal Cost ($ per unit)
100	1,000	900	1,900	19.00	9.00
200	1,000	1,600	2,600	13.00	7.00
300	1,000	2,200	3,200	10.67	6.00
400	1,000	2,800	3,800	9.50	6.00
500	1,000	3,400	4,400	8.80	6.00
600	1,000	4,050	5,050	8.42	6.50
700	1,000	4,750	5,750	8.21	7.00
800	1,000	5,550	6,550	8.19	8.00
900	1,000	6,500	7,500	8.33	9.50
1,000	1,000	7,650	8,650	8.65	11.50
1,100	1,000	9,050	10,050	9.14	14.00

on the assumption that decisions are made for batches of 100 units each. The second column shows the fixed costs, which are $1,000 a month at all levels of output. This $1,000 pays the rent on the plant, interest on borrowed investment, taxes, insurance, executive salaries, and other items that do not vary with changes in the level of output. The third column shows the variable costs for each level of output: wages of hourly employees, raw materials, and other types of expenditures that directly reflect the level of production in the plant. The remaining columns are derived from these.

Now let us consider how these costs are influenced by the level of output. At the very lowest level, variable costs amount to $900 a month, so that total costs (the sum of fixed and variable costs) are $1,900 a month (fourth column). Since 100 units are being produced, the cost per unit, or *average cost,* is $19 (fifth column). The marginal cost of the first batch is recorded as $9 per unit. Strictly speaking, this does not conform to our definition but if, as is likely to be the case, work orders are issued in lots or batches of 100 units each, the decision to order one batch instead of none increases total costs by $900, or $9 per unit ordered. There are no data available on how much the production of a single unit would add to costs; very likely the paper work involved in ordering one unit would cost more than the actual processing. Accordingly, we have estimated the marginal cost to be one-hundredth of the addition to total costs caused by increasing output by one batch. (The data that businessmen and economists have to work with are frequently this crude—sometimes cruder.)

If, now, the rate of output is increased to 200 units a month, fixed costs will not be affected, but variable costs will increase to $1,600 a month, shown on the second line of the variable-cost column, and total costs will increase to $2,600. With 200 units of output, this comes to an average cost of $13 per unit. The increase in cost imposed by the second batch of 100 units is $700, so marginal cost is estimated as $7 per unit at that rate of output.

Perhaps we had better pause here to restate the three cost concepts that we shall be using repeatedly:

1. The *total cost* of any level of output is the total expense of obtaining it. It is the sum of the fixed costs and the variable costs at that level of output. Denoted $TC(x)$.

2. The *average cost* of any level of output is the total cost divided by the output. In other words, it is the per unit cost. Denoted $AC(x)$. By definition $AC(x) = TC(x)/x$.

3. The marginal cost at any level of output is the increase in total cost that would be imposed by producing one more unit. Denoted $MC(x)$. By definition $MC(x) = TC(x + 1) - TC(x)$. And by simple algebra [6] $MC(x) = AC(x + 1) + x[AC(x + 1) - AC(x)]$.

[6] See appendix to this chapter for details.

These three cost concepts are illustrated by the computations in Table 3–3. The figures given there for total and average costs follow the definitions exactly; the marginal-cost figures are only approximations, as we have noted.

The mathematical relationships among total, average, and marginal costs are explained in the appendix to this chapter. Here we want to concentrate on how all of them evolve when the level of output changes.

The active component of total, average, and marginal costs is variable costs. Notice that according to the table the first 100 units required variable costs of $900, but the second 100 units added only $700 to that amount. Why should the second 100 units require less by way of man-hours, raw materials, and other variable inputs than the first? The answer is that once the work has been set in motion for manufacturing the first 100 units of a commodity, a great deal of the work required for the second 100 units has already been accomplished. The purchase orders have been written, the job assignments have been made, the machines have been set up and adjusted.[7] All that is needed to increase the output is to write the orders for larger quantities and to let the machines run somewhat longer.

The third batch of 100 units adds $600 to the cost of operation, bringing variable costs to $2,200, total costs to $3,200, and the average cost to $10.67. The marginal cost of producing the third batch is $6 per unit, which is a lower figure than that for either of the preceding batches, and one indicative of still further economies through increased mass production. (These come about because production can be organized more efficiently as the level of output increases: men can be assigned to more specialized jobs, and the different phases of the work can be better coordinated, with less slack, waste, overlap, and so on.)

The fourth and fifth batches of 100 units cause the same increase in costs as the third, indicating that all the advantages of mass production have been gained at the output of 300 units a month. The fourth batch, though raising variable cost to $2,800 and total cost to $3,800, continues the decline in average cost; and the fifth batch, which again raises variable and total costs by $600 each, causes the average cost to fall even lower. (Why does average cost keep on going down although marginal cost is holding steady?)

With the sixth batch, however, a critical change occurs: this batch adds $650 to the variable and total costs, indicating a new marginal cost of $6.50 per unit. The cause of this jump in costs can be traced to difficulties that are beginning to arise on the production floor. Every plant has a certain capacity or rate of output that it can maintain conveniently. Oftentimes this economical capacity can be stated explicitly in numbers (as are the capacity of a power

[7] Job printing provides a striking example. For a small number of copies, nearly all the cost is for setting the type and making the press ready. The number of copies can be increased simply by using more paper and running the press longer, with no increase in the heavy expenses. Nearly all production processes display this same distinction between setting-up costs and running costs.

plant, and the load and speed restrictions assigned to an aircraft)—but these are seldom truly rigid figures; stated capacities of plants more often than not can be exceeded. The trouble is that when this is done, operating costs are likely to rise sharply.

Indeed, the marginal costs in a plant are likely to begin to rise well before its theoretical capacity is reached, and that is what we observe in the table. It is easy to see why this should be so. When a plant's output is comfortably below its capacity, every facility is in ample supply: there is plenty of room to work in and plenty of storage space to keep tools and materials just where they are needed; and machines can be shut down regularly for oiling and maintenance because there are reserve machines to take their places. (By the same token, production schedules are easy to keep even if a machine breaks down, because the reserve equipment *is* on hand.) But even before the nominal capacity of a plant is reached, this luxurious slack begins to disappear. Shelves and work spaces become crowded, tools have to be kept in inconvenient places, parts begin to get lost and broken. When a single machine breaks down, the work schedule may be seriously disrupted. Men and machines stand idle waiting for delayed subassembles, thus delaying later stages of the production process. Inferior, standby machinery is brought into use. Some work has to be done on overtime. In short, costs rise (marginal costs, that is)—at first almost imperceptibly, but then by leaps and bounds—as the sources of annoyance, inconvenience, and waste take more and more wind out of the sails of increased production.

Typical of the complaints when this state of affairs is reached are two reported in a prominent business paper:

> We are working 24 hours a day and in some cases six days a week . . . costs are rising faster than sales. Not only must we pay heavy overtime, but inflated production schedules are causing more defective parts that have to be either reworked or scrapped.
>
> Where we should keep standby equipment for short runs, we've got to put it in the mainstream, and this pushes costs up. . . . Maximum capacity is not the most efficient rate—if we had our choice we'd drop back.[8]

All these sources of expense are reflected in the marginal-cost column of the table. The increase from 500 to 600 units a month causes only a little disruption: marginal cost rises there only 50 cents a unit. But the step from 700 to 800 units is more costly, and thereafter marginal costs rise swiftly indeed.

Now follow down the rest of the table. As marginal costs rise, the increase in variable and total costs accelerates and the decline in average cost decelerates; in fact, the decline comes to a full stop and then reverses itself.

The relation of costs to the level of output is displayed most vividly by a graph of the cost curves, such as Fig. 3–1. The last two columns of Table 3–3 are plotted in that graph, and the tendency of average costs first to fall as output increases, and then to rise, is clearly shown. This tendency arises, as we

[8] *The Wall Street Journal,* September 16, 1965, p. 1 (slightly paraphrased).

have seen, from a contest between two conflicting forces. At low levels of output, variable cost per unit is low because each worker is able to work efficiently without encountering congestion or delays. But fixed costs per unit are high because the expenses of providing the fixed facilities are spread over a meager output. At the other end of the scale, fixed costs per unit are low but the inefficiencies of working in a congested plant push variable costs way up. Somewhere between the two extremes lies the happy medium where neither fixed costs per unit nor variable costs per unit are as low as possible, but the sum of the two is. This happy medium plays an important role in our subsequent analysis.

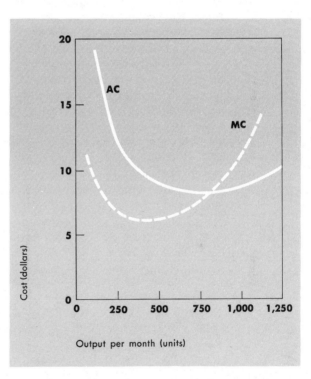

FIG. 3–1 Average- and marginal-cost curves. As output increases, average and marginal costs first fall, then rise, like a "U."

Output per month (units)

THE SUPPLY CURVE FOR AN INDIVIDUAL FIRM

Now that we have seen how a firm's costs are influenced by the level of its output, we have done most of the work required to understand its supply decisions. Remember that the firm is seeking the level of output that will afford it the largest profit when it sells its products at market prices. Which output this is can be determined by comparing the marginal-cost curve with the market price. Suppose, for example, that at the ongoing level of output the marginal

51

cost is less than the market price. Then it would pay the firm to increase its level of output by one unit at least, because the increase in expenses (= marginal cost) would be less than the amount that the resultant output could be sold for (= price). In fact, it would be best for the firm to continue increasing its output until it reached the level at which price and marginal cost were equal—up to this point, each unit of increase would add more to sales revenues than to costs. On the other hand, if the marginal cost at the ongoing level of output is greater than the price, the firm could increase its profits by reducing its level of output by one unit at least, for then the reduction in monthly expenses would be greater than the resultant reduction in the value of sales. In this case the firm would be best off if it reduced its output to the level at which price and marginal cost were equal. Taking these two cases together, we confirm our earlier conclusion that:

> The most profitable level of output for a competitive firm is the one at which the marginal cost is equal to the market price.

This, of course, establishes the firm's supply curve. Confronted with any market price the firm would want to produce and sell the quantity for which the marginal cost of production is equal to that price. In other words, a firm's marginal-cost curve is also its supply curve. That is why the marginal-cost curve is so important.

The output that maximizes profit at any market price can be found by a direct computation; this is done in Table 3–4 for a price of $10 a unit. There the value of sales (= $10 × the output) is shown in the second column, total cost according to Table 3–3 is shown in the third column, and monthly profit (the difference between sales value and total costs) is in the last column. A glance shows that 900 units a month is the most profitable output at this price.

To find the most profitable level of output by direct computation, a table similar to Table 3–4 would have to be constructed whenever the market price changed. But a table or graph of marginal costs gives the correct level without any additional calculations. The marginal-cost column of Table 3–3 shows that output can be increased from 800 to 900 units at a marginal cost of $9.50 a unit. At a market price of $10 a unit, that increase would be worthwhile—in fact, it should increase profits by 50 cents × 100 = $50. (Check this on Table 3–4.) But the marginal cost of the next batch is $11.50 a unit, which is not worthwhile at that market price. Hence the profit-maximizing output is found without any calculation to be 900 units.[9]

It is clearly more convenient to determine the levels of output that firms will offer at various prices by using the marginal-cost data rather than direct

[9] Notice that in this solution the marginal cost is not exactly equal to the market price. Exact equalities are a luxury reserved to mathematicians and theorists; businessmen and practical economists have to be content with approximations.

Table 3–4   RELATION OF PROFITS TO OUTPUT IN A HYPOTHETICAL FIRM

(Price = $ 10 per unit)

Monthly Production (Units)	Sales Value ($)	Total Cost ($)	Profit ($)	Monthly Production (Units)	Sales Value ($)	Total Cost ($)	Profit ($)
100	1,000	1,900	900*	700	7,000	5,750	1,250
200	2,000	2,600	600*	800	8,000	6,550	1,450
300	3,000	3,200	200*	900	9,000	7,500	1,500
400	4,000	3,800	200	1,000	10,000	8,650	1,350
500	5,000	4,400	600	1,100	11,000	10,050	950
600	6,000	5,050	950				

* Loss

computation, and just as accurate. As we reasoned above, the quantity that the firm will offer at any market price is the quantity for which the marginal cost is equal to that price. This firm's supply curve is shown in Fig. 3–2.

It is worth noting that the most profitable level of output depends on prices as well as on costs, and therefore is not necessarily the level for which average cost is lowest. In this example, average cost is lowest at an output of 800 units a month, where it equals $8.19 a unit. The most profitable output when the price is $10 a unit is 900 units a month, with an average cost of $8.33. (What will be the average cost when the price is $12 a unit?)

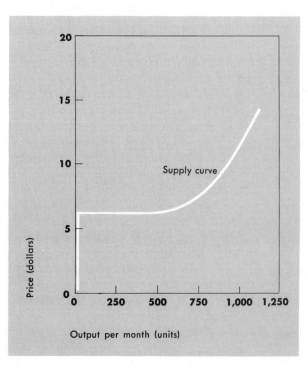

FIG. 3–2   Individual firm's supply curve. It coincides with the firm's marginal-cost curve for prices above the lowest possible variable cost. For lower prices the supply offered is zero.

All the foregoing deals with profitable states of affairs. But if the price were lower than the lowest possible average cost, the firm would have to lose money. For example, there is no possible output at which the illustrative firm could cover its costs if the price were $8 a unit. Our reasoning applies nevertheless: losses are inevitable in such a case, but they will be as small as possible at the output for which marginal cost equals the price, an output of 800 units in this instance. There are, however, prices so low that if they reigned, it would not be worthwhile for the firm to produce at all. The price of $6.75 is such a price in our example. If that were the market price and if the firm produced 600 units, its sales revenue would be $4,050, which would just cover the variable costs at that level of output (see Table 3–3). At any other level of output, variable costs would be greater than sales revenue at a price of $6.75 or less. Look, for example, at the variable costs for an output of 1,000 units. They are $7,650, which is considerably more than 1,000 times $6.75. Accordingly, at that price and at lower ones the firm will not offer any supply.

Thus our conclusion that a firm's supply curve is the same as its marginal-cost curve is valid for all prices that are high enough to cover the variable costs of production at some level of output. At lower prices the firm will not offer any supply.

THE SUPPLY CURVE FOR THE INDUSTRY

The firm's cost curves determine its supply curve, that is, the amount it will supply at every possible price. (Actually, its marginal-cost curve is the *same* as its supply curve unless the price is so low that variable costs cannot be covered at any level of output. At such low prices, the firm produces nothing.) The firm's supply curve, in turn, helps determine the industry's supply curve, for the supply of a commodity at any price is simply the sum of the offerings at that price of all the firms that produce it.

The supply curve for the industry will have the generally upward-sloping shape that we assumed in the last chapter, since this is the shape of the supply curves for the individual firms that comprise the industry. At every level of the price, each firm will want to sell the amount for which its marginal cost of production is about equal to the common market price, provided that this price at least covers its average variable costs. Consequently, the higher the price, the larger the amount of the commodity that each firm will offer; thus the expected shape will be imparted to the industry supply curve.

The interaction between the price (set by the firms) and the quantity sold (decided by the purchasers) is complex, as we have seen. When the firms find themselves selling amounts far from their supply curves they are strongly tempted to adjust their prices, and they do so. As a result, except in times of violent market disturbance, most firms produce at levels fairly close to those indicated by their supply curves. Consequently:

The price of a product sold in a competitive market tends to be equal to the marginal cost of every firm in the industry or, in short, to the marginal cost of producing the product.

This is so because every firm in the industry will want to sell the quantity for which its marginal cost is equal to the common market price. However, if the quantities offered in response to the market price do not add up to the amount demanded at that price, the price will change (as we have seen in Chapter 2), and the offerings will change accordingly. When equilibrium is again established, the cost of an additional unit produced by any firm will be equal to the new market price.

The marginal cost will thus be about the same for all firms in the industry, though their cost curves may differ substantially. If the firms are operating efficiently, so that each one is producing its output at the lowest possible cost, the industry as a whole will also be producing its total output at lowest possible cost. This follows because when marginal costs are the same for all firms in the industry, the industry's costs cannot be reduced by shifting some of the production from one firm to another. The reduction in costs in the firms that reduce output would be just about offset by the additional costs in the firms that increase output to compensate. In other words, the industry's production task is distributed among the firms in the most efficient manner, and without any centralized direction. This is one of the self-regulating properties of the market economy.

But, be warned, this conclusion is not valid for other than competitive markets, as we shall see presently. It depends on the presence of effective pressures to bring the marginal costs in the individual firms into line with the market price.

In summary, both the firm's and the industry's supply curves result from profit-maximizing decisions of businessmen according to the principles just described. The supply offered by the industry in response to any market price is just the sum of the supplies of the firms in it, each producing the amount for which the marginal cost is equal to that market price. This behavior determines the point on the supply curve corresponding to that price.

If the quantity thus offered corresponds also to the point on the demand curve for that price, consumers will be satisfied and that market price will persist. Otherwise the kinds of adjustment described in Chapter 2 will ensue until a price is established at which supply and demand are equal. In this situation each firm is making the highest possible profits given the market price, consumers' demands are being satisfied, and the total output of the industry is being produced at the lowest possible cost given the current outfit of plant and equipment in the industry.

But this is only a temporary achievement. The market processes we have discussed lead the industry to make the best use of its current stock of productive equipment. But that stock of equipment may not be appropriate to the current state of demand: the industry may be either overequipped (as in the case of coal) or, more usually in a growing economy, underequipped (as in the case of color television). Then long-run adjustments are induced. We turn to them now.

INVESTMENT DECISIONS

We have been analyzing the most profitable level of output of a firm, regarding its current plant and organization as given. The decisions discussed in this context therefore concern the economical use of the plant and equipment currently available to a company or, to take a larger view, of a whole industry or economy. But the growth and prosperity of a company, or the development of an economy and the wealth of its members, depend on a different kind of decision, decisions to invest and thereby to enlarge the stock of fixed capital. These are the decisions that really have the far-reaching and long-lasting consequences.

A full-fledged discussion of the causes and consequences of investment decisions would carry us far beyond the scope of this book, into the realms of dynamic economics and growth theory. But some of the most important investment decisions are within our scope and, indeed, have to be discussed because they are part of the market adjustment process that is our central concern. These are the decisions that determine the long-run supply curves of established industries.

The problem can be posed by considering how the adjustment process described in the preceding sections sets the stage for investment decisions. Suppose that an industry and the firms in it have attained the equilibrium price and output relative to their current stock of fixed capital. The situation of a typical firm might be as shown in Fig. 3–3. The figure shows the average- and marginal-cost curves, the current price, and the average variable-cost curve, labeled *AVC*. The last is a new concept, but obvious. Average variable costs are variable costs per unit of output, or variable cost divided by output.

Clearly the industry is prospering. This is shown by the fact that the price is well above average cost at the most profitable level of output (1,050 units, where marginal cost equals price). At that level of output average costs are substantially above their lowest level, and so are average variable costs. This indicates that the current plant is too small to produce the profitable rate of output without incurring some costs due to congestion and overloading. The obvious way to avoid the costs and headaches of an overworked plant is to enlarge it. The stage is set for deciding whether to enlarge the plant and, if so, how much.

The decision is reached by balancing the favorable and unfavorable effects of plant enlargement. The favorable effects are to reduce the bottlenecks, crowding, and general overworking of the plant, which will be reflected dia-

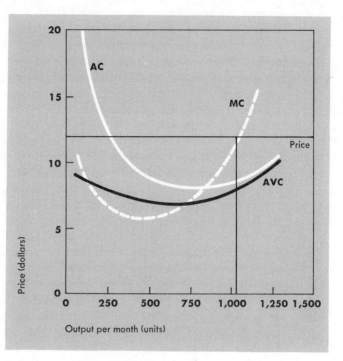

FIG. 3–3 Short-run equilibrium of the firm. Marginal cost equals price, but average cost can be lower.

grammatically in a reduction in average variable costs. How much these costs are reduced depends on how much the plant is enlarged. At the extreme, which is not likely to prove economical, it appears from the graph that they could be reduced to as little as $6.75 a unit. This would save about $1.15 a unit, amounting to $14,500 a year.

The unfavorable effects can be regarded in either of two ways which, correctly analyzed, should lead to the same decision. Basically, plant expansion costs money. In the first place there is the capital cost of building the plant and buying the equipment. After that there is a continuing flow of fixed expenditures for property taxes, insurance, and the like. We shall refer to this continuing flow as the associated fixed costs.

So far we have that if the firm enlarges its plant it will realize an annual saving equal to the reduction in variable costs minus the associated fixed costs, but also it will have to pay for this saving by incurring the capital cost at the time of the expansion. Now we are up against the fundamental question of investment decisions: Is the saving large enough to justify the capital cost? Is, for example, a prospect of saving $12,000 a year big enough to warrant an investment of $36,000? The essence of the question is how to compare an expenditure that would have to be incurred now with savings that will accrue over a long period, perhaps 15 years.

There are, as we said, two ways in which this can be done. One is to convert the anticipated flow of savings into a single sum of money that represents how much that flow is worth to the company, that is, how much it would be willing to pay to obtain those savings. This sum is called the "present value" of the savings and can be compared directly with the capital cost. The alternative is to convert that capital cost into an annual flow that can be compared directly with the savings. This is the alternative that we shall choose because it explains the depreciation accounts in the income statements and is essential to understanding the concept of fixed cost. The two approaches, of course, lead to the same decision in the same circumstances.

To understand how a capital cost can be converted to an annual flow of fixed costs we start with the easiest case, indeed a trivial one. This is the case of fixed capital that lasts only one year, for example an automobile purchased by a car-rental company that retires its cars each year. Let us enumerate the costs of owning and operating a car on the supposition that it costs $3,000 new and has a year-old resale value of $1,800. First, there is the depreciation, the $1,200 decline in value. Then there are insurance, taxes, license fees, and so on, in short, the associated fixed costs. Then, the money for buying the car is likely to be borrowed; if so, the interest on the purchase price is part of fixed cost. But interest is part of fixed cost even if the company finances the purchase from its own resources, for if the company buys the car with its own funds it loses the interest that those funds would have earned if lent out, invested in a bond, or used in any other profitable way.[10] These are the major components of fixed cost. Notice that they include depreciation and interest but not the purchase price itself. In addition, there are all the variable costs of operating the car.

In short, if the car is to be worth purchasing, the company must anticipate that it will earn sufficient gross revenues to cover the variable costs of operation, plus the associated fixed costs, plus interest on the investment, plus the depreciation. Otherwise the company would be better off without the car. Thus the relevant comparison to be made is the revenues net of variable costs on the one hand with the sum of associated fixed costs, interest, and depreciation on the other.

The next step introduces and solves the essential difficulty. This is the case of deciding on the purchase of an asset that last two years.[11] To be concrete, suppose that the asset is a taxicab that costs $3,000 and is resold after two years for $800. All the components of fixed cost are arrived at just as before, except depreciation. Over the whole period the cab depreciates by $2,200, but how much should be counted as part of fixed cost in the first year, and how much in the second? We answer this question with the aid of two principles:

[10] Here is one point where accountants and economists diverge. Accountants include only contractual interest, interest on borrowed funds, in their records. But when businessmen make decisions about investments they recognize, as economists do, that an asset is not worth acquiring unless it promises to earn enough to cover the interest on its full cost along with other expenses.

[11] Years are significant not because they span the four seasons, but because they are the basic accounting period for which fixed costs and other accounting concepts are estimated.

first, the depreciation charge should be the same in all (two) years, and second, it should be chosen so that if the asset earns just enough to cover the variable and fixed costs, it should be barely worth owning. To this end we imagine that each year a certain sum, called a sinking-fund contribution, is set aside and that the sinking fund is allowed to accumulate until, at the asset's retirement date, it amounts to the total lifetime depreciation. For with such a sinking fund, on retirement date the company will be able to recover its initial investment in the asset, and if all the other expenses have just been met, the asset will have barely paid its way. In the case of the taxicab, if the interest rate is 6 per cent, the annual sinking-fund depreciation charge is $1,068, as can be seen from the calculation in Table 3–5. This sinking-fund contribution appears in the books of the company as depreciation expense.[12]

Table 3–5   SINKING FUND DEPRECIATION OF A TWO-YEAR ASSET

(6% interest assumed)

Year	Contribution or Depreciation Charge	Years Held	Accrued Interest (at 6%)	Value on Retirement Date
1	$1,068	1	$64	$1,132
2	1,068	0	0	1,068
Total fund				2,200
Resale value				800
Total				$3,000

The same general principles apply no matter how long an asset lasts. There is an annual depreciation expense in each year of the asset's life, which it must earn enough to cover, along with other expenses, if it is to be worth having. This depreciation expense, accumulated at interest, is just sufficient to enable the firm to recover its original investment at the end of the asset's life. We have explained the sinking-fund method for computing the annual depreciation expense. There are other methods, but this one is sufficiently accurate for all our purposes. Interest-rate tables, which are widely available, make it easy to compute the sinking-fund contributions in practical applications.

Now we have provided an implementable definition for fixed cost. It is the sum of associated fixed costs, interest on the value of the investment, and depreciation expenses. This sum can be compared with the annual savings or earnings of an investment to determine whether it is worth undertaking.

[12] Accountants and businessmen often use "straight-line depreciation," which is slightly simpler. According to this method the annual depreciation charge for an n-year asset would be one nth of its lifetime depreciation. Straight-line depreciation for the taxicab would be $1,100, which is slightly too high because it neglects the interest earned by the depreciation reserve or sinking fund. There is not much harm in slight errors, but for a building that costs $100,000, lasts 40 years, and has no scrap value, the sinking-fund contribution is $646 and the straight-line depreciation is nearly four times as great. So there is danger of substantial error.

In summary, we have arrived at a simple rule for making investment decisions. It is: First, estimate the annual earnings (after allowance for variable costs) or savings that would result from the proposed investment. Second, estimate the increase in annual fixed costs that would be caused by it, as the sum of its associated fixed costs, interest cost, and depreciation charges. Then the investment is advisable if the annual earnings or savings exceed the increase in fixed costs; otherwise not. Notice that the decision depends only on the annual earnings and the fixed costs. The initial capital outlay influences the fixed cost but does not enter the comparison directly.

This rule, of course, is deceptively simple. It is often very difficult to make the estimates. The future earnings and resale values cannot be foretold with accuracy or certainty. Even the appropriate interest rate is sometimes difficult to estimate. So the rule provides a framework for analysis rather than a definite formula ready for mechanical application. It organizes the considerations rather than solves the problem, and a good deal of sophisticated economics, business judgment, and investment analysis is likely to be required to apply it in any practical instance. But it will suffice for our expository purposes.

LONG-RUN COSTS AND COST CURVES

The foregoing analysis of investment decisions has important implications for production costs and production decisions. Let us put it back into the framework with which we started, the question of expanding a plant that is overloaded at the currently profitable level of operation. Figure 3–3 shows the average cost curve in the firm's current plant. That curve is repeated in Fig. 3–4, where it is labeled "C." Figure 3–4 also shows some of the alternatives open to the firm. By investing $18,000 in plant expansion it can eliminate some of the currently expensive bottlenecks. The increase in fixed costs that this plant expansion would entail can be calculated by the methods just discussed.[13] The plant designers can estimate the average variable costs of the enlarged plant at various levels of output. Adding the average variable costs and the average fixed costs of the expanded plant for a range of output levels produces the average-cost curve for that plant. This is shown by the curve labeled "18." Similar calculations have been made for investments of $36,000 and $72,000 and are shown in the figure.

Notice how the four curves, each corresponding to a plant of different size and cost, behave. At low levels of output the larger plants have higher average costs, because they have high average fixed costs and the congestion they are

[13] As a rough calculation: Insurance, taxes, and so on amount to about 3 per cent of capital cost, interest is 6 per cent, sinking-fund contributions, assuming a 15-year life, are 4.3 per cent, totaling fixed costs of 13.3 per cent of the capital cost. For an investment of $18,000, this is $2,400 a year or $200 a month. At an output of 1,050 units a month, this adds $.19 a unit to the average fixed costs resulting from the plant already owned.

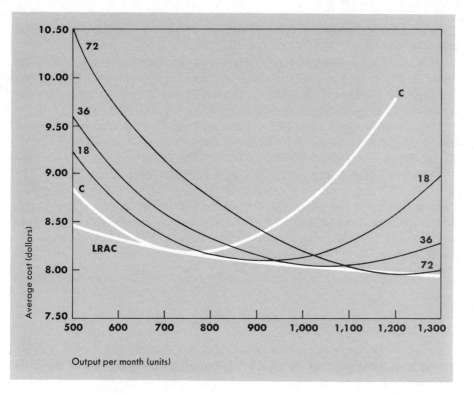

FIG. 3–4 Short-run and long-run average-cost curves. For each level of output the long-run curve touches the short-run curve that is lowest for that output.

intended to avert would not occur in any event. But at high levels the order is just reversed; the fixed costs are spread out over a large number of units and the bottlenecks encountered in small plants are severe.

Which plant to choose depends on the anticipated level of output. The best plant is the one with lowest average costs at that level. Because: if you compare that plant with a smaller one with higher average costs, the fact that average costs are higher shows that the reduction in fixed costs is overwhelmed by the increase in variable costs at the anticipated level of output. Similarly, if you compare the plant with lowest average costs with a larger plant, the rise in average costs indicates that fixed costs increase more than the saving in variable costs, at that level of output, can justify.

Thus, to every level of output there corresponds a best plant for producing that level; the plant that produces it at lowest average cost. The average cost of producing any output in the best plant for that level is known as the *long-run average cost.* In the illustrative case the best plant for producing 1,050 units a month is the one that costs an additional $36,000, and the corresponding long-run average cost is $8.02.

The diagram shows the best plants and the long-run average costs for other levels of output. For 700 units a month the current plant is best and the long-run average cost is $8.21. For 1,300 units a month the plant requiring an additional $72,000 is best, and the average cost is $7.97. And so on.

If we string together the long-run average costs of all the different significant levels of output, we obtain the *long-run average-cost curve,* shown in the figure by the heavy line. Hereafter we shall distinguish the previous cost curves from this one by referring to them as short-run average-cost curves.

So we emerge with the concept of the long-run average-cost curve, defined as the curve that shows the average cost of producing each level of output in the plant best adapted to it. This curve is fundamental to understanding the long-run behavior of industries and markets, just as the short-run curves were fundamental to understanding short-run market adjustments and price determination.

LONG-RUN MARKET BEHAVIOR

The long-run cost curves we have just deduced are the key to long-run market behavior and to the broad, enduring characteristics of the price structure. They have no simple relationship to the short-run cost curves that determine the supply responses in short-run market adjustments. The short-run curves describe the costs of producing various levels of output in a given plant, whereas the long-run cost curves arise from considering the costs of producing specified outputs in plants of different size and design.[14] Long-run cost curves are the appropriate concept when possible new investments are being considered. Those decisions depend on envisaging probable levels of output and then planning the facilities that will operate at those levels as economically as possible.

If a firm's average costs in its current plant are higher than those that could be attained in a plant adapted to its current and prospective levels of output or, in other words, if its current average costs are higher than its long-run average costs at prospective output levels, then that firm is not in long-run equilibrium; it could increase its profits by altering its plant. How such a firm, or an industry made up of such firms, will respond depends on the shape of the long-run average-cost curve. Three cases have to be distinguished.

---

[14] It is not even true that the bottom of a short-run average-cost curve indicates the average cost of producing that output in a plant of most appropriate size. The plant whose lowest average cost occurs at 1,000 units a month is not necessarily the same as the plant that can produce 1,000 units a month most cheaply.

Constant Long-Run Costs

Constant long-run costs occur when the long-run average cost is the same at all levels of output except, perhaps, the very lowest. It is characteristic of many small- and medium-scale manufacturing industries where plant expansion takes the form of replicating existing facilities. A large cotton mill is very much like a small one, except that it has more spindles. If a small mill is being overloaded, expanding it will permit average costs to be reduced. But the average costs of the enlarged plant at its most efficient level of operation will be about the same as those of the smaller plant operating at its most efficient level. The common sense of this is that twice as many men using twice as many spindles with twice as much cotton can make twice as much thread—doubling output by doubling the amount of every input leaves average costs unchanged.

In an industry with constant long-run costs neither a small nor a large firm has any particular advantage. Such an industry tends to be made up of a large number of firms of varying size. When the industry expands, the established firms in it grow and it is easy for new firms, usually of small to middling size, to enter the industry and compete on equal terms with the old ones.

Figure 3–5 represents the relationship between the short-run and the long-run average-cost curves in a constant-cost industry. The long-run average cost is $15 a unit. Short-run average-cost curves are shown for a small, a medium-

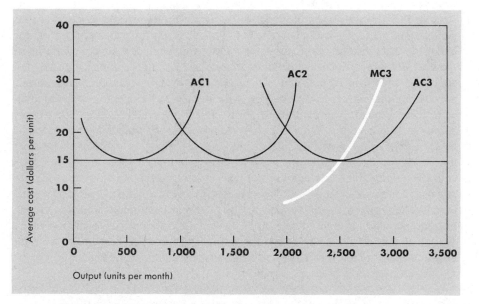

FIG. 3–5 Constant long-run cost curve. All levels of output can be produced at the same average cost by using plants of proper size.

sized, and a large firm, and the marginal-cost curve for the large firm is shown. The industry will be in long-run equilibrium if the price is $15, and at that price the small firm will be selling 500 units a month, the medium firm 1,500 units, and the large firm 2,500 units. Though their outputs would be different, each firm would be incurring the same average costs, all equal to the long-run average cost.

If the industry's demand curve should shift, say upward, the equilibrium will be disturbed. In the very first instance the firms would find themselves selling more at $15 a unit than before and their marginal costs would rise. This would induce an increase in the price and, in due course, a short-run equilibrium with a price above $15 and outputs on the rising portions of the average-cost curves.

Such a short-run equilibrium cannot endure very long. The firms will be encountering the bottlenecks and congestion problems we have described and will be under strong inducement to expand their plants until they can produce the larger output at an average cost of $15. But this will not restore the equilibrium. When the larger plants come into operation, the short-run industry supply curve will shift to the right, in accordance with the marginal-cost curves of the enlarged plants. A new short-run equilibrium will be established with a somewhat lower price and a somewhat higher output than had obtained before the plants expanded. At this new level of output the firms will again be encountering bottlenecks (though less severe than at first) and will be under a renewed incentive to expand.

In fact, the industry will not be in full equilibrium until the price has fallen to $15. The situation is depicted in Fig. 3–6. The industry demand curve, the long-run average-cost curve, and two short-run industry supply curves are shown. As long as the industry supply curve is like supply curve 1 in the diagram, the short-run equilibrium will require the firms to produce on the rising portions of their average-cost curves, which is an inducement to expand their plants. The industry will continue to grow until it has a supply curve like supply curve 2, which corresponds to an industry capacity sufficient to meet the demand evoked by a price equal to long-run average cost without overloading the plants.

Hence the long-run equilibrium of a constant-cost industry is at a price equal to long-run average cost and an output equal to the corresponding demand. The price will not be affected by the state of demand except to the extent that when the industry grows, it bids up the prices of some of its factors of production, thus raising the level of the average-cost line. The price of the products of such industries need not increase in the long run, even though the demand for their products grows.

Decreasing Long-Run Costs

In many manufacturing industries, in transportation, and in some other fields, the techniques used by a large firm are radically different from those

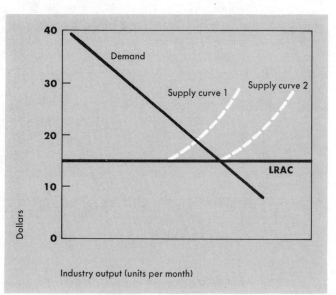

FIG. 3–6 Equilibrium of a constant cost industry. In equilibrium the price, long-run average cost, and marginal cost are all equal.

available to small enterprises. Automobile manufacture is a dramatic and famous example. Practically speaking, no small automobile manufacturers exist in the United States. They simply could not afford the expensive presses, special-purpose automatic machine tools, or automated assembly lines that the giant firms employ. Where there are real advantages of mass production, so that large plants with intricate machinery can undersell smaller ones, there are *decreasing long-run costs*.

The firm discussed in connection with Fig. 3–4 had mildly decreasing long-run costs. Figure 3–7 shows a more striking example. The curve labeled *AC*1 is the average-cost curve for a small plant that operates most efficiently at an output of 550 units when its average cost is $8 a unit. *AC*2 is the average-cost curve of a middle-sized plant that can produce 900 units a month at an average cost of $4.70. The third cost curve is for a large plant that can achieve average cost of $3 a unit for volume of 1,350 a month. The dashed line is the long-run average-cost curve. It shows, for example, that an output of 750 units a month can be produced most economically in a plant with average-cost curve *AC*2, where the cost will be $5 a unit.[15] Similarly every other point on this dashed curve shows the average cost of producing the stated output in the best possible plant for that output.

Large firms are the rule in decreasing-cost industries. Table 3–6, compiled by Professor Joe S. Bain, shows the situation in a number of industries. Notice

[15] A small paradox: The middle-sized plant is the best one for producing 750 a month (at $5 a unit), but it is not the best one for producing 850 a month, although its average costs there are lower (about $4.70). The best plant is the one, not shown, whose short-run average-cost curve touches the long-run curve at 850 a month.

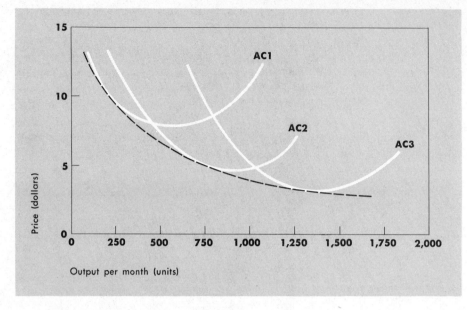

FIG. 3–7 Short-run and long-run cost curves for a decreasing-cost industry. Firms with large plants can sell at lower prices than smaller firms.

that in the gypsum, cigarette, and typewriter industries a single firm, to be fully efficient, must be large enough to supply a fifth or more of the entire national market. Such an industry therefore contains room for only a small number of large firms.

Table 3–6 PERCENTAGE OF MARKET SUPPLIED BY MINIMUM-SIZE EFFICIENT FIRM

Industry	Percentage
Gypsum products	22–33
Cigarettes	15–20
Typewriters	10–30
Tractors	10–15*
Copper	10
Steel	2–20
Soap	8–15
Automobiles	5–10*
Fountain pens	5–10
Rayon	4–6*
Canning, Petroleum refining, Flour, Distilled liquor, Metal containers, Farm machinery, Tires and tubes, Shoes, Meatpacking	3 or less

* Size of efficient plant; minimum efficient firm may be larger. (The minimum size required for a firm to be efficient is different in different industries, but as a rule the firm rarely is large enough to supply more than a minor share of the market.)

Source: Joe S. Bain, *Barriers to Competition* (Cambridge, Mass.: Harvard University Press, 1956), p. 86.

An actual long-run average-cost curve, for the cement industry, is shown in Fig. 3–8. Each dot shows average costs in some plants of similar size. Small plants, with outputs below 500 barrels a year, are 50 per cent more expensive, per unit of output, than the large plants, with outputs above 1,500 barrels a year. After that level the decrease in costs appears to level off, as indicated by the curve drawn through the empirical data. Thus, this is a decreasing-cost industry for small and middle-sized plants, and a constant-cost industry for larger sizes. This general behavior is quite typical.

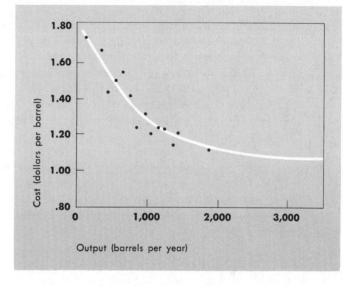

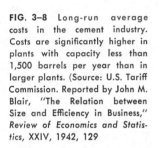

FIG. 3–8 Long-run average costs in the cement industry. Costs are significantly higher in plants with capacity less than 1,500 barrels per year than in larger plants. (Source: U.S. Tariff Commission. Reported by John M. Blair, "The Relation between Size and Efficiency in Business," *Review of Economics and Statistics,* XXIV, 1942, 129

The long-run adjustment process of a decreasing-cost industry would be similar to that described for a constant-cost industry if it were not for one feature: the smallness of the number of firms. When an industry comprises only a few firms it is an oligopoly and, as will be discussed more fully in Chapter 6, the members of an oligopoly do not follow their marginal-cost curves the way firms in a competitive industry do. If the demand for the product of such an industry should increase, the firms would, naturally, increase their output from their current plants and raise their prices. Their average costs would increase and this would stimulate plant expansion, just as in the constant-cost case. But here the similarity ceases. For when the new productive capacity comes into use, the oligopolists will not cut their prices in order to sell in accordance with their new marginal-cost curves; each one is too keenly aware that if he cuts his price, his competitors will follow suit. Instead they will retain the price that induced the new capacity, and sell a smaller output at a higher price than firms under competition would sell. Price will remain above long-run average cost, and the firms will retain oligopolistic profits.

The ability of oligopolists to maintain a price higher than long-run average costs is, however, limited by two considerations. The greater the discrepancy, the more tempting it will be for each firm to shade its price and enjoy the profits of larger sales. There are limits to mutual forbearance or even fear of retaliation, so that the "discipline" of the industry will break down if prices are being held very far above long-run costs.

The other restraining consideration is the prospect of invasion. No profitable industry, other than a legal monopoly, is secure from it because firms in other industries, large as well as small, are constantly on the lookout for profitable opportunities. For example, the Ford Motor Company and the Honeywell Manufacturing Company (which produces industrial control equipment) both invaded the electronic computing industry. Both the prospect and the reality of such formidable invasions moderate the cupidity of oligopolists.

Figure 3–9 shows the demand curve and the long-run average-cost curve for a decreasing-cost industry. If the firms behaved competitively, the industry would reach equilibrium at the price and output indicated by the crossing of the two curves, just as in the constant-cost case. But they do not. The growth process will be arrested at some price like p. Industry capacity will be adequate to produce q units a month at the lowest possible average cost. The "supply curve," in quotes, shows the quantity the industry would supply at various prices if it behaved competitively, that is, if each firm produced until its marginal costs were equal to the price. The stickiness of prices here indicated is characteristic of oligopolistic, decreasing-cost industries. It will be discussed further in Chapter 6.

Increasing Long-Run Costs: Rent

In some industries firms cannot acquire new facilities that are as productive as the ones already in use. Mining is a case in point. A mining firm can increase its rate of output by digging new shafts, but these are likely to be less rich or less easily worked than the ones already operating. Law firms encounter a similar obstacle. A successful law firm finds difficulty in growing because it cannot attract personnel of the high quality that originally distinguished it. And there are a considerable number of other such industries, typically in the agricultural, lumbering, and extractive sectors. In all of them the firms cannot expand their outputs, even by acquiring new facilities, without increasing their costs of production. The firms in these circumstances are said to experience *increasing long-run costs*.

The distinguishing characteristic of increasing-cost industries is that they rely on some resources or inputs whose units vary in quality, just as farmland, ore veins, or lawyers do. Such industries cannot be analyzed in the way that we have been following, by conceiving them to consist of a number of firms with fairly similar productive opportunities. Instead it is best to regard an increasing-cost industry as comprising a number of productive units of differing quality, which cannot be varied in size. An example of a productive unit would be a

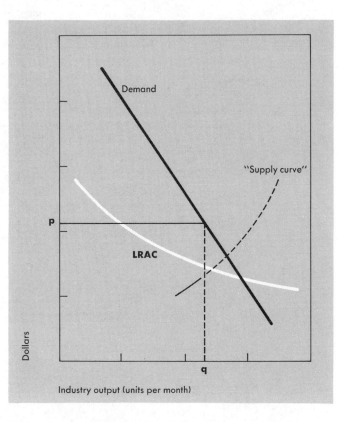

Demand

"Supply curve"

p

LRAC

Dollars

Industry output (units per month)

q

particular farm or a single mine shaft. A firm in the industry can own and operate one or several productive units. The analysis runs in terms of the outputs of productive units and the number of productive units employed in the industry rather than in terms of the outputs of entire firms.

Figure 3–10 shows the behavior of an increasing-cost industry in which only three productive units are available. For each productive unit the marginal-cost curve is shown and also a curve labeled AOC (for average operating cost), which is the same as the familiar average-cost curve. We shall see below why average operating costs have to be distinguished from average costs in this case. Notice that the best unit has lower average operating costs than either of the other two at all levels of output.

Each productive unit will be operated so that its marginal cost is equal to the market price. If the market price is p_1, the best unit will be used to produce x_1 units of output, the second best unit will produce x_2 units, and the worst unit will not be operated at all—it may not even exist—since that price is not high enough to cover the average operating costs of producing with it. The industry supply will be simply $x_1 + x_2$.

If the price should rise to p_2, the outputs of the best two units

69

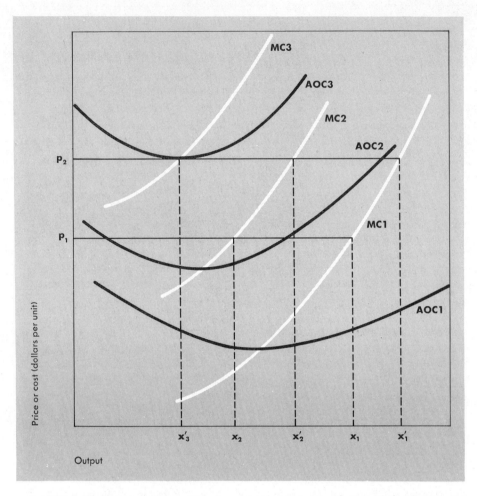

FIG. 3–10 Cost curves for an increasing cost industry. Each productive unit has its own cost curves, which cannot be altered.

would rise to x'_1 and x'_2. In addition, either a new firm would enter the industry or one of the old firms would acquire the worst productive unit and use it at level x'_3. Industry output would then be $x'_1 + x'_2 + x'_3$.

Now this is a highly simplified schematic example. In any real industry there would be far more than three productive units and the average operating-cost curves of units of neighboring quality would not be as dissimilar as those shown. But the industry supply curve would be generated in just the same way. As the price rose, productive units already in operation would expand their outputs according to their marginal-cost curves, and new productive units would be brought into the industry, by new firms or old, when the price became high enough to cover their average operating costs. The shape of the industry supply curve would depend on the number of productive units of each quality that were available in the economy.

Each productive unit has a supply curve, corresponding to the marginal-cost curve of producing on it. The whole industry has a supply curve that reflects, for each price, the output elicited from each productive unit by that price and the number of productive units of each quality that would be employed in the industry. The shape of the industry supply curve would depend on the marginal-cost curves of the productive units and on the number of productive units of each quality available in the economy. In contrast to what we found in the other two cases, this would be a normal-looking, upward-sloping curve, indicating that higher prices are necessary to elicit greater output and that no long-run adjustments are possible to reduce the cost of producing large outputs.

Increasing-cost industries differ from the other two types in some essential respects. In constant- and decreasing-cost industries all the firms are likely to enjoy roughly similar profits per unit of output and to expand their plants so as to have similar production costs along similar long-run cost curves. In increasing-cost industries, where the basic productive units are not expandable, each productive unit has its unique cost curve and unique profit margin for any market price. In Fig. 3–10, for example, when the price is p_2 the best productive unit is highly profitable, whereas the poorest is barely worth operating. An investor, therefore, would be willing to pay a good deal more for the high-quality resource that accounts for the profitability of the best unit than for the mediocre one that characterizes the worst unit. In technical terms, the high-quality resources would command a differential rent or differential value. That is why good farmland is more expensive than poor.

Now we have encountered an important and pervasive phenomenon: the value of productive resources or units whose qualities cannot be duplicated. Ricardo made this phenomenon one of the cornerstones of his theory of market prices in the early days of economics. His reasoning, in modern dress, was as follows. Suppose that the three productive units of Fig. 3–10 are farms and that the demand for their product is $x'_1 + x'_2 + x'_3$ when the price is p_2. Then all three farms will be operated, but the poorest one will not be valuable—in technical terms it will be a marginal farm, one that is barely worth cultivating because when the price is p_2 the operator of that farm will just be able to cover his operating costs without paying anything for the use of the farm. He could not afford to pay rent for its use, and if he were to buy it he would not earn any return on its purchase price.

But the other two farms would be valuable. The owner would be able to charge a rent equal to the difference between the price and the average cost of operation, multiplied by the volume of output. No farm operator could afford to pay more than that for the use of the good farm, but if the rent were lower the operator of the poorest farm would be better off hiring a good farm than working the marginal one, and he would bid the rent up in his effort to lease it.

Now, from the point of view of the farm operator, this rent is a component of fixed cost and therefore of average cost. That is the new ingredient that distinguishes average cost in an increasing-cost industry from the average operating cost, which includes only the familiar components of cost. When rents are included, average costs are pushed up, and unit profits down, until they are the same on the best land as on the poorest land in use.

Notice that it makes no difference (except to the farmer) whether he rents his land or owns it. If he rents the farm, his rental payments are clearly part of his cost of production. If he owns the farm, then he relinquishes the income he could obtain by renting it to someone else, and that is a cost to him. Notice, also, that the rents do not affect the supply curve and do not increase the market price, as other components of cost do. The good land commands a rent because the price is higher than the operating cost of producing on it; the price is not high because the rent has to be paid.[16] This remark dispels a common fallacy. It is not true, for example, that the prices charged in stores in the central business district are high because the desirable retail-stores sites are so expensive. On the contrary, the good sites are expensive because the stores located on them are so productive.

The phenomenon of rent also shows why farmers are so vulnerable to price fluctuations. They have purchased their farms, almost invariably with mortgages, at land prices that are predicated on current produce prices. When farm-product prices fall, they find themselves unable to meet the operating costs and mortgage payments that would have been reasonable at the higher prices. But rent does not attach to land alone. It is earned by all high-quality productive units or resources. Well-located urban properties, mineral deposits, entertainment stars, eminent lawyers, skilled executives are only a few examples of rent-commanding resources.

Overview of Long-Run Adjustments

The three types of cost curves lead to radically different behavior in the long run. Yet there are certain elements in common. The situation can be summarized by considering the long-run supply curves for the three cases, the supplies that would be offered at each price when the firms had had time to adapt their plants fully to demand at that price. Notice that this definition is a modification of the concept of a supply curve that was appropriate in short-run analysis. In the short-run the supply offered at any price depended only on the price itself and on the applicable cost curves. In the long-run the supply offered at any price depends also on the quantity demanded at that price because the quantity demanded influences decisions about plant expansion and contraction.

In constant-cost industries we found a very peculiar long-run supply curve. We found that an indefinitely large quantity will be offered at any price above long-run average costs, and none at lower prices. There was, therefore, no rea-

---

[16] Thus Ricardo concluded that the incomes of the landed gentry did not increase the price of the workingman's food. Nevertheless he deplored those unearned incomes. The only corrective he could see was, in effect, to increase the supply of good-quality land used to feed England, by reducing the impediments to food imports.

son for the price to rise or fall, in the long run, in response to changes in demand conditions. That conclusion is valid for most constant-cost industries but is subject to some amendment. Constant-cost industries prevail in the manufacturing sectors, and such industries obtain their raw materials from agricultural, lumbering, and mining industries where increasing costs are the rule. If a large constant-cost industry (for example, construction) increases its scale of operation, it is likely to bid up the prices of the raw materials that it purchases from increasing-cost industries. The long-run average-cost curves, as we constructed them, did not allow for possible increases in raw material and factor prices, but if they occur, they will impart an upward slope to the long-run average-cost curve and to the industry's supply curve. This complication does not arise in the case of comparatively small industries. The output of wooden toys could expand enormously without affecting the long-run average-cost curve, but the output of frame houses cannot.

The long-run supply curves in decreasing-cost industries are quite different, and they help explain why the price of a newly introduced plant (such as television sets) is likely to fall sharply during its early years. Look again in Fig. 3–9 and imagine a demand curve well to the left of the one drawn there. It would intersect the long-run average-cost curve at a much higher cost and smaller quantity. This means that the industry would attain equilibrium with smaller and higher-cost plants (because demand was not sufficient to justify the fixed costs of large, efficient plants) and perhaps fewer of them. Generalizing from this, the amount that the industry offers depends not only on the price but on the position of the demand curve. If demand grows, the price will fall—for a while at least. Eventually, of course, all the advantages of large-scale production will be enjoyed and the industry may bid up the prices of its raw materials.

The supply curve of an increasing-cost industry is, as we noted, normal and upward sloping throughout its range.

The common thread in all these cases is the response of industry capacity to demand conditions and the close tie (even in oligopolistic industries) between the price and long-run average costs. In every case the industry adjusts its plant so as to be able to produce its equilibrium output at the lowest possible average cost, and this cost governs the equilibrium price. This is most striking in constant-cost industries, where the price may not vary at all in response to changes in equilibrium output but holds in all the cases.

An unimportant instance will illustrate the strong gravitational pull of long-run costs. When ball point pens were first introduced, the Reynolds Pen Company, relying on a patent that proved to be shaky, priced them at $15, which was at least ten times their long-run production cost. This wide discrepancy was too attractive to be resisted. Other firms entered, the patent was challenged, and in scarcely a year the price was down to $2.50 and falling rapidly. The worst intentions in the world seem unable to preserve a wide discrepancy between production costs and prices for very long.

THE CONCEPT OF COST

We began this analysis of cost and supply curves by adopting the accountants' definition of costs. But as the analysis proceeded we became increasingly uncomfortable about that definition, and little by little we departed from it. We saw, in agreement with the accountants, that many business costs correspond to payments incurred for the use of various factors of production—labor, raw materials, power, and the like. But we saw also that some disbursements do not correspond to costs, as when a long-lived asset is acquired, and that many components of production cost do not give rise to explicit payments. Depreciation expense was of that sort, and also interest on the firm's own capital, rent for the premises it owns, and, often, the time and labor of the firm's owners.

A firm's books of account record its monetary expenditures and receipts plus a conventional allowance for depreciation. Now we are aware that these sums are not the same as the costs that it has incurred, and that it can be misleading to interpret them as a measure of costs or to use them as a basis for business decisions.

But if we cannot accept the accountants' practical definition of costs, what definition can we accept? A single standard has been implicit in all our analyses: it is the sum that would have been available for other purposes if the production had not been undertaken. Out-of-pocket expenses are clearly part of cost by this standard. So are the interest on own capital used in production, rents on owned land, and the value of the time and labor of proprietors.

Depreciation expense is a little more subtle. We defined it to be the amount that has to be put aside each year to have a fund sufficient to replace the asset on its retirement date. To see that this conforms to our standard, consider an asset that is financed entirely by borrowing. Then the purchase does not initially preclude any expenditures for other purchases, but it does require periodic provision for ultimate repayment of the loan, and in just the amount of the depreciation expense. If the asset had not been purchased (or if it never wore out), those funds would have been freed for other purposes. So depreciation expense, too, measures the reduction in the firm's unobligated resources entailed by acquiring an asset for production.

This standard is known as the *opportunity-cost* or *alternative-cost* principle. This principle holds that the economic cost of producing anything is the most highly desired other goods and services that could have been produced with the resources that the production absorbs. At first glance, it seems peculiar and circular to say that the cost of a television set consists of the radios that could have been produced with the same resources, but in truth we habitually recognize that cost is merely a synonym for sacrifice, as when we say, "Swete is love of damosele; ac hit askith costes feole." In monetary terms the opportunity cost of producing anything is the value of the resources that it absorbs, because that value reflects the usefulness of those resources in other employments.

A simple example may emphasize how misleading it can be to deviate from this concept of cost. Suppose that a truck farmer sells his produce for $2,000 a month more than the total of his cash expenses and reasonable depreciation on his farm equipment. Suppose also that he could lease his farm to a suburban developer for $1,500 a month and take a job as a produce buyer for $1,000 a month. Is his farm profitable? His books of account would show that he is making a good living from the farm, but in fact he is losing $500 a month by farming, since he could increase his income by that much if he rented out the farm and took the job. All things considered, he may prefer farming, but he is paying $500 a month for the privilege.

Now this farmer is not a rare fellow. Every firm has its own funds invested, funds that could be loaned out at interest, or otherwise used to produce income for the owners, if the money weren't tied up in the business. Those funds are just like the farmer's land, and the income that they could earn, if not used in the business, is part of the cost of operating the business. But accountants don't include this forgone income in their books, because it is invisible.[17]

In unincorporated businesses, the wages of the owners are not included among the bookkeepers' records of expenses. The fact is that they are every bit as much expenses as are the wages paid to the employees. If the owner did not attend to his business, he could earn wages by working for some other firm. These forgone wages are a reduction in his income just as truly as the wages he pays to his employees. All these invisible expenses, and others like them, are included in the concept of opportunity cost.

All this discussion of costs may strike you as being excessively business-like. After all, the economist's job is not to tell businessmen how to make money, but among other things, to tell an economy how to make socially useful products and distribute them equitably. The point of this concern with profitable business operation is twofold. First, as a matter of description and prediction, if we understand how businessmen should act in order to make profits, we have a first approximation to how they will act. Second, from the viewpoint of economic policy, to the extent that businessmen use resources profitably they also use them efficiently to produce the things that consumers want and are willing to pay for. We shall see in the last chapter that there are some differences between sound business accounting and economic accounting, but fundamentally they are the same.

[17] This quirk of accounting has an implication for tax policy. When a firm borrows money to invest in its business, the interest on the loan is a tax-deductible expense. When it invests its own or stockholders' money, no tax deduction is permitted for forgone interest. This presents firms with an incentive to invest with borrowed funds instead of with their own capital.

SOCIAL IMPLICATIONS

Let us set aside for the present the possibility that some of the industries in an economy may operate under conditions of decreasing costs, or may be not competitive for some other reason. Then the main results of this chapter can be expressed as two propositions:

1. In the short run, the price of every commodity and the marginal cost of producing it tend to be equal.
2. In the long run (to which the above proposition also applies) every industry tends to have the stock of plant and equipment that makes the average cost of producing its output as low as possible.

These two conclusions are of the utmost importance because of what they indicate about the allocation of the economy's resources among its industries and commodities.

An economy can be visualized as a vast workshop in which all commodities are produced and in which a great pool of resources is allocated among all the tasks of production. When the two conditions stated above are satisfied, this work is being organized as efficiently as possible—that is, the economy is obtaining the largest flow of commodities that can be obtained with the use of its resources. This is seen most clearly by considering the division of resources between two commodities that are not too dissimilar in their resource requirements. Let us consider automobiles and typewriters, both of which use steel, labor, power, and a large number of other inputs. In short-run equilibrium, the marginal cost of producing either will be equal to its price. Recall that the marginal cost of producing anything is the cost of producing one more unit with the given fixed plant, so that it consists entirely of the costs of the steel, labor, and other variable inputs needed for a unit increase in output. This means, for present purposes, that an automobile selling for $3,000 will require $3,000 worth of these variable inputs.

Now suppose that by the mandate of some high authority the production of automobiles were cut back by one unit and that the variable inputs that would have been used to make that automobile were transferred to the typewriter industry. Then, if a typewriter is priced at $300, those resources would suffice for producing ten typewriters at most.[18] This is true because if $3,000 worth of additional resources could be used to produce *more* than ten typewriters, the marginal cost of a typewriter would be *less* than $300. This transfer could not, then, increase the value of the goods in the economy. By the same argument, the same is true for a transfer of resources between any other pair of industries.

What's so good about that? Well, the price that an individual is willing to

[18] We say at most because the resources released by the automobile industry would probably not be just the kind that can be used to manufacture typewriters most efficiently.

pay for a commodity is a measure of its importance or desirability to him. (Although common sense alone tells us this, we shall look into the matter further in Chapter 5.) In a somewhat looser way, the prices of different commodities also measure their social importance, even when they are not all purchased by the same individual. (This is discussed more thoroughly in Chapter 7.) So if it were possible to transfer resources between a pair of industries in such a way that the increase in the output of the receiving industry was valued more highly than the decrease in the output of the donating industry, then that transfer would be socially beneficial. And if no such transfer is possible, then the economy's resources are already distributed among industries in the most efficient manner.

That is the social implication of the first proposition. It tells us that the forces of competition lead to an optimal distribution of variable resources in the short run. It is important to note that to arrive at this conclusion we have had to exclude the possibility of decreasing-cost industries, in which competition is likely to break down.

Now we turn to the significance of the second proposition. Let us remain in the short-run framework and suppose that in the automobile industry the plant is the correct one for producing at lowest possible average cost, but that in the typewriter industry the plant is smaller than it should be. This would indicate that somewhere along the line a mistake has been made in the direction of investment; a mistake, that is, from the social point of view.

We argue as follows. When the plant in an industry is such that average costs could not be reduced by changing its size, then the decrease in variable costs that would be permitted by a small investment in that industry would be just counterbalanced by the increase in fixed costs. Suppose, for example, that investment in the automobile industry had been $100,000 smaller than it was. The cost of the capital invested in an industry does not enter directly into the total cost of a year's operation or the average cost of a unit of its output. What enters directly is depreciation of the machinery, interest on the capital tied up, insurance, and similar expenses of maintaining and using fixed assets. Say that these come to $25,000 a year on the $100,000 investment. Then if the investment had not been made, these fixed costs would not have been incurred, and the variable expenses in the automobile industry would have been $25,000 a year greater than they are with the investment, since, by assumption, total costs cannot be reduced below their current level.

Now let us again turn to the typewriter industry, in which we assume that average costs can be reduced by additional investment. If the $100,000 investment had been made in the typewriter industry, variable costs in that industry, at the same level of output, would fall by more than $25,000 in comparison with their level without the investment. That is where the mistake lies. If the $100,000 had been invested in typewriters instead of in automobiles, the society could have the same number of typewriters and of automobiles as under the assumed circumstances, with a smaller expenditure of variable resources in the two industries together. The resources so saved could be used to increase the output of typewriters, of automobiles, or of some third commodity.

This argument is of course perfectly general, because although it is especially easy to visualize the transfer of resources between two ferrous metal-fabricating industries such as typewriters and automobiles, the common pool of resources in an economy is so flexible in the long run that such shifts can be made between practically *any* pair of industries if the transfers are socially beneficial. But the second proposition, you will recall, asserts that competition leads to an allocation of investment among industries that does not permit any socially beneficial reallocation. Thus the automatic, competitive direction of investment is in the social interest.

Let us be careful not to claim too much, because we have not by any means covered all aspects in our discussion. We have neglected, for instance, the impact of decreasing long-run costs (though we shall go into that in Chapter 6). We have neglected some other things of importance, too. The trickiest, perhaps, is that market prices are often not a true reflection of social costs. For example, the automobile would cost society more than the $3,000 shown by the manufacturer's average cost curve if the waste from the paint shop polluted a river and forced someone else to devote resources to cleaning it up.

But, postponing such questions, we have found that competitive inducements guide investment so as to make average costs in all industries as low as possible when those industries are using established techniques and confronting fixed demand curves. But demand curves are always changing, not only fortuitously but also systematically as population grows and the economy becomes more wealthy. Techniques of production are always changing, too, and so are the supply curves of the ultimate resources of production—labor, crude fuels, metallic ores, and the like. And the allocation of capital that is ideal for any one set of conditions will soon become obsolete and inappropriate. All we can conclude so far about investments (our analysis did not deal with the efficiency of investment in the dynamic context that actually exists) is that competitively guided investment will not be far from appropriate if conditions are not changing too rapidly.

In point of fact, businessmen have more wisdom (business acumen) than our simplified analysis gives them credit for. Certainly the considerations of immediate profitability that we have analyzed weigh heavily in their decisions, but, being forward looking, they also take account of changes that they see imminent. We certainly cannot claim that businessmen's decisions are invariably ideal when they are caught up in a dynamic business context, but they are likely to be as sound as is humanly possible. In view of the limited ability of even shrewd businessmen to foresee the future, it seems unlikely that any other system for directing investments could perform better.

Some other necessary qualifications to the conclusions of this section will be pointed out in Chapter 7.

SUMMARY

The material in this chapter can be divided into two broad topics: short-run behavior of firms and industries (that is, decisions in which firms' plant, equipment, and central management are regarded as unchangeable) and long-run behavior. In the short run the firm's crucial decision is the price to charge for its product; in the long run it is the size and type of plant to build and maintain.

Businessmen and accountants appraise a firm's performance by means of rather elaborate accounts, particularly the income statement and the statement of operating costs. Economists view the firm rather differently. They simplify the accounts by classifying all the components of cost into two broad groups, fixed costs and variable costs. And they focus attention on the effect of different possible decisions on the firm's revenues and these categories of cost. Thus the analysis depends heavily on the response of fixed and variable costs to changes in the level of output (in the short run) and in plant (in the long run). These changes are shown by the various cost curves.

In the short run, fixed costs do not vary. Average costs are high for very low levels of output, decline for a while, and then rise again at high levels of output that press hard on the productive capacity of the plant. The active component is marginal cost; the most profitable level of output for any price is the level for which marginal cost is equal to that price. So the marginal cost curve is also the firm's supply curve, except for prices that are too low to justify any production at all. The industry's supply curve is the sum of the supply curves of the firms in the industry.

If the market price for a competitive industry is such that each firm can sell approximately the corresponding amount on its supply curve—so that it is about equal to marginal cost for all the firms in the industry—no firm has much incentive to change its price, and the industry is in short-run equilibrium. This is simultaneously a profitable state of affairs for the firms and an efficient utilization of resources from the social point of view. If this condition is not met, some firms are either making sales on which they lose money or else failing to make sales that would be very profitable. In either case, firms are under strong incentives to change their prices in the direction of the equilibrium price.

Turning to the long run, firms invest in expanding their plant when the saving in variable cost at anticipated levels of output is greater than the increase in fixed cost that the expansion entails. The increase in fixed cost consists largely of interest on the capital required for the new investment and depreciation charges that enable the firm to recover this capital at the end of the plant's useful life.

Long-run behavior of an industry depends on the shape of its long-run average cost curve. In a constant-cost industry, competition is likely to prevail, and the price of the product does not vary with the output except to the extent that the industry bids up the (long-run) price of its raw materials when it grows. In a decreasing-cost industry, a few large firms are likely to dominate the market. Nevertheless, the price will tend to reflect the economies of large-scale production. In an increasing-cost industry, increases in demand will engender increases in price even in the long run, and favorably situated units of production will receive rents. In all cases, resources will tend to flow to the industries whose products consumers value most highly.

MAIN CONCEPTS INTRODUCED

The principal concepts in this chapter relate to the idea of cost in its manifold aspects. Costs may be fixed or variable, total or marginal or average, or short-run or long-run, all in various combinations. The main variants are:

COST OR TOTAL COST. The value of the resources consumed in producing a given amount of output. Best measured by the value of the most valuable alternative commodities that could have been produced by those resources. When measured in this way called OPPORTUNITY COST.

MARGINAL COST. The increase in cost that would be required to increase the volume of output by one unit.

AVERAGE COST or UNIT COST. Total cost divided by the volume of output.

FIXED COST. The sum of those components of total cost that do not vary appreciably with temporary fluctuations in the volume of output. AVERAGE FIXED COST is fixed cost divided by the level of output. MARGINAL FIXED COST is zero by definition; therefore, this concept is never used.

VARIABLE COST. The sum of those components of total cost that change significantly when the level of output changes. MARGINAL VARIABLE COST and AVERAGE VARIABLE COST are defined analogously with marginal and average cost. Marginal variable cost always equals marginal cost.

LONG-RUN COST. The long-run cost of producing any level of output is the total cost of producing it in the plant that is most economical for that level. LONG-RUN MARGINAL COST and LONG-RUN AVERAGE COST are defined correspondingly. Thus LONG-RUN MARGINAL COST is the increase in long-run cost that would result from increasing the steady level of output by one unit, enlarging the plant appropriately to do so.

SHORT-RUN COST. Same as cost as defined above. Used in some contexts to emphasize distinction from long-run costs. SHORT-RUN MARGINAL COST and SHORT-RUN AVERAGE COST correspond to it.

RENT. Payment for the use of irreproducible resources. Occurs particularly in increasing-cost industries.

DEPRECIATION. An annual charge for the use of fixed plant and equipment, calculated so that the charges accumulated over the plant's useful life, with allowance for interest, add up to the cost of the plant.

SINKING FUND. The sinking fund at any date is the sum of the depreciation charges accumulated at interest up to that date. When the plant is retired, the sinking fund equals its cost less its salvage value.

APPENDIX: RELATIONS AMONG THE COST CURVES

The three cost curves introduced in this chapter describe the same physical data and are therefore related mathematically. Let $TC(x)$ be the total cost of producing output x in a certain firm with a given plant. Then the average cost of output x, $AC(x)$, is defined as *the total cost divided by the amount produced,* or

$$AC(x) = \frac{TC(x)}{x} \tag{1}$$

Marginal cost, $MC(x)$, is defined, precisely enough for our purposes, as *the increase in total cost imposed by a unit increase in output.* Therefore:

$$MC(x) = TC(x+1) - TC(x)$$

Making use of equation (1) we can also write:

$$MC(x) = (x+1)AC(x+1) - xAC(x)$$
$$= x[AC(x+1) - AC(x)] + AC(x+1)$$

Hence:

$$AC(x+1) - AC(x) = \frac{MC(x) - AC(x+1)}{x}$$

Suppose now that output x lies in the range in which average costs are falling. Then the left-hand side of this equation is negative, implying also

$$MC(x) < AC(x+1) < AC(x)$$

In words: If average costs are falling, then marginal costs are less than average costs.

By similar reasoning, if average costs are rising, making the left-hand side positive, $MC(x) > AC(x+1) > AC(x)$. Thus, average costs rise when and only when marginal costs are above average costs.

Finally, from the facts that average costs are above marginal costs when average costs are falling, and average costs are below marginal costs when average costs are rising, it follows that the two curves must cross where the average-cost curve bottoms out—that is, where average costs are at their minimum.

Behind the Cost Curves:

Production Choices and Costs

CHAPTER FOUR

We have just seen that the cost of producing a given quantity of a commodity depends upon the plant in which it is produced. It may be turned out in a small plant with low fixed costs and a great deal of handwork, or alternatively in a large, mechanized plant with high fixed costs and a small amount of labor. In the long run, when the firm can choose its plant, it will select the one in which production costs are lowest.

This choice between incurring fixed and variable costs is one instance of a problem that businessmen constantly face: how to produce their products as cheaply as possible. They search incessantly for economical methods of operation. This search results, of course, in efficient operation of their plants. But it also has two other consequences, which will be explained in this chapter. One result is the efficient distribution of labor and other resources among plants and industries (which is not the same thing as their efficient utilization within plants). The other is an impact, on the markets for labor and other resources, which helps determine wages and the prices that resources command. This chapter is devoted to the consequences of businessmen's searches for the cheapest methods of production. But first, we must describe the search.

FINDING THE CHEAPEST METHOD:
AN EXAMPLE

Because every branch of production is based on some specialized technique, examples of production choices that are not entangled in technicalities are rare. But one class of production problem is so frequent and important that it has a name, and it isn't very technical. This is the "lot-size problem," and we choose it as our illustration.

The issue is this: most manufacturing processes are carried out in "lots" or "batches" in which a number of identical articles are produced, after which the machinery used is cleaned up, readjusted, and prepared for the manufacture of something else. For example, a paint manufacturer will mix a certain number of gallons of one color, then clean his vats and use them to mix another color. Or a steel-rolling mill will produce a certain number of tons of one thickness, then stop, be readjusted, and be used for steel of a different gauge. This is the most common mode of operation in manufacturing.

Setting up equipment for a particular job is expensive, so it is desirable to produce a large lot once the machinery is prepared. On the other hand, storing things is expensive, so it is desirable to produce small lots frequently, in order to avoid having to store a large stock. The lot-size problem is the problem of finding the best resolution of these conflicting considerations.

To be specific, suppose that an electronic firm requires 500 chassis of a certain type each year (as a component for its final product) and that each chassis stored requires a square foot of storage space renting for $2.50 a year. If the chassis are produced in two lots of 250 each, the firm will have to rent storage space for 250 chassis, at a cost of $625 a year. Suppose that to set up the drills for manufacturing a lot of chassis (that is, a batch of 250) requires ten hours of skilled labor costing $5 an hour, or $50 for each batch. Then, the setup and storage costs for two batches a year would amount to $625 + $100 = $725. The cost of materials, manufacturing labor, and so forth are irrelevant for this problem, since they are the same for 500 chassis irrespective of the number of batches into which they are divided.

Another possible choice is to make ten lots of 50 chassis each. Then, storage space for only 50 chassis would be needed, costing $125, but there would be ten setups, costing $500. The total cost for this choice would be $625. Clearly this is better than manufacturing two batches, but is it the best possible decision?

We analyze this problem by means of a convenient and flexible scheme.[1] Two resources are involved here: storage space and skilled labor. The amounts used can be represented in a graph (like Fig. 4–1), wherein the amount of labor is plotted vertically and the amount of storage space horizontally. Each point in the diagram represents a certain pair of amounts of the two factors. For example, point A represents 20 hours of labor and 250 square feet of storage space; point B represents 150 hours of labor and 40 square feet of storage.

Now, the desired 500 chassis can be produced by using 20 hours of labor and 250 square feet of storage space, or 100 hours of labor and 50 square feet

[1] Actually, this is not the best method for solving this particular problem, but it is the most instructive for the purpose of economic analysis.

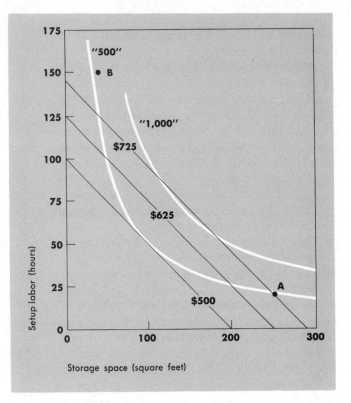

FIG. 4–1 Isoquant diagram for the lot-size problem. Two isoquants and three isocost lines are shown. The solution occurs where an isoquant touches an isocost line.

of storage, or any of many other combinations.[2] The curve labeled "500" passes through all the combinations that just suffice for producing 500 chassis. Point *A* lies on this curve; point *B,* whose quantities are sufficient for 600 chassis, lies above it.

Such a curve is known as an *isoquant* (from the Greek *iso* = equal, and *quantus* = how much). An isoquant for a given level of output is a specification of all the combinations of factors of production that are just adequate for producing that output.

An isoquant exists and can be drawn for every level of output. Two are shown in Fig. 4–1: the one for 500 chassis a year and the one for 1,000. Each isoquant displays graphically all the combinations of storage space and setup labor that can produce the specified output but no more. Our problem is to find the cheapest combination on the isoquant for 500 units.

Each point on the diagram has a certain cost of attainment. For example, point *A* costs $725: $100 for 20 hours of labor, plus $625 for 250 square feet of space. We can connect all the points that cost $725; this is done in the dia-

[2] In fact, any combination will do for which number of square feet $\times$ hours of labor = 5,000.

gram by the line labeled $725. Such a line is an *isocost line*. An isocost line shows all combinations of factors of production that cost the same amount in toto.

The isocost lines have a very easy formula. The equation for the isocost line for $725 is

$$2.5X + 5Y = 725$$

where X is the number of square feet of storage space and Y is the number of hours of setup labor. (Where does the 2.5 come from?) Similarly, the isocost line for any other level of cost will have the formula

$$2.5X + 5Y = \text{cost.}$$

Because the coefficients on the left-hand side are the same for all isocost lines, they form a family of parallel lines. Three are shown, and their costs are indicated.

The problem is solved by finding the lowest isocost line—that is, the lowest member of this family—that touches the isoquant for 500 units. This turns out to be the isocost line for $500 (look at the graph), which just touches the isoquant at the point representing 50 hours of labor and 100 square feet of storage space. Thus we have found the cheapest production plan and its cost.

This example, incidentally, throws additional light on why average costs fall as volume grows, until the plant becomes congested. With a little arithmetic (such as solving the same problem for a use rate of 1,000 a year) you can see that the setup plus storage costs per unit produced diminish as the use rate grows. (We found them to be $1 per unit for a use rate of 500 a year; they are about 71 cents for a use rate of 1,000 a year.) This contributes to the declining trend in average costs at low levels of output for all commodities produced in batches.

IMPLICATIONS OF THE SOLUTION

The batch-size problem, simple though it is, illustrates some of the most fundamental characteristics of production. Everything that is produced requires the use of some inputs, or factors of production. If we know the technology of production and the amounts of the different factors available, we can compute the greatest amount of the product that can be made. But we cannot reason so sharply in the other direction: if we know the quantity of the product to be manufactured and the technology, we still cannot compute unambiguously the amounts of the different factors that are required, because any volume of output can be produced in numerous ways, each requiring a different combination of inputs. The variety of ways for producing each level of output is specified by the corresponding isoquant.

The method that will be chosen for producing any level of output is the cheapest method on its isoquant. This depends on the shape of the isoquant (that is, the technology of production) and the prices of the different factors of production—in general, just as in our example. These considerations provide a clearer insight into the origin of the cost curves used in the last chapter. Suppose, for simplicity, that only two factors are involved, though in general there will be many more than that. There is an isoquant corresponding to every level of output. Each point on that isoquant specifies a quantity of factor 1, say x, and a quantity of factor 2, say y, that together will just suffice to produce that amount of output. If the prices of the two factors are p_1 and p_2, the cost of producing the output by that method will be $p_1x + p_2y$. This cost can be calculated for as many points on the isoquant as desired, and by trial and error, or by graphical methods, or by algebra the cheapest x, y combination on that isoquant can be found and also the corresponding cost. The result is the total cost of producing that output, and if we divide it by the volume, we get the average cost.

In Chapter 3 we presumed that this computation had been performed for every possible output, and graphed to give the average-cost curves used there. Because the lowest achievable cost had been found for each output, the average cost for each output was an unambiguous number, although, in fact, each output could be produced by a variety of different factor combinations.

In summary, the average cost of producing any output in a given plant is the unit cost of producing it when the cheapest possible combination of factors is used. This cheapest combination can be found neither from the isoquant diagram or by some other method. Naturally, the cheapest combination and the average cost will change if either the technique of production or the price of any of the factors changes.

In the batch-size problem the choice that ultimately determined the quantities of the two inputs took the form of deciding on the sizes and frequency of the production batches. In other circumstances the details of the choice are very different. One additional example will help to indicate the variety of possibilities. In cutting cloth for clothing manufacture, the major factors of production used are cloth and cutters' labor. The critical man in the process is the patternmaker—his task is to arrange the pieces into which a bolt of cloth is to be cut so that the job can be done as cheaply as possible. If inexpensive cloth is being used, he arranges the patterns loosely so that the cutters can work quickly. If the cloth is expensive, he places the pattern pieces tightly together to reduce the amount of cloth wasted as trim and scraps. In the latter case the cutters have to work more slowly and carefully, but they use less cloth per garment. (An extreme instance of this tradeoff between care and material occurs in diamond cutting, where days of planning may be lavished on a single uncut stone to make sure that as little as possible is wasted.)

Figure 4–2 illustrates how businessmen adapt their methods of production to the prices of the different factors that they use. Offhand, there would not seem to be much room for choice between using electricity and gas as a source of industrial heat and power, and there isn't much scope once a plant has been constructed. But before a plant is constructed, and particularly before its location has been determined, there is opportunity to take the relative costs of gas and electricity into account in planning methods of production. The diagram shows how responsive businessmen are to such price considerations. Each dot in the diagram represents a state. The ratio of the price of a therm (100,000 BTU's) of gas to the price of a kilowatt-hour of electricity is plotted vertically; the ratio of the amount of gas used by industrial firms to their purchases of electric power is plotted horizontally. For example, the dot in the upper left-hand corner represents a state where a therm costs about 20 times as much as a kilowatt-hour. Industrial firms in that state use a miniscule amount of gas—perhaps 1 per cent as much gas as electricity. At the other extreme there is a state where a therm costs only twice as much as a kilowatt-hour. The firms in that state use slightly more gas than electric power. The dots between the two extremes show the general tendency that we should expect: broadly speaking, the lower the ratio of gas to electric prices, the higher the ratio of gas to electric usage.

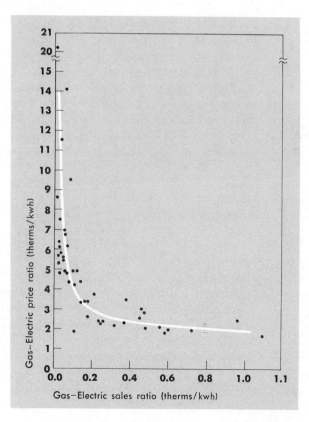

FIG. 4–2 Industrial use of gas and electric power, by states, 1961. Firms use more gas in proportion to electricity in states where the price of gas is lower relative to the price of electric power. (Source: J. R. Felton, "Competition in the Energy Market between Gas and Electricity," *Nebraska Journal of Economics and Business*, 4 (Autumn 1965), 7.

SUBSTITUTION AND FACTOR PRICES

We have seen that the best way to produce a given output depends on the prices of the factors used, for these prices determine the isocost lines. Now we want to look more closely at the relationship between the factor prices and the choice of input combination. The batch-size problem will bring out this relationship if we approach it from a slightly different point of view, namely the marginal analysis that we applied in the last chapter.

Consider again the decision to manufacture two lots of 250 chassis each, the plan requiring 20 hours of setup labor a year and 250 square feet of storage space. But now, instead of opening the field up wide, we compare that plan with others that are not very different, for example, producing 2½ batches per year [3] of 200 units each. This plan also would satisfy a demand for 500 chassis a year, but it would reduce the requirement for storage space to 200 square feet and would increase the amount of setup labor to 25 hours a year. We concentrate now on these changes in factor requirements and designate them by the Greek letter delta, Δ.[4] If S stands for the amount of storage space used and L for the amount of labor, the change from 2 lots a year to 2½ results in $\Delta S = -50$ square feet and $\Delta L = 5$ hours of setup labor. The practical effect of the change is to substitute ΔL hours of setup labor for ΔS square feet of storage space, without affecting the rate of output.

The possibility of such substitutions of dissimilar factors of production is the key to keeping production costs down. It is expressed in general by the *marginal rate of substitution* of one factor for another, abbreviated *MRS*. Formally: the marginal rate of substitution of factor X for factor Y, written $MRS(X:Y)$, is the number of units of factor X needed to replace one unit of factor Y with the rate of output remaining the same. As a formula

$$MRS(X:Y) = -\frac{\Delta X}{\Delta Y}.$$

We have found

$$MRS(L:S) = -\frac{\Delta L}{\Delta S} = \frac{5}{50} = \frac{1}{10}$$

when 20 hours of labor and 250 square feet of storage are being used.[5] Though this substitution does not affect the rate of output it does affect the cost. Saving 50 square feet of storage space saves $125, while adding 5 hours of setup labor costs $25, for a net saving of $100. Clearly, the plan of making two batches a year is far from economical.

---

[3] There is no reason to restrict ourselves to round numbers. Two and one-half batches a year (of 200 chassis each) is the same as five batches in two years, and can support a use rate of 500 a year.

[4] $\triangle$ is used frequently in economics, as in mathematics, to denote a finite change in some quantity.

[5] Our result is only approximate because the curvature of the isoquant introduces some error. The smaller the changes considered, the more accurate the approximation.

The general principle at work here is that costs can always be reduced if the *MRS* at the combination selected is not equal to the ratio of the prices of the factors. This is easy to see. Suppose that the prices are p_x and p_y. A substitution that does not change the output consists of reducing the use of factor Y by one unit (saving p_y) and increasing the use of factor X by $MRS(X : Y) = \Delta X/\Delta Y = X/1 = \Delta X$ units, which will cost $p_x \Delta X$. The net result will be to reduce cost if the saving in expenditures on factor Y, or p_y, is greater than the offsetting increase in expenditures on factor X, amounting to $p_x \Delta X$. Indeed, the net saving will be $p_y - p_x \Delta X$.

If this net saving is positive, then the use of factor Y should be reduced by one unit, at least, and the requisite number of units of factor X should be substituted for it. On the other hand, if the net saving is negative, costs can be reduced by increasing the use of factor Y and cutting back on the use of factor X. The only time when costs cannot be reduced is when the net saving is zero, or, equivalently, when

$$\frac{p_y}{p_x} = MRS(X : Y).$$

This equation, then, specifies the relationship between the prices of the factors and the marginal rate of substitution between them when the most economical combination is being used. We have arrived at an important general principle: When the cost-minimizing combination of factors is used, the *MRS* of any pair of factors is equal to the ratio of their prices.

You can check this, if you like, by computing the *MRS* (storage : labor) at the cost-minimizing combination (50 hours, 100 square feet), but it is more instructive to confirm it graphically. Graphically, the kind of substitution we are considering consists in moving from one point to another on the isoquant for 500 units, since none of these substitutions changes the output. The *MRS* is the ratio of the changes in the quantities of the two factors; in other words it is the slope of the chord connecting the combinations before and after the change. For very small changes this chord is to all intents and purposes the tangent to the isoquant, and it is best to think of it as such. Thus the slope of the isoquant at any point is the graphic representation of the *MRS* there.

But the price ratio is the slope of the isocost line, and this also is easily seen. Suppose, as before, that the prices are p_x, p_y. If the firm buys one unit less of factor Y, it will have p_y more to spend on factor X without changing its total expenditure on the two factors. This amount will buy p_y/p_x units of factor X. The isocost line then moves p_y/p_x units to the right whenever it moves one unit down, and this is its slope.

So when the *MRS* is equal to the price ratio, the isoquant has the same slope as the isocost lines. We can now rephrase our conclusion to say: The cost-minimizing combination of factors for any output is given by the point on the isoquant for that output at which the slope is equal to the slope of the isocost lines. At this point an isocost line will be tangent to the isoquant.

Figure 4–1 shows that this relationship holds for the lot-size problem. This problem, or any other one of the same type, can be solved by following the isoquant until we find the point at which it has the proper slope.

Businessmen, of course, do not follow isoquants, or even draw them. But they do, by their own devices, strive to minimize their costs of production. When they do so, no matter how, they arrive at a combination at which the relationships deduced in this chapter hold—at least approximately. That is why we are interested in these relationships.

THE "LAW OF DIMINISHING RETURNS"

Our whole argument and its conclusions depended heavily on the shape of the isoquant that we deduced for a very special problem. In particular they depended on the fact that the isoquant curved up so that its tangents lay below it. (Why was this important? Where would the cost-minimizing point be if the isoquants had a different shape?) In mathematical language, we found that the isoquants were *convex*.

Granting that the isoquants for the lot-size problem are convex, can we rely on finding that same property in general? There is no general principle that says we can. Whether the isoquants pertaining to any particular production situation are convex is a matter of fact that depends on the relevant technology. But there are good reasons for thinking that isoquants usually have this shape, and that is what we shall argue in this section. Actually, we shall argue it in two stages: first we shall explain the "law of diminishing returns," and then we shall derive from that "law" the convexity of isoquants in normal circumstances.

The "law of diminishing returns" is one of the oldest and most fruitful insights in economics. It arose from observation of the production conditions in agriculture. Suppose that a farmer is cultivating an acre but is using very little fertilizer. Then he is likely to obtain a very meager crop because of nutritional deficiencies in the soil. But if he applies a little more fertilizer, say five pounds per acre, the half-starved plants will show a sharp increase in growth. A second dose of five pounds will increase growth still further, but not as much as the first dose. As successive increments of five pounds each are applied, each will contribute less to growth than its predecessor, until finally, when the soil is provided with all the nutrients that the plants can take up, further doses are both figuratively and literally fruitless.

This sort of behavior is not peculiar to fertilizer; it is the same with seed, with water, with the labor of cultivation, and with every other input to agricultural production: whenever the amount of one input is increased, the first additions yield greater responses than the later ones. Nor is this phenomenon restricted to agriculture. Consider the cloth-cutting example. If a bare minimum of cloth is used, the patterns must be placed very close together and the cutters must work very slowly around awkward corners. If a bit more cloth is used, the worst corners can be eliminated and the output of the shop, per week let us say, will go up. Another bit of cloth will permit a little more improvement, but not as much as the first, because the worst impediments have already been eliminated. And so it will go as the amount of cloth is increased foot by foot, until finally the ultimate in convenience is achieved, and having more cloth is only a nuisance.[6]

Although these observations and many more like them do not constitute a proof of anything, they do suggest very strongly a general principle: If the amount of any one factor of production is increased in successive equal doses, the amounts of the other factors remaining the same, then successive increases in output will be obtained, up to some limit, but each increase will be smaller than its predecessors.

This is the "law of diminishing returns"—which, as you may already have surmised, takes quotation marks (instead of being capitalized or italicized) because it is not really a law; there are exceptions to it. Exceptions granted, however, sufficient universal truth remains within this "law" to have established it as one of the basic guides that determine the efficient use of economic resources.

The importance of the "law of diminishing returns" may be more properly emphasized by stating it in a slightly different way that has the advantage of introducing a very important concept, the concept of *the marginal product of a factor*. The marginal product of a factor of production is the increase in output that results when one more unit of that factor is employed, the quantities of all other factors remaining the same.[7]

The importance of this concept is that the marginal product of a factor measures its usefulness in terms directly pertinent to economic decisions. For instance, the cost of using an additional hour of labor is the hourly wage. The gain from using that hour, in a competitive industry, is the marginal product of labor (the amount of the product produced by that man-hour) times the price of the product. If the marginal-product times price is greater than the hourly wage, profits can be increased by employing more labor. Very simple. Also very important, and we shall follow up its implications in a later section. Now we can state what the "law of diminishing returns" asserts about marginal products: As the amount of any one factor is increased, the amounts of all other factors remaining fixed, the marginal product of the factor that varies will fall.

[6] This suggests another aspect of the "law of diminishing returns." If the amount of any one factor is increased without increasing the amounts of the others, it will eventually become deleterious. Too much water is a flood, too much fertilizer burns the soil, too much cloth becomes an unwieldy tangle. Then the returns to increases in the varying factor are worse than small; they are negative.

[7] Students often become confused about the directions of the changes used in definitions like this one, and in the definition of the MRS. Why isn't the marginal product the *decrease* in output that results when one *less* unit of a factor is employed? The answer is that it doesn't make any difference. For small changes you get about the same result, in whichever direction you take the variation. So we shall not pay any attention to this distinction, and shall take the marginal product to be either the increase resulting from one more unit, or the decrease resulting from one less, whichever is more convenient at the moment. The same goes for the MRS, marginal cost, and other definitions relating to the effects of small changes.

The "law of diminishing returns" does not establish that isoquants are convex, since it deals only with the consequences of varying factor inputs one at a time—but it supports the belief that they are. Any of our examples will show why. In the cloth-cutting example, suppose that a choice has been made on the isoquant for some quantity, near the end representing high inputs of cloth and low inputs of labor, as at point *A* in Fig. 4–3. If, now, the amount

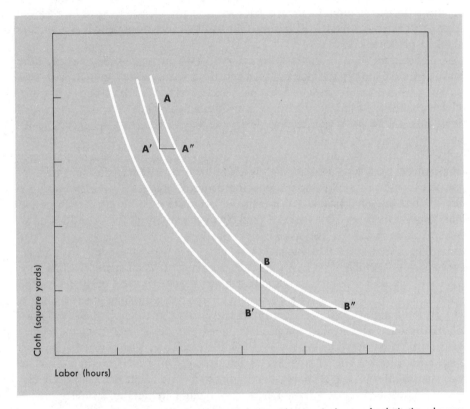

FIG. 4–3 Effect of substitution between two factors. The marginal rate of substitution changes along an isoquant, making it convex.

of cloth to be used per week is slightly reduced, the amount of labor remaining the same, the patterns can be arranged somewhat more tightly so as to keep the same number of cutters busy on the smaller quantity of cloth. Output per week will fall, because the cutters have to work a bit more slowly, but it will not fall much because the amount of cloth after the change is nearly as ample as it was before. This is in accordance with the "law of diminishing returns." Graphically, the decrease in the use of cloth moves us to point *A'*, on a lower isoquant than point *A* but not much lower.

If the original rate of output is to be restored by increasing the amount of labor, only a small increase in labor time will be necessary because the deficiency to be made up is small and because, with so much cloth to work with, the additional cutters can still work fast. This also is in accordance with the "law of diminishing returns." Such a restoration returns us to the original isoquant at point A''. The two changes together constitute a substitution of labor for cloth along the isoquant. The chord from A to A'' approximates the slope of the isoquant, or the MRS, which is seen to be high.

Contrast this with the same operations departing from point B, where the supply of cloth is already so short that a great deal of labor is required to attain the isoquant. Reducing the amount of cloth (that is, moving from B to B') now increases the amount of slow and delicate cutting and reduces the weekly output more than the reduction considered before. Point B' accordingly lies on a lower isoquant than point A'. The return to the original isoquant (at point B'') consequently requires a large increase in the use of labor, both because a large decrease in output has to be made up and because the output per man-hour is low on that part of the isoquant. Hence the chord BB'' is flat. All this means that as we move down an isoquant it becomes flatter, as drawn, or that it is convex.

This discussion indicates that the isoquants descriptive of cloth-cutting technology are likely to be convex; we cannot establish anything more than that. But since the influences that determine the shape of the isoquants in cloth cutting are so similar in their general nature to the influences operative in other technologies, it seems reasonable to conclude that isoquants will in most instances have this same general shape.

MARGINAL PRODUCTS AND FACTOR PRICES

The marginal rate of substitution between two factors is closely related in the marginal products of the two factors individually. We shall work out this relationship now, and then use it to get some new and useful formulas for the cheapest way to produce an arbitrary output and also for the most profitable output to produce.

Recall that the marginal product of a factor is the amount by which output would be increased if one more unit of the factor were employed, the use of all other factors remaining the same. The amount by which output would decline if one less unit of the factor were used, other inputs remaining unchanged, is approximately the same. We shall denote the marginal product of factor X by MP_x.

Now suppose that certain amounts of two factors, X and Y are being used, and consider the effects of varying their quantities. If the amount of Y is reduced by one unit, output will fall by MP_y units, where MP_y denotes the marginal product of Y. Now suppose that the use of X is increased by u units. Output will increase uMP_x units if u is small enough so that the marginal

93

product of X doesn't change appreciably as a result of the variation. The net effect on the output of these two changes is

$$- MP_y + uMP_x.$$

Finally, choose u so that the change in output is zero. We obtain

$$u = \frac{MP_y}{MP_x}.$$

But this is the marginal rate of substitution of X for Y, the number of units of X that can replace one unit of Y without affecting output. Thus we have found that the marginal rate of substitution between two factors is the ratio of their marginal products.

That conclusion is true, mathematically, whatever combination of factors is being used. We found above that when the cost-minimizing combination is used, the MRS is equal to the ratio of the prices. Putting these two facts together we find that when the cost-minimizing combination is used

$$\frac{MP_y}{MP_x} = \frac{p_y}{p_x}$$

for any two factors of production. That is to say, when any quantity of output is being produced in the cheapest possible way, the marginal products of the factors used are proportional to their prices.

Let us check on this conclusion in the batch-size example. The cheapest combination for producing 500 chassis a year was found to be 50 hours of labor and 100 square feet of storage, that is, to produce 5 batches a year. An additional square foot of storage would therefore permit batch size to increase to 101 chassis, and output to be increased by five units a year. The marginal product of storage space is 5 chassis. If the use of setup labor were increased by 1 hour without increasing storage space, the batch size would have to remain at 100 but the number of batches could be increased to $5\frac{1}{10}$ per year. The increase of a tenth of a batch means that output would be increased by 10 chassis, which is thus the marginal product of setup labor. The marginal product of setup labor is thus twice that of storage space. Now, if you will look back at the data of the problem, you will confirm that the ratio of their prices was $5.00 : 2.50 = 2$, just as our theorem predicted. The theorem holds whenever a cheapest combination of factors is used, which is a condition that businessmen strive to achieve.

An immediate consequence is that if output is to be increased by one unit or other small amount it doesn't matter which input is used to obtain the increase. For suppose that output is to be increased one unit by using more of factor X. One additional unit of factor X will increase output by MP_x units; therefore a unit increase in output requires $1/MP_x$ additional units of factor X. The cost of achieving the increase is then p_x/MP_x.

Similarly, if the increase in output were achieved by using more of some other factor Y, the cost would be p_y/MP_y. But our proportionality formula shows that these two costs are the same. You can verify this for yourself, using the data of the batch-size problem.

This finding ties right in with the analysis of costs in Chapter 3. There we defined the marginal cost of a commodity to be the cost of increasing its rate of output by one unit. Now we find that the marginal cost of a commodity is p_x/MP_x, where p_x is the price of any factor used to produce the commodity and MP_x is the marginal product of that factor. It doesn't matter which factor we use for this computation, since the ratio is the same for all (when the least-cost combination is used). For example, taking factor X to be labor, the marginal cost of an electronic chassis when 500 are being produced is $5/10 = \$.50$.

Finally, we recall from the last chapter that when the profit-maximizing output is produced, the marginal cost is equal to the price of the product. Denoting the product's price by p_o this can be written:

$$p_o = \frac{p_x}{MP_x}$$

or more conveniently:

$$p_x = p_o MP_x.$$

Since this is a condition that businessmen aim to maintain, we conclude that businessmen will employ factors in such quantities that the wage or price of each factor equals its marginal product times the product price, or the value of its marginal product.

Hardly any principle in economics is more important than this one, for the simple reason that hardly any question that economics deals with is more important than the determination of the wages of labor and payments to other factors of production. We shall discuss it further below.

THE PRODUCTION FUNCTION

So far in this chapter we have used three main concepts: isoquants, marginal rates of substitution, and marginal products. All describe aspects of the broad relationship between quantities of inputs and quantity of output. They can be related to each other and remembered most easily by thinking of them in the context of this broad relationship, called the *production function*. The production function for any firm summarizes its technological data by stating the greatest output it can obtain from each possible combination of quantities of inputs.

A production function can be stated in many ways. Frequently it takes the form of a mathematical formula. It is easy, for example, to find the formula for the production function in the lot-size problem. Suppose that Q denotes the annual output. Then Q equals the number of batches, say N, multiplied by the batch size, say B, or $Q = NB$. Each batch requires ten hours of setup labor, so we can write $N = \frac{1}{10}L$. The greatest possible batch size is equal to the storage space, so $B = S$. Substituting for N and B, we get the production function

$$Q = \frac{LS}{10}$$

for the greatest output that can be obtained with L hours of setup labor and S square feet of storage space. This formula can be used, along with a little calculus, to derive all the results we have obtained for this example.

An isoquant diagram, such as Fig. 4–1, is another method for expressing the production function, since the maximum output obtainable from any pair of input quantities can be read off it. Of course, this method is limited to those rare instances where only two factors of production have to be taken into account.

Perhaps the most vivid way to show a production function when only two inputs have to be considered is to draw a "production hill." This requires three dimensions: one for each of the two inputs and one for the output.[8] Such a

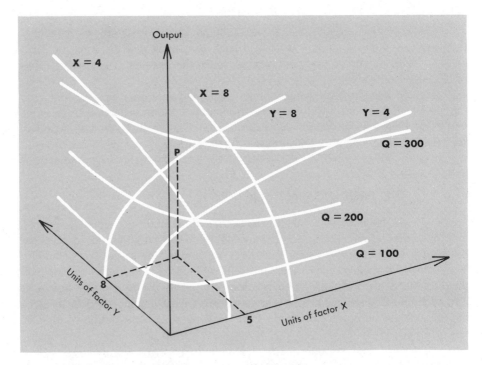

FIG. 4–4 A production function for two factors. The height of the "hill" above any point shows the level of output attainable using the factor quantities for that point.

[8] A production hill can be drawn only when there are two factors of production to be considered, but the concept of a production function encompasses any number of factors.

production hill is shown in Fig. 4–4. Quantities of two factors, X and Y, are shown horizontally and the resultant output is measured vertically. Thus, point P in the diagram represents the output when five units of factor X and eight units of factor Y are used. The whole curve labeled $Y = 8$ shows the results of using eight units of factor Y in conjunction with various quantities of factor X. The curves labeled $Y = 4$, $X = 4$, and $X = 8$ are interpreted similarly. These curves form a kind of network etched on the surface of the production hill, by means of which the whole shape of the hill can be visualized.

The diagram also shows a few isoquants, combinations of inputs for which the quantity produced is the same. The curve labeled $Q = 100$ shows all combinations of factors that produce 100 units of output, and similarly for the curve labeled $Q = 200$. The marginal product of X is shown by the steepness with which the hill climbs as you move from left to right, parallel to the X-axis, that is, by the steepness of such curves as $Y = 4$ and $Y = 8$. The marginal product of Y is shown by the steepness of curves such as $X = 4$ and $X = 8$. The hill shows the phenomenon of diminishing marginal productivity that we discussed above: it is steeper when the quantities of the inputs are smaller than when they are large.

The isoquant diagrams are, in effect, an alternative way to depict the production hill. You may have noticed that the isoquant diagrams are very similar in construction to the contour maps used by geographers to represent terrain features and especially altitudes. Just as the geographer does, we can visualize an isoquant diagram as the two-dimensional representation of a hill in which the quantities of two factors of production are plotted instead of latitude and longitude, and the quantity of output is plotted in place of altitude. The isoquant diagram corresponding to a production hill similar to Fig. 4–4 is shown in Fig. 4–5. There the isoquant for 200 units of output is shown and the isoquant for every 10 units thereafter, up to 390 units. Every fifth isoquant is emphasized for clarity.

One of the two salient features of this isoquant map has already been discussed: the isoquants are all convex. The other significant feature is that the isoquants are densely clustered toward the bottom of the "hill" and spread apart near the top. Every user of Geological Survey maps knows that tightly clustered contour lines indicate a steep climb for him, while spread-out lines signify easy going. The interpretation of the isoquants on the production "hill" is similar: at the bottom of it a small increase in the use of either factor will increase output the 10 units from 200 to 210; output there climbs steeply in relation to input. At the top, however, a large increment in either factor is required to increase output those last 10 units from 380 to 390. There, the level of production climbs slowly in relation to increases in the use of the two factors.

Each of these isoquants corresponds to a certain total cost which could be ascertained by drawing in the isocost line tangent to it.[9] Where the isoquants are close together, the increase in total cost between any one and the one

[9] The isocost lines have been omitted to keep the diagram uncluttered.

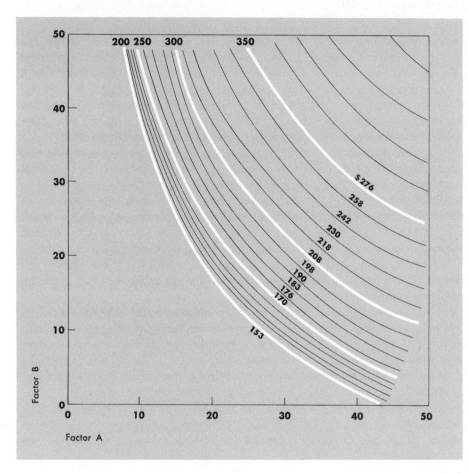

FIG. 4–5 Isoquant diagram to represent the production function. Each isoquant is an altitude contour of the production hill.

above it is small. Since the isoquants are drawn for constant increments of output (ten units), this means that marginal costs are low. Where the isoquants are far apart, a large increase in total cost is needed to increase output by ten units; marginal costs are high. Thus the spreading-out of the isoquants is another mode of expression for the increase in marginal costs at high levels of production.

To facilitate the following step, we have written next to some of the isoquants in Fig. 4–5 the total cost of attaining them.[10] Note that the increase in output from 200 to 250 units costs $17, the increase from 250 to 300 units costs $38, and the increase from 300 to 350 costs $68. Marginal costs are increasing as predicted. To find the best isoquant, or the best quantity to produce,

[10] That is, the cost of the cheapest combination of factors, using prices of $5 for factor A and $3 for factor B.

we have only to compare marginal cost with the price of the product. Suppose, for example, that the price of the product is 70 cents. We note from the diagram that the increase in output from 260 to 270 units costs $7, so that the marginal cost when 260 units are being produced is about 70 cents. Then 260 units is the best output to produce, in accordance with the findings of Chapter 3.

Though the production function is a very informative concept as a theoretical tool, it is not of much value to the businessman in making his practical decisions. Even the smallest firm is too complicated to have its workings summarized conveniently in this form. For one thing, there is no such thing as a firm that uses one, or two, or a handful of factors of production. But, more fundamentally, the relationships between inputs and output in any actual firm are exceedingly complex. The batch-size problem with which we started is only a tiny part of the production function of the electronics firm. Similar problems arise in the fabrication of every component of its product. They arise even in the administration of the firm, but who can tell the relationship between the number of bookkeepers employed and the number of chassis that can be produced?

In practice, a businessman knows only a few bits and pieces of his production function; his foremen and department managers know other bits and pieces. All together they know enough to employ their resources relatively efficiently. And that is sufficient for our purpose, which is to explain the principles relating the use of factors to their market prices.

PRODUCTION FUNCTIONS AND SUPPLY CURVES

The most important applications of production functions are to help explain the supply curves for products and the demand curves for factors of production. These are the topics of this and the following sections.

The production function in any of its forms is a purely technological datum. It tells how much product can be obtained by the use of any combination of factors of production. But, given the prices of the different factors, the production function can be used to determine the cheapest way to produce any quantity of output. We have seen how the isoquant version can be used for this purpose. The total-, average-, and marginal-cost curves are all consequences of this calculation (made implicitly or explicitly by businessmen) and so, also, is the supply curve.

Ultimately, then, the supply curve of any commodity is derived from its production function and the prices of the factors of production employed in its industry. The various cost curves of the preceding chapter are no more than convenient summaries of these fundamental, underlying data. They change whenever any of the underlying data, such as factor prices, change; we have already seen illustrations of that. But now we can see that the effect of a change in a factor price is more complicated than the cost curves reveal.

In Chapter 2,[11] we considered the effect of the increase in the price of a raw material on the supply curve of a commodity that uses it. But there we were forced to postulate without explanation the effect of the increase in the material's price on the average cost of the product. Now, by using the production-function concept, we can calculate the effect of the price increase on the cost curves. It consists of two parts, which oppose each other: a direct effect and a substitution effect.

The direct effect is the increase in average cost that would result if the combination of factors used to produce each level of output did not change in consequence of the price increase. It is simply the amount of price increase multiplied by the number of units of the raw material used per unit of product.

But the factor combination will change, and this gives rise to the substitution effect. This can be seen clearly in Fig. 4–6, which is a less cluttered reproduction of Fig. 4–5. Two isocost lines have been added, both touching the isoquant for 200 units. Isocost 1 is drawn for the situation in which factor A costs $5 a unit and factor B costs $3. At those prices the cheapest combination for producing 200 units consists of 18 units of factor A and 21 units of factor B, costing $153 in all. The average cost is then 76 cents.

If the price of factor B should rise to $4, the total cost of that same input combination would increase to $174, and the unit cost to 87 cents. The direct effect of the price increase is thus 11 cents a unit.

But at the higher price for factor B, isocost line 1 is no longer applicable. Isocost line 2 is drawn to correspond to the new prices, and shows that the cheapest combination has become 21 units of factor A and 16 of factor B, costing $169. Average cost is 85 cents a unit, and the substitution effect is a saving of 2 cents a unit.

Estimating the effects of an increase in material or factor prices without allowing for the substitution effect, as is frequently done, will overstate the effect of the change, sometimes to a significant extent.[12] But the most important consequence of the substitution induced by a change in the price of a factor is its effect on the demand for the factors, to which we now turn.

DEMAND CURVES FOR FACTORS

The demand curve for any factor of production tells how much of it will be used in the economy, as influenced by the price or wage of that factor. It answers a rather more complicated question than does the demand curve for an ordinary consumer good. The demand curve for an ordinary good tells how consumption of it will be affected if its price changes while all other prices in the economy remain fixed. But in the case of a factor of production it is irrelevant and unreasonable to expect all other prices to remain constant if its

[11] Page 25ff.

[12] Similarly this same simplification applied to a decrease in the price of a factor will understate the reduction in average costs. Why?

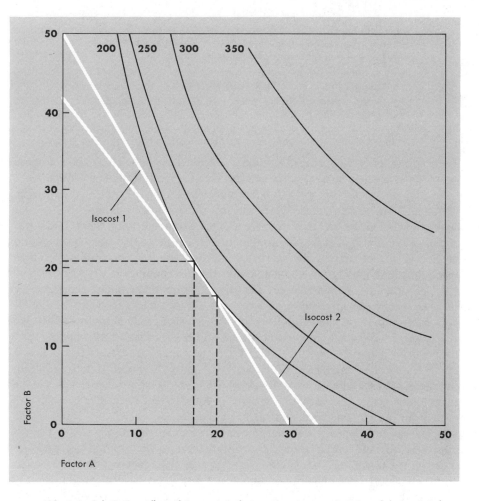

FIG. 4–6 Substitution effect of increase in factor price. Increase in price of factor B induces firm to use more A and less B in producing same output.

price changes. At the very least, the prices of products made with that factor are almost sure to change if the factor's price does.

The chain of consequences touched off by an increase in the price of a factor of production is likely to be quite complicated. The major reverberations are these:

- The average cost curves of the products made with that factor shift upwards, in about the amount of what we have called the direct effect. The marginal cost curves also probably shift upwards.[13]

[13] We say probably because there are some rare, and rather abnormal, production functions for which this does not happen.

- The upward shift in the marginal cost curves (to concentrate on the preponderant case) carries the supply curves with them. The equilibrium prices of these commodities then rise (but by less than the increase in marginal costs) and the equilibrium quantities purchased fall.
- In consequence, the employment of the factor whose price has risen (and other factors in the same industries) will fall.
- The factor whose price has risen has become more expensive relative to other factors used in the same industries. Other factors will be substituted for it, reinforcing the decline in employment of the initiating factor, but offsetting partially the decline in employment of the substitutable factors.

There are other consequences, too, but these are the major ones, and the more remote ones are most unlikely to counterbalance or greatly alter their effects.

The difficulties of the bituminous-coal industry illustrate in a general way this chain of causation. When miners' wagers were raised in the thirties largely by union action, they carried the price of coal with them. This was one of the circumstances that led to the diminished use of coal for the generation of electric power and to the increased mechanization of coal mining. These two trends have greatly reduced employment in coal mining.

Because the demand curves for factors of production are generated by such a complicated array of considerations—the demand curves for commodities, the amount of substitution permitted by the production functions, the supply curves of substitutable factors, and so on—it is not worthwhile to spell them out in detail. It is clear enough from the foregoing considerations that a rise in the price of any factor will cause the quantity demanded to fall. Whatever the price of the factor, we already know that the quantity demanded will be such that the value of its marginal product is equal to that price. The complexities arise from the circumstance that many of the data on which the value of the marginal product depends will change when the factor price does.

The demand curve alone does not determine the equilibrium price or wage of the factor, or the amount employed in the economy. But is is often useful on its own account. For example, it throws a good deal of light on the common question, "Can unions raise wages?" In a certain sense they undoubtedly can. If factor B in Fig. 4–6 is a unionized craft, a sufficiently strong union could insist on a contract that would raise the wage from $3 to $4 an hour. But if it did so, the value of the marginal product of this craft at the level of employment corresponding to a $3 wage would be less than the current wage. Other factors would be substituted for this one and, since the wage increase would be likely to raise the marginal cost of the product, the level of output would probably fall. For both these reasons, members of the craft would be thrown out of work. At the same time, the increase in the wage would, if anything, increase the number of men desiring work in the craft. The union would then have difficulty in maintaining the increased wage, unless it could persuade employers to retain men whose marginal productivity was low (hence "featherbedding" rules), and could exclude nonunion members who wanted work in the trade (hence apprenticeship rules, closed-shop contracts, and similar devices). Clearly, strong pressures have to be resisted in order to maintain a wage substantially higher than what the value of the marginal product of the craft would be if all men desiring work in it were employed.

In general, an increase in the price of a factor starts a chain of consequences, all of which tend to reduce the employment of that factor. Unless the supply of the factor has been reduced correspondingly, the higher price is not likely to persist.

SOCIAL IMPLICATIONS

All the discussion in this chapter has been from the point of view of the businessman—his endeavor to produce the most profitable level of output at the lowest possible cost, and the consequences of this endeavor for the demand for factors of production. This effort leads businessmen in competitive industries toward the key relationship among factor prices, product prices, and marginal products:

$$p_x = p_o MP_x.$$

In words: actuated by their own interests and pressed by their competitors, businessmen will try to use factors in such quantities and proportions that the value of the output produced by a unit of each factor is equal to that factor's wage or other reward. In working toward this result, businessmen bring together their own knowledge of their production functions, contained in MP_x; the social values of the factors of production, contained in p_x (for that is what determines what the employer has to pay for his factors); and the desirability of the product to purchasers, contained in p_o.

When businessmen in all industries have accomplished that, it will not be possible to transfer a factor from one industry to another where it will produce an output that consumers desire more than the output that has been sacrificed. The factors will then be allocated efficiently among industries from a social point of view. The ingenious feature of this mechanism is that all a businessmen has to know, in order to do his part, is his own production function and the prices relevant to him.

The rewards to owners of factors of production are a by-product of this allocation process, and the consequences can be capricious. A man whose livelihood is derived from an inefficient factor used in producing a low-valued product can have a hard time of it, unless his income is supplemented in some way. The obvious remedy, requiring that "adequate" compensation (a "living wage") be paid to owners of low-valued factors of production, raises serious problems. It can be regarded as a hidden tax on consumers of the products made by the inadequately compensated factors. Alternatively, the inadequate compensation can be regarded as concealed subsidy on the consumption of those products, cruelly extracted from the factor owners.

But, moralizing aside, artificial floors to factor payments are likely to result in decreased employment of the very factors they are intended to help. A better corrective appears to be to leave the signaling system of the economy intact and to loosen the tie between individuals' incomes and the values of the resources they happen to own. But of that, more in the final chapter.

SUMMARY

The motivating idea of this chapter is that businessmen determine the cost of attaining any output by choosing the combination of factors with which to product that output. Their range of choice is described by an isoquant, which shows the combinations of quantities of different factors of production required to produce the specified quantity of output. In general, the isoquant can be conceived of for any number of factors of production, but it can be shown graphically only for two factors, and we have concentrated on such cases.

Isoquants can be compared with isocost lines, which specify the quantities of different factors of production that can be procured at a constant aggregate cost. The cheapest combination of factors for producing a given output corresponds to the point where the isoquant for that output touches, and is tangential to, the lowest possible isocost line.

The slopes of the isocost lines represent the ratios of the prices of the factors of production. The slope of an isoquant at any point represents the marginal rate of substitution between the factors there—that is, the number of units of one factor needed to compensate for the loss of one unit of the other, leaving output unaffected. When the cheapest combination of factors is used to obtain any output, the marginal rate of substitution between any pair of factors is equal to their price ratio.

When the price of any factor rises in proportion to the prices of the others, the least-cost combination for any output will change. Less of the more expensive factor will be used in proportion to the others than in the preexisting least-cost combination.

The isoquant map, the diagram showing isoquants for different levels of production, is the fundamental datum underlying both cost curves and supply curves. It can be used to determine the most profitable level of output as well as the least-cost method for producing that output. The isoquant diagram is simply a convenient way of showing the production function when only two factors of production are under consideration. The production function incorporates all the technical data about production; it shows the greatest amount of output that can be obtained by the use of every possible combination of input quantities.

The marginal product of a factor is the increase in output that results when one more unit of that factor is used, all other factor quantities remaining the same. It, too, can be read off the isoquant map. When the least-cost combination of factors is being used, the marginal cost of the product equals the ratio of the price of any factor to the marginal productivity of that factor, this ratio being the same for all factors. This is so because the number of units of a factor required to produce one more unit of output, other factor quantities remaining constant, is the reciprocal of the marginal product. Multiplying the number of units of the factor required by the price of the factor gives marginal cost. The significant fact is that the cost of a small increase in output is the same no matter which factors are varied to secure it, provided that the starting point was the least-cost combination.

Even more can be said when the firm is producing the most profitable output in the cheapest way. Since under those circumstances marginal cost equals price, we can assert that a dollar's worth of any factor will produce a dollar's worth of output.

The marginal products of the factors are the foundation of the demand curves for them. If the price of the factor varies, the quantity employed will vary, too, so that in every firm that uses it, a dollar's worth of the factor will produce a dollar's worth of the product—or, in fancier language, so that the value of the marginal product will remain equal to the price of the factor. This is the basis of the marginal-productivity theory of factor pricing, which is useful in understanding wages and other factor prices even though it does not provide a complete explanation.

The "law of diminishing returns" helps justify the shape of isoquants and isoquant maps. It asserts that the marginal product of any factor tends to decline when more of it is used in proportion to the factors that cooperate with it. Our explanation of the tendency of short-run costs to rise with increases in output is an instance of this general phenomenon. The convexity of isoquants in general is a consequence of this same principle.

Throughout this summary, and in fact throughout this chapter, we have indulged in some verbal shorthand. For example, we have stated firmly that the price of a factor is equal to the value of its marginal product. The truth is that this and many similar assertions hold only in certain restricted circumstances— though it should be emphasized that they are circumstances that competitive markets tend strongly to bring about. All these statements, in fact, are statements of equilibrium conditions (that is, of conditions that will obtain only *after* firms, their customers, and their suppliers have had time to adjust to changes in circumstances). This detracts somewhat from the exactitude of our assertions, but it does not diminish their importance.

MAIN CONCEPTS INTRODUCED

ISOQUANT. A specification, usually graphic, of all the combinations of quantities of factors of production that are just sufficient to produce a given level of output.

ISOCOST LINE. A specification of all the combinations of quantities of factors of production that cost a given amount in toto.

MARGINAL RATE OF SUBSTITUTION. The marginal rate of substitution of factor X for factor Y, denoted $MRS(X:Y)$, is the number of units of factor X that can be used to replace one unit of factor Y, leaving the level of output unchanged.

MARGINAL PRODUCT. The marginal product of factor X, denoted MP_x, is the increase in the level of output that would result from employing one more unit of X, the quantities of the other factors remaining the same.

PRODUCTION FUNCTION. A specification of the greatest amount of output producible with any given quantities of inputs. It expresses all the technological data about the production process. It presumes that standard and available techniques are used and that the firm's management operates at a good, ordinary level of efficiency.

Behind the Demand Curves

CHAPTER FIVE

The past few chapters have explained the considerations that determine the supply of a commodity: the amount that will be produced and offered in response to any market price. But we should not forget that the main purpose of production is to satisfy consumers' wants. Now we turn to the study of demand, which is the mechanism by which consumers' wants and tastes find expression in the market-place and thereby become known to producers. The importance of the demand curves is that they tell producers how strongly consumers desire each commodity, relatively to others.

The significance of this information becomes apparent if we think of the predicament of people who have to make decisions about non-market goods and services. There are many nonmarket goods in our economy, mostly provided by the government and given away without charge or with only nominal charges. Measures for the control of water pollution are typical. They are expensive, and they are provided, usually, by state and local governments. When a decision has to be made about how much to spend on water treatment, the city fathers or other officials use their own judgment and talk to various people. If the possible expenditure is great, they may hold public hearings. From all this they will learn that the manufacturers in town feel that very modest expenditures will be adequate and will be all that the city can afford, while the sport fishermen and the members of the Audubon Society give fervent support to very high and expensive standards of water treatment. But there is no way for the responsible officials to find out how much the citizens at large are willing to contribute to improve the quality of the water. They have to decide the amount to be spent, and they have nothing more than hunches and rhetoric to go on. There is no reason to think that these decisions, usually made anxiously and earnestly, conform at all closely to the amount that the citizens would like to see spent on water improvement. The trouble is not that the politicians don't care about what the people want; it is that they have no way of finding out in the absence of a market and a demand curve that will enable each taxpayer to demonstrate in earnest what the abatement of pollution is worth to him. The salient advantage of economic markets lies just here: they enable consumers to vote with their dollars on just how much should be spent on producing each good and service that enters into the market economy. How the demand curves elicit this information is what we now have to elucidate.

The demand for a commodity is the amount that purchasers choose to buy. It therefore depends ultimately on how consumers make up their minds, and on all the attitudes, customs, fashions, and other influences that affect purchasing decisions. Clearly, just what a consumer decides to purchase is a very complicated matter whose full explanation requires all the knowledge that psychologists, sociologists, and other experts on behavior can muster. Economists, however, do not purport to explain purchasing decisions in their full richness and complexity. They undertake a different task: without attempting to account for tastes, they ask how consumers with given wants and preferences allocate their expenditures among the different commodities that they might purchase. They ask also how changes in prices and in consumers' incomes affect this allocation. In short, they concentrate on only one factor that influences purchasing decisions: how much the commodity costs in relation both to the costs of other things and to what the consumer can afford. They do not do this because prices are the most important influences on consumers' decisions (usually they are *not*), but because the consumers' decision to buy or not at given prices is the main channel by which consumers communicate their desires to the rest of the economy.

One consequence of this concentration is that economists ignore many aspects of consumers' decisions that are of engrossing importance to other people, such as sociologists and advertising experts. Some time ago, for instance, the psychologists who advise the tea importers' association concluded that tea sales suffered because Americans (in contrast to Englishmen) regarded tea as a sissy's drink. The tea importers consequently spent large sums trying to erase this "image" of effeteness associated with their product. Now, although the question of whether tea is a he-man's drink is undoubtedly important from some points of view, to an economist it is irrelevant simply because it throws no light on the operation of the economic system; he is willing to take such attitudes, preferences, and customs as his primary data. Taking such attitudes, and so on, as given, his concern instead is with the answer to the question: How are consumers' decisions affected by changes in prices and in incomes? This will be our question, also. We shall attempt in answering it to show how the economic system responds, within the limits of its productive capabilities, to give consumers what they want.

CHOICE BETWEEN TWO COMMODITIES: UTILITY MAXIMIZATION

Our analysis begins with a very simple question. Supposing that a consumer has a given amount of money to spend, how should he divide his expenditures among different goods so as to achieve maximum satisfaction? In other words, what must he do to get the most for his money?

To answer this question, let us make up an example that we shall study in some detail. Mrs. X, a remarkably systematic housewife, has already decided to spend exactly $50 on frozen foods for the coming month. The question that now confronts her is how much of that to spend on meat (costing $1 a pound) and how much on vegetables (costing 40 cents a pound). Notice that the total amount she has to spend, and the two prices, delimit her range of choice. She could spend her whole $50 on vegetables (obtaining 125 pounds of them), or all of it on 50 pounds of meat. Of course, she is not very likely to do either of these; instead, she will probably buy some number of pounds of meat, say x (somewhere between 0 and 50), and some number of pounds of vegetables, say y (somewhere between 0 and 125), chosen so that her total bill will not exceed her limit of $50. That is, her choice can be described by two letter symbols, x and y, delimited by the condition

$$x + .40y = 50$$

—a range of choice depicted by the straight line in Fig. 5–1.

More generally, if a consumer has $\$B$ to spend on two commodities whose prices are p_1 and p_2, his range of choice is given by all combinations of x and y, such that

$$p_1x + p_2y = B.$$

Such a range of choice, corresponding to a given budget and prices, is called a *budget line*.[1] The budget line shows how prices and the budget limitation jointly define the range of choice open to the consumer. Algebraically, this limitation is expressed by a linear equation; geometrically, it corresponds to a straight line. But the budget line gives no information about which pair of quantities, satisfying the budget equation, the consumer will choose.

Indifference Curves

Conceptually, we can split the problem of consumers' choice into two parts. One part, solved by the budget line, is to describe the range of choice open to the consumer. The other part is to determine which combination of commodities, of all those on the budget line, the consumer will pick. The first part incorporates the basic economic data, and for it the economist assumes full

---

[1] If there were three commodities, the equation for the budget line would be (let us say) $p_1x + p_2y + p_3z = B$, where x, y, and z denote the quantities purchased of the three commodities. The extension of this concept to larger numbers of commodities is obvious.

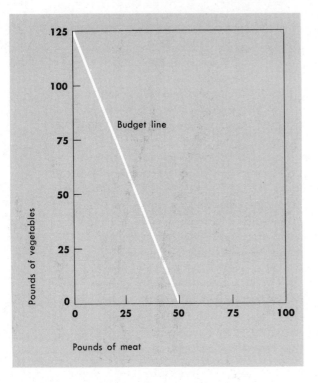

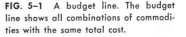

Budget line

Pounds of vegetables

Pounds of meat

FIG. 5–1 A budget line. The budget line shows all combinations of commodities with the same total cost.

responsibility. The second part depends on psychological data, and concerning it the economist can say only that the consumer will pick the combination on the budget line that he likes best. This apparently feeble response to the second part of the problem means that the budget line alone does not determine consumers' decisions; that more data are needed—data about preferences of consumers. We now set about introducing these data.

Suppose that last month Mrs. X had bought 50 pounds of vegetables and, therefore, 30 pounds of meat (point *A* on Fig. 5–2), and suppose that she had run short of vegetables before the end of the month. Then as she made this month's choice, she would judge market basket *A* to be less desirable than other combinations that include more vegetables, such as 55 pounds of vegetables and 22 pounds of meat (which costs the same). In this way her tastes and experiences enable her to compare mentally the desirabilities of any pair of market baskets.

To the practical Mrs. X the contemplation of any combinations of amounts of vegetables and meat other than those she can afford would seem a waste of time. But let us disregard that practical consideration for a moment, and think of comparisons among *all conceivable* market baskets of meat and vegetables. Then, taking market basket *A* as a point of departure, every other conceivable market basket will be a member of one of three classes: (1) the class of

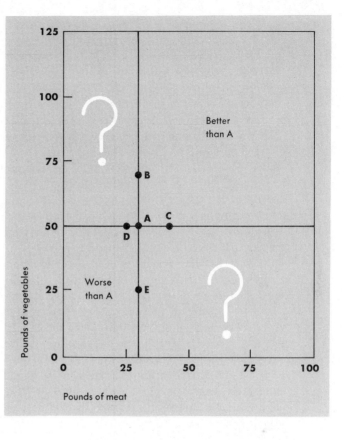

FIG. 5–2 Comparative desirability of some market baskets.
Consumer prefers one with more
of either commodity and no less
of the other.

market baskets that are preferred to *A;* (2) the class of those that are inferior to *A;* and (3) the class that are as satisfactory as *A* (meaning, for this class, market baskets that Mrs. X deems to be about as desirable as market basket *A,* but no more desirable).

So much is empty classification. To give our reasoning substance, we must notice some prevalent characteristics of consumers' preferences.

In the first place, if a market basket has more of either commodity than *A* and no less of the other, it will be preferred to *A*. On this basis, market basket *B* (30 pounds of meat, 70 pounds vegetables) would be preferred to *A* (30 pounds meat, 50 pounds vegetables), and so would market basket *C* (35 pounds meat, 50 pounds vegetables). In fact, any market basket that lies in the area to the north and east of *A* in Fig. 5–2 would be preferred to market basket *A*. By the same reasoning, market basket *D* (25 pounds meat, 50 pounds vegetables) is inferior to *A*. So is market basket *E* (30 pounds meat, 25 pounds vegetables), and, in general, any market basket southwest of *A*. (We cannot yet say anything about market baskets to the northwest or southeast of of *A*.)

111

The assumption we have just made is known as the *postulate of nonsatiation.* It asserts that consumers normally prefer more to less—or, less tersely, that if a consumer can obtain more of one commodity without having to give up any of any other, he will do so.

In order to eliminate the "?" marks from Fig. 5–2, we have to make some more refined comparisons. This is done in Fig. 5–3, where the same data are recorded. Return to market basket *D,* which contains less meat than *A.* Suppose we add a pound of vegetables to it, to obtain a market basket a slight distance up along the arrow drawn through *D* in Fig. 5–3. The result will be a market basket that is preferred to *D,* by the nonsatiation postulate, and that may or may not be preferred to *A.* If this new market basket is still judged inferior to *A* (judged by Mrs X, that is), add another pound of vegetables to it, thus moving to a basket farther up the arrow. It is reasonable to suppose that as we move up the arrow we shall eventually come to a market basket, say *A′,* that Mrs. X would feel is as satisfactory as *A.*[2]

This reasoning has introduced a second assumption, called the *substitutability postulate.* This postulate holds that if a small amount of one commodity is subtracted from a market basket, the deficiency can be made good by an adequate increase in the amount (or amounts) of the other commodities. By virtue of the substitutability postulate there is a point on the upward arrow through market basket *D* which is just as satisfactory as market basket *A.* We have already called this point *A′.*

We can make a similar analysis for market basket *C,* which contains more meat than *A* and is therefore superior to it. This time, though, we shall have to move downward to find the point, called *A″,* at which our basket would contain five pounds more meat than *A* and just enough fewer vegetables so that it would be just as satisfactory as *A.*

There was clearly nothing special about points *D* and *C.* If we start with any market basket on the horizontal line through *A* (except one unduly close to *F*), we can move upward or downward as is appropriate (that is, add or subtract vegetables) to find a point like *A′* or *A″* that is as satisfactory as *A.* If we do this a large number of times, and string all those points together, they will form a curve like the curve drawn through *A′, A, A″* with the characteristic that any point on it represents a market basket that is as satisfactory as the market basket represented by point *A.* This curve is called the *indifference curve through A.* (It could as well be called the indifference curve through *A′.*) An indifference curve consists of all points that represent market baskets that a consumer regards as equally satisfactory.

Clearly such an indifference curve can be drawn through any market basket represented in the diagram by drawing a horizontal line through it and

[2] This is not inevitable, however. Suppose we start from F, the market basket with as much in the way of vegetables as A but with no meat at all. It is quite possible that no matter how many vegetables you load onto it, you will not get a market basket that Mrs. X would feel is as good as A; her family would rather have a skimpy diet with some meat than a lavish vegetarian menu.

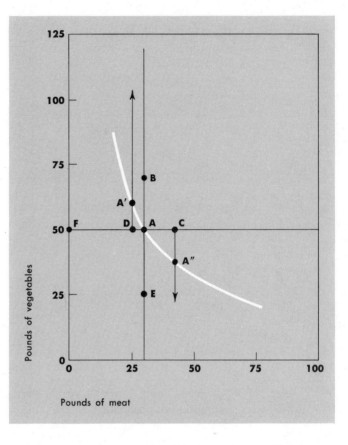

following the same reasoning. That is to say, corresponding to every market basket there is a family of alternative market baskets that are just as satisfactory to Mrs. X as it is, and these can be strung together on an indifference curve similar to the one that we found for market basket A. These indifference curves incorporate all the psychological data that are pertinent to the consumer's choice, just as the budget line incorporates all the relevant economic data. We must therefore point out a number of the characteristics of these curves.

Figure 5–4 shows three of this infinite number of indifference curves, one through market basket B, one through A, and one through E. These curves are, in essence, a scale for ranking the desirabilities of the different market baskets. For example, basket B is superior to basket A (by the nonsatiation postulate); and any market basket on the curve through B is as satisfactory as B (by construction) and is therefore superior to any market basket on the curve through A—and, all the more, to any market basket on the curve through E. (It follows at once that the indifference curves cannot cross each other; draw a

113

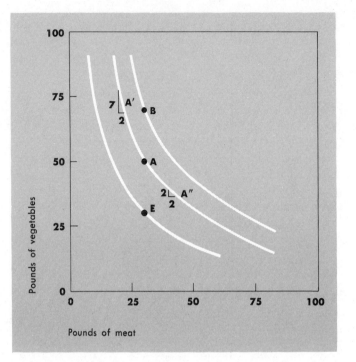

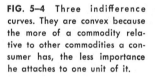

FIG. 5–4 Three indifference curves. They are convex because the more of a commodity relative to other commodities a consumer has, the less importance he attaches to one unit of it.

diagram in which two indifference curves *do* cross, and you'll see that you have violated the nonsatiation postulate.)

Notice in Fig. 5–4 that the indifference curves slope downward to the right (and recall, incidentally, that since *A'* has less meat than *A,* if it is rated as desirable as *A* it must have more vegetables). Note also that the indifference curves curl upward, or, in mathematical language, are convex. This characteristic reflects a new psychological assumption. Suppose that two pounds of meat are taken out of market basket *A',* shown by the short horizontal line marked "2." Market basket *A'* did not contain very much meat to begin with, so a large offsetting increase in the amount of vegetables (marked "7") is needed to produce a market basket that has two pounds less meat than *A'* but is just as desirable. On the other hand, if basket *A",* which has a large allotment of meat, is taken as a point of departure, it seems reasonable that only a small increase in vegetables (also marked "2") is needed to compensate for a two-pound reduction in the amount of meat. The psychological assumption that underlies this reasoning is called the *postulate of diminishing marginal substitutability.* The postulate of diminishing marginal substitutability asserts that the more a market basket contains of one particular commodity in proportion to others, the smaller will be the increases in the amounts of other commodities needed to compensate psychologically for a unit decrease in the amount of that one.

There are many exceptions to this postulate, but it does express the quite usual fact that the more a consumer has of anything, the less importance he attaches to having one unit more or less of it.

Now we can bring together the psychological data contained in the indifference curves with the economic data contained in the budget line. See Fig. 5–5, where the budget line is shown together with four indifference curves labeled I, II, III, and IV. Mrs. X cannot afford any market basket on indifference curve I because it lies entirely above the budget line, which shows the greatest quantity of vegetables she can afford in conjunction with any given quantity of meat. But she can afford at least one market basket on each of the other indifference curves shown. She will choose a market basket on the highest indifference curve she can afford—namely, indifference curve II. This follows from the postulate of nonsatiation because each indifference curve contains a market-basket point that is directly above some point on every lower indifference curve. Each indifference curve therefore designates a family of market baskets, each of which is preferable to every market basket on every lower

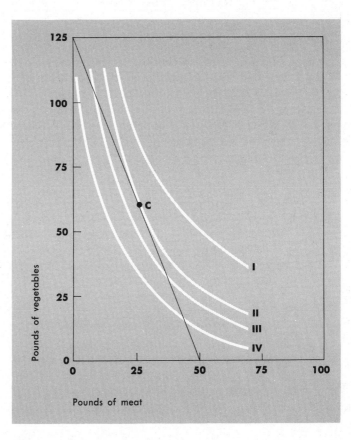

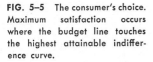

FIG. 5–5 The consumer's choice. Maximum satisfaction occurs where the budget line touches the highest attainable indifference curve.

indifference curve. Because of the shapes of the indifference curves, market basket C (26 pounds meat, 60 pounds vegetables) is the only combination on curve II that she can afford. Accordingly, she will select it. Her decision is determined.

Thus the problem of consumers' choice with given budget, prices, and tastes is solved—though one property of the solution deserves particular emphasis. Notice that the budget line is tangent to the indifference curve through the market basket chosen, market basket C. Because this is the only point on the budget line where this relationship holds, we can summarize our result by saying that the consumer will choose the combination of goods at which the budget line is tangent to an indifference curve.

You have a poor memory if the indifference curves don't remind you of isoquants and if the budget lines don't seem like isocost lines. Indeed, the economic problems of the consumer trying to get the most satisfaction for his money and the producer trying to get the most output for his are fundamentally the same. The diagrams and the underlying logic are virtually identical, and, we shall see, the major conclusions are strongly analogous. Thus there is an underlying logical symmetry between the demand side and the supply side of any market.

The principal differences between the theories of production and consumption, aside from mere terminology, are two. First, the consumer's total expenditure is constrained by his income, while the producer is free (within wide limits) to choose the most profitable level of expenditure on factors of production. Second, the producer endeavors to maximize his profits, which are an objective and measurable quantity, whereas the consumer tries to maximize the satisfaction he derives from his consumption, which is a most subjective and unmeasurable magnitude. Virtually all the differences between the two theories stem from these circumstances. In particular, the theory of production is much more concrete than the theory of consumption because profits are much more concrete than satisfactions.

So far we have been looking mostly at the geometry by which consumers' decisions can be analyzed. The economic meaning of our conclusion—that the consumer will choose the market basket for the point where the budget line and an indifference curve have the same slope—follows from the economic interpretation of these two slopes. We turn to that now.

SOME TECHNICAL CONCEPTS

The economic meaning of the slope of the budget line is elementary. Starting from any point on the line, if Mrs. X buys one less pound of meat she will save $1, with which she can buy 2½ pounds of vegetables. Therefore, the line climbs 2½ units every time it moves one unit to the left. In general terms, if the price of the commodity plotted horizontally is p_1 and that of the commodity plotted vertically is p_2, buying one unit less of the horizontal commodity will save p_1, with which p_1/p_2 units of the vertical commodity can be bought. The slope of the budget line will therefore be p_1/p_2 and it depends entirely on the ratio of the prices.

The interpretation of the slope of the indifference curve at any point is almost as easy. Remember that in the small triangles drawn in Fig. 5–4 (which show the quantity of vegetables needed to compensate for a small decrease in the amount of meat) two of the vertices of the triangle drawn at A' lie on the indifference curve through A'. The chord drawn through those two vertices is an approximation to the tangent at A', and the approximation will become better and better as we think of drawing smaller and smaller triangles. In fact, the tangent is the mathematical limit of those chords as the triangles diminish in size. But the slope of each such chord is the number of pounds of vegetables (the vertical leg) needed to compensate Mrs. X for relinquishing the number of pounds of meat represented by the horizontal leg, or the compensating number of pounds of vegetables per pound of meat forgone. This is a very important concept in economics, known as the *marginal rate of substitution* (abbreviated *MRS*). More explicitly, in this example the slope of the indifference curve is Mrs. X's marginal rate of substitution of vegetables for meat, which can be abbreviated $MRS(V : M)$.

> The marginal rate of substitution of any commodity V for any other commodity M is the number of units of V needed per unit of M to compensate the consumer for forgoing a small quantity of M. It is represented graphically by the slope or tangent of an indifference curve.

For example, at point A' in Fig. 5–4, seven pounds of vegetables are required to compensate Mrs. X for losing two pounds of meat. The *MRS* of vegetables for meat at that point is 3.5 approximately.[3]

In short, the slope of the budget line shows the ratio at which the commodities can be exchanged for each other at market prices, and the slope of the indifference curve shows the ratio at which the consumer would be just willing to exchange them for each other, that is, the number of units of one that he could exchange for one unit of the other and be neither better nor worse off. At the market basket chosen these two ratios are equal or, symbolically

$$MRS(V : M) = \frac{p_1}{p_2}.$$

Verbally: in allocating his budget between two commodities, the consumer will choose the market basket on his budget line for which the *MRS* between the two commodities is equal to the ratio of their prices.

In spite of the forest of technicalities, this is only common sense. Consider

---

[3] We say "approximately" because the slope of the chord is only approximately the slope of the tangent.

any point on Mrs. X's budget line for which the *MRS* of vegetables for meat is not 1 : .40 = 2.5—say, a point at which it is 3.0. At that point 3 pounds of vegetables would be needed to compensate her for giving up one pound of meat, or one pound of meat is as desirable to her as 3 pounds of vegetables. But she can obtain an additional pound of meat by giving up only 2½ pounds of vegetables. If she found herself at such a point, she would move to a higher indifference curve by buying 2½ pounds fewer of vegetables and one pound more of meat, and she would continue to improve her position by moving southeast along her budget line until she reached the point where her *MRS* was equal to the price ratio.

The same is true for market baskets on the other side of the optimal point. At a point where the *MRS* is 2.0, 2 pounds of vegetables would be as valuable in her esteem as one pound of meat. But she can obtain 2½ pounds of vegetables by reducing her purchase of meat by one pound and, again, she would not choose such a point. The only point at which she cannot improve her position by reallocating her purchases is the one at which her *MRS* is equal to the ratio of the prices.

Still another way to express the same conclusion is to say: in allocating his budget between two commodities the consumer will choose the market basket on his budget line at which an additional dollar's worth of one commodity is just as desirable as an additional dollar's worth of the other.

This conclusion says exactly the same thing as went before, but in simpler language: we can expect the consumer to shift his dollars from one commodity to the other as long as he can increase his satisfaction by doing so—unless he is at the point where he's indifferent between additional dollar's worths of the two commodities. This is the same as our earlier conclusion (that a dollar's worth of one commodity would be deemed just as desirable as a dollar's worth of the other), because if we measure quantities in dollars' worth rather than in pounds, the price ratio is by definition 1 : 1, and we have asserted that in that case the *MRS* for the market basket chosen must be 1 : 1.

If the upshot, then, can be reduced to such common-sense, self-evident terms, why all the falderal about indifference curves, marginal rates of substitution, and all that? There are two reasons. First, we have been forced to make explicit many of the assumptions that lie hidden behind common-sense reasoning, and so have a better idea of when it is applicable and when not.[4] Second,

---

[4] Just to indicate how easy it is to slip assumptions in unnoticed, here are some others that were used implicitly in our reasoning. (1) *Completeness:* that the consumer can compare any two bundles and decide which is preferable or whether they are equally satisfactory. He never "just doesn't know which he prefers." (2) *Transitivity:* that if A, B, and C are three bundles of goods, any consumer who prefers A to B and B to C also prefers A to C. This is an obvious prerequisite to making consistent decisions. (3) *Continuity:* that if bundle A is preferred to bundle B we can take away a very small quantity of any commodity from bundle A and have left a bundle that will still be preferred to bundle B. This disallows the preferences of a drunkard, for example, who might prefer a quart of whiskey and a small hamburger to 31 ounces of whiskey and the most delicious dinner conceivable.

For a somewhat more rigorous treatment of consumption theory see our companion volume, *The Price System,* in this series. For a still fuller discussion see Peter Newman, *The Theory of Exchange* (Englewood Cliffs, N.J.: Prentice-Hall, Inc., 1965), or any other good intermediate text on economic theory.

we have laid a foundation for the analysis of consumers' responses to changes in the size of their budgets or in the prices of the things they buy.

EXAMPLES: SUBSTITUTES AND COMPLEMENTS

A couple of examples will show how this method of analysis works and how the indifference curves reflect consumers' tastes. In Fig. 5–6 the topmost diagram is my indifference diagram for two brands of gasoline. It happens that I don't care at all what brand of gasoline I use. If I am deprived of one gallon of either brand, I can get back on to the same indifference curve by replacing it by one gallon of the other. Therefore the indifference curves are straight lines that make 45-degree angles with the two axes. Four of these in-

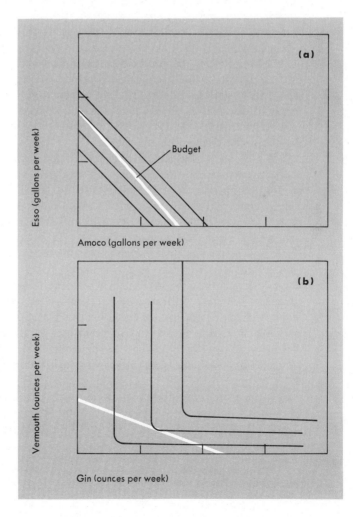

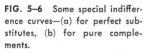

FIG. 5–6 Some special indifference curves—(a) for perfect substitutes, (b) for pure complements.

difference curves are shown. A budget line is drawn, which is slightly steeper than the indifference curves, indicating the Amoco is slightly more expensive than Esso. It isn't tangent to any of the indifference curves anywhere, but it attains the next to highest indifference curve at a point that indicates that I will fill my tank with Esso and not buy Amoco.

If I had happened to prefer one brand, say Amoco, the diagram would have looked a little different. Suppose that I were willing to pay 10 per cent more (about 3 cents a gallon) for Amoco than for the other brand. Then one gallon of Amoco would be worth as much to me as 1.1 gallons of Esso or, if I were deprived of one gallon of Amoco, I could get back on the same indifference curve by replacing it by 1.1 gallons of Esso. The indifference curves would be steeper but they would still be straight lines.[5] And I should still fill my tank with one or the other, depending on whether the price differential was more or less than my degree of preference.

In either version of this example the two brands of gasoline are said to be *perfect substitutes.* (In the second version, 1.1 gallons of Esso is a perfect substitute for 1 gallon of Amoco, even in common parlance.) The defining characteristic of perfect substitutes is that the marginal rate of substitution between them is the same for all market basket combinations of the two. The geometric representation of this fact is that the indifference diagram for the two is a family of parallel straight lines. One economic consequence is that the consumer is likely to spend his entire budget on one or the other, and to shift abruptly if the price ratio changes only slightly.

The lower diagram in Fig. 5–6 shows my indifference map for gin and vermouth. These are *complementary goods,* that is to say, they are consumed in rigidly fixed proportions. This is shown by the indifference curves, which are shaped virtually like reverse "L's." Once I have gin and vermouth in the right proportions, more of either without more of the other leaves me on the same indifference curve. Large changes in the price ratio will not change the proportions in which I consume them appreciably. This is characteristic of complementary goods.

Perfect substitutability and perfect complementarity are extreme forms of consumer preference. Most goods are related in some intermediate fashion, as indicated by the more gradual curvature of the earlier diagrams.

We have now answered our preliminary question: How will a consumer with a given amount of money to spend divide his purchases among different goods so as to obtain maximum satisfaction? But the answer—to equate his *MRS* to the ratio of the prices—was derived from an example using only two goods: meat and vegetables. Now we must do three things. (1) We must extend this answer to the more realistic case where numerous goods are involved. (2) We must ask how the consumer's spending will be affected if the amount of income at his disposal is changed. (3) We must ask how his pur-

[5] Trigonometric exercise: verify that in this case the indifference curves make an angle of 48 degrees with the horizontal axis.

chases will be affected if the relative prices of different goods change. (This last question, indeed, will lead us to a central objective of this chapter—namely, the derivation of demand curves.) We shall take up each of these matters in turn, and all our reasoning will depend on the logical apparatus we have developed to answer the preliminary question.

MORE THAN TWO COMMODITIES

Of course, neither our Mrs. X nor any other consumer normally is concerned with a choice between just two commodities. The importance of the above analysis lies in the fact that the concepts there expounded are applicable no matter how many commodities are involved in the consumer's decision. If a budget is to be allocated among any number of commodities, there is a budget line determined by the total budget and the prices of all the commodities. Preferences among market baskets can be described by indifference curves, no matter how many different commodities are represented in each market basket. There is a marginal rate of substitution between every pair of commodities in a market basket and, when a sensible selection has been made, the *MRS* for every pair must be equal to the ratio of their prices. All this is just as in the two-commodity case, but the argument behind these assertions cannot be reduced to a problem in plane geometry when more than two commodities are involved. Since the argument requires new technicalities but no essential new ideas, however, we shall omit it.

RESPONSE TO CHANGES IN THE BUDGET

Thus far we have seen how a consumer permitted to spend a given budget divides it among commodities at given prices. It is at least as important to economic analysis to see how consumers respond to changes in these data, to which we now advance.

The amount that a consumer spends on any commodity depends on the total amount of money that he is permitted to spend: his budget. When consumers' incomes change, causing changes in their consumption budgets, their demand curves for commodities shift, with important impacts on commodity markets. Consumers in advanced, wealthy countries divide their budgets quite differently from consumers in poor, less-developed countries. Expenditure patterns are not the same in prosperous times as during depressions. These are the phenomena that the theory of the present section illuminates.

We can regard any single purchase decision as a choice between just two commodities. This may seem surprising, when there are so many commodities in the world, but let us look closely at a purchase decision and see what the issues are. Suppose that Mrs. X, our typical consumer, has $50 to spend on

121

all foods, including meat, and that she is now standing before the meat counter. The issue that confronts her is simply that the more she spends on meat, the less she will have left over for everything else on her shopping list. She confronts, at that moment, a two-commodity problem, the two commodities being meat and money left over for other things (*MLO* for short). This choice can be represented on the now-familiar two-commodity diagram, remembering that, by definition, the price of *MLO* is $1 per unit.

Taking this point of view, the two-commodity diagram makes it easy to represent the effect of changes in Mrs. X's budgetary allowance on her purchases of meat. Let x stand for the number of pounds of meat purchased, y for the amount of *MLO*, and B for Mrs. X's total budget. Then, since the prices of a pound of meat and of a unit of *MLO* both happen to be $1, Mrs. X's budgetary constraint or budget line is

$$x + y = B.$$

This line is shown in Fig. 5–7 for three levels of B—$40, $50, and $60. Note that the three budget lines are parallel to each other because the slope of the line depends on the ratio of the prices of the two "commodities," and not at all on the amount of money available for expenditure.[6] In terms of the diagram, a change in the amount available for expenditure shifts the budget line vertically up and down, and has no other effect on it.

Mrs. X's psychological preferences are expressed by indifference curves in which the appropriate commodities now are meat and *MLO*. To be sure, *MLO* is an artificial or composite commodity. The desirability of y of *MLO* is simply the desirability of the best combination of foods other than meat that Mrs. X could buy with $y. But this does not affect our reasoning, and there exist indifference curves between *MLO* and meat just as between vegetables and meat.

Whatever may be the value of B, Mrs. X will select the point on the corresponding budget line at which it touches the highest accessible indifference curve. (Three indifference curves and the consumption choices that they determine are shown in the figure.) When Mrs. X has $40 to spend on food she buys 21¼ pounds of meat; when she has $50 she buys 25 pounds; when she has $60, 29 pounds. We can think of drawing budget lines for other budgetary limits (for example, $45) and of determining the corresponding purchases of meat. Finally, we can think of connecting by a line all the points so determined. This line, called Mrs. X's *expansion path* for meat purchases, is drawn in the figure. It shows how her purchases of meat are influenced by changes in the budget available to her.

As drawn, the expansion path has a slight downward curvature. This shape is characteristic of the expansion paths for luxury goods because it indicates that out of every successive $1 increment in budget a slightly larger pro-

[6] If meat were to cost $1.25 a pound, the equation of the budget lines would be 1.25 x + y = B and the slope of the budget lines would be different from the one shown. But, for the moment, we are not assuming this to be the case.

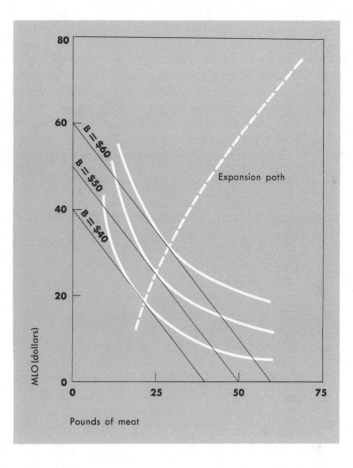

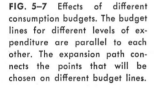

FIG. 5–7 Effects of different consumption budgets. The budget lines for different levels of expenditure are parallel to each other. The expansion path connects the points that will be chosen on different budget lines.

portion will be spent on meat than was spent from the previous increment.[7] The expansion path for a necessity would curl upward because as a consumer's budget is increased gradually the proportion of each successive increase spent on necessities diminishes. It is even possible for the expansion path to turn back on itself—that is, although it must start out (for very low incomes) pointing generally northeast, it may curve upwards until eventually it points northwest. This would indicate that actually less of the commodity in question is purchased at high incomes than at some lower ones. Such commodities are known as *inferior goods*. Familiar examples are cheap grades of clothing, poorer cuts of meat, visits to lower-class resort areas.

Figure 5–7 shows how a consumer's tastes, described by his indifference curves, determine the amount of a commodity that he purchases at different levels of consumption expenditure. Since the total budget is not one of the axes

[7] Check this for yourself: If the expansion path became horizontal, the entire increment in income would be spent on meat.

in this diagram, however, the actual relationship between it and purchases of a specific commodity is shown more clearly by another type of graph, known as an *Engel curve*. The Engel curve corresponding to Fig. 5–7 is shown in Fig. 5–8. The total budget is there plotted horizontally, and the amount of meat purchased is plotted vertically. For example, a purchase of 21¼ pounds of meat is shown corresponding to a food budget of $40. Figure 5–9 shows empirical Engel curves, based on a survey of American consumption habits. The curve for food consumed at home displays the shape characteristic of necessities; the curve for meals eaten out is typical of purchases of luxuries.

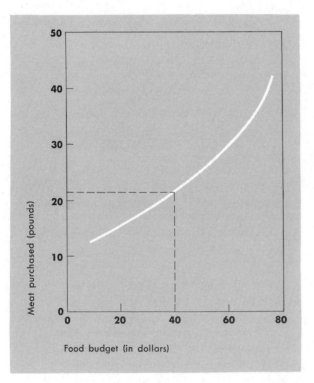

Food budget (in dollars)

FIG. 5–8 An Engel curve. Consumption of this commodity is higher for higher consumption budgets.

One peculiar kind of behavior is illustrated in Fig. 5–10. We include it partly because this case is of some interest in more advanced economic analysis, but mostly to show that it is quite possible to draw indifference maps that make no sense psychologically. In this figure *MLO* is plotted vertically and the quantity of some commodity *A* horizontally. The indifference curves are parallel; they are vertical displacements of each other. The budget lines tangent to the indifference curves are shown. Because the indifference curves are parallel, each of the budget lines is tangent to an indifference curve at the same quantity of

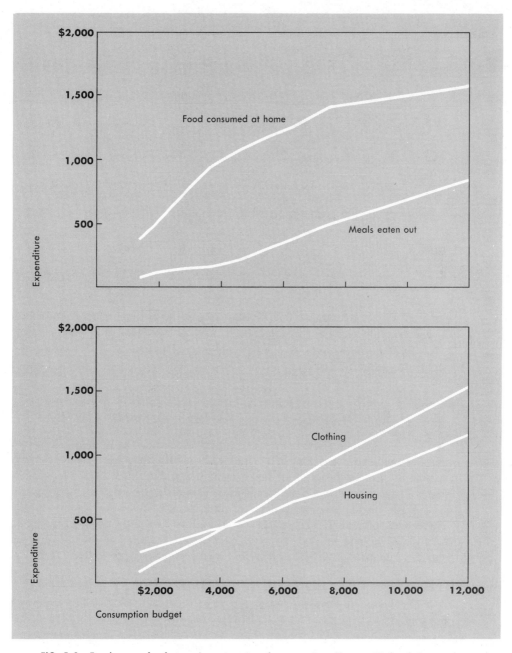

FIG. 5–9 Engel curves for four major categories of consumption. (Source: *Study of Consumer Expenditures, Incomes, and Savings,* University of Pennsylvania Press, 1957.)

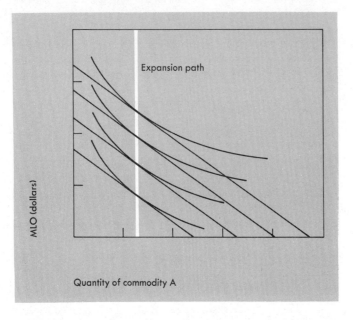

Expansion path

MLO (dollars)

Quantity of commodity A

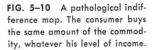

FIG. 5-10 A pathological indifference map. The consumer buys the same amount of the commodity, whatever his level of income.

commodity A as the others. This consumer buys the same amount of commodity A whatever his income. His expansion curve is a vertical line and his Engel curve for this commodity is a horizontal line. There is no real consumer or commodity like this.

RESPONSE TO PRICE CHANGES: DEMAND CURVES

Common sense leads us to expect that when the price of a commodity rises consumers use less of it, and when it falls they use more. Like most common-sense conclusions, this one is usually true, but not always. The concepts that we have been developing permit us to gain a deeper insight as to why.

Figure 5–11 shows again Mrs. X's indifference curves for meat and *MLO*. Three budget lines are shown, all corresponding to a total expenditure of $50 on food. The one labeled "$p = \$1$" is already familiar; it is the one that applies when meat costs $1 a pound, and corresponds to the formula.

$$x + y = 50.$$

The higher line applies when the price of meat is 75 cents a pound; its formula is

$$.75x + y = 50.$$

The lower line applies when meat costs $1.25 a pound. (What is its for-

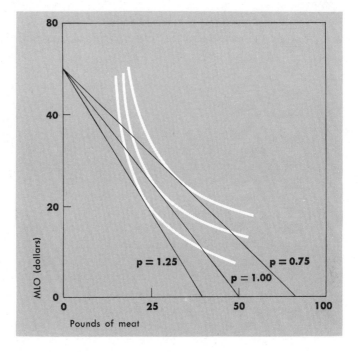

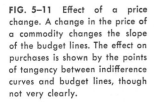

FIG. 5–11 Effect of a price change. A change in the price of a commodity changes the slope of the budget lines. The effect on purchases is shown by the points of tangency between indifference curves and budget lines, though not very clearly.

mula?) Note that these three budget lines form a cone emanating from the point for no meat, $50 *MLO*. The other ends of the lines show how much meat can be purchased if the entire budget is spent on that commodity. The geometric effect of an increase in the price of meat is simply to make the budget line steeper, rotating it around its left end point.

When Mrs. X stands at the meat counter she makes her decision in the light of the price of meat, among other things. To each price of meat there corresponds, as we have just seen, a budget line, and (without thinking of graphs, of course) she chooses the point on that budget line where it just touches the highest accessible indifference curve. The indifference curves and decision points corresponding to three prices of meat are shown in the figure. Mrs. X's decisions accord with our expectations: at a price of $1.25 per pound she buys 23 pounds; at $1 a pound she buys 25 pounds; at 75 cents a pound she buys 29 pounds.[8]

An increase in the price of a commodity has two effects on a consumer: an *income effect* and a *substitution effect*. The income effect is illustrated by the fact that the higher prices of meat, corresponding to the steeper budget lines,

---

[8] This result is not, however, inevitable: you can easily draw indifference curves according to which Mrs. X will buy less meat at 75 cents a pound than at $1 a pound. Of course, they will represent *different* tastes, but they will represent *possible* tastes.

force Mrs. X down to lower indifference curves, just as a reduction in her budgetary allowance would. In a real sense they impoverish her. We already know that, inferior goods apart, a reduction in the budget induces a reduction in consumption of a commodity. The substitution effect arises directly from the increasing steepness of the budget line as the price increases. We also already know that this consumer will choose the point on her budget line where the *MRS* of *MLO* for meat is equal to the price of meat (the price of *MLO* being always 1). If the price of meat rises, the *MRS* of *MLO* for meat at the choice point must rise, too. But the *MRS* rises as we move to the left along an indifference curve or budget line, that is, in the direction of buying less meat. Thus, normally, an increase in the price of a commodity induces a decrease in purchases of it in two ways: first, by forcing the typical consumer to a lower indifference curve; and second, by inducing the consumer to substitute other things for it, as indicated by a movement to the left along the highest indifference curve that can be reached.[9]

The relationship between price and the amount purchased is not shown very clearly in Fig. 5–11 because the price is indicated there only by the slope of the budget line. But the same data can be displayed, as in Fig. 5–12, by plotting prices vertically and showing for each price the quantity that Mrs. X will purchase at that price. For example, Fig. 5–11 shows that Mrs. X will choose 23 pounds of meat when the price is $1.25 a pound; this datum is shown on Fig. 5–12 by the highest of the three emphasized points. The budget line for $1 a pound on Fig. 5–11 shows that Mrs. X will buy 25 pounds at that price. This information is transcribed onto Fig. 5–12 and is represented by the middle emphasized point. In this way, each possible budget line on Fig. 5–11 gives rise to a single point on Fig. 5–12, the point which shows how much meat Mrs. X will buy at the price corresponding to that budget line. When all these points are strung together, the result is Mrs. X's demand curve for meat. It shows vividly how the quantity she buys diminishes as the price increases, and summarizes both the economic and the psychological data that determine her decisions at different possible prices.

MARKET DEMAND CURVES

So much for Mrs. X. We have analyzed her purchasing decisions in some detail, but they are not of much practical importance except to her immediate family. What is important is that Mrs. Y, Mrs. Z, and all the other ladies who buy meat (and shoes, and sealing wax) have indifference curves too,

---

[9] In the case of an inferior good, the first effect (the income effect) of the increase in price will tend to increase consumption of the good, and in extreme instances this will outweigh the second (the substitution) effect. This is how an increase in price can lead to an increase in purchases. The good in question, however, must be both an inferior good and such an important item of consumption that the income effect is substantial.

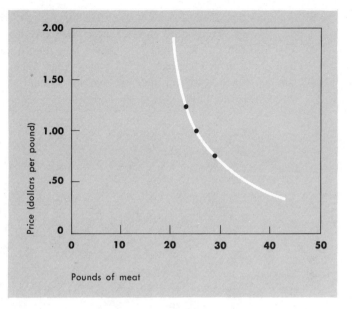

from which their individual demand curves can be determined. These individual demand curves add up to a market demand curve just as, on the other side, the supply curves of individual firms add up to a market supply curve. For example, we know that at $1.25 a pound Mrs. X will buy 23 pounds of meat. Suppose that Mrs. Y, whose husband avoids potatoes, will buy 25 pounds (of meat) at that price, and that Mrs. Z, confined by a more stringent budget, will buy 22 pounds, and that somehow these three constitute the entire market. Then the market demand at a price of $1.25 will be 70 pounds. In the same way, at a price of $1 a pound, Mrs. X will buy 25 pounds of meat. If Mrs. Y then buys 26 pounds and Mrs. Z 24 pounds, the total market demand will be 75 pounds at a price of $1 a pound. Continuing thus, we can ascertain the market demand at every possible price simply by adding up the demands of individual consumers at that price. The result, when graphed, is the market demand curve that we set out to explain.

Now the time has come to look at a real demand curve. It is manifestly impractical to build up the demand curve for a commodity by duplicating our conceptual procedure—that is, by ascertaining the budgets and indifference maps of individual consumers and working from there out. In actual practice, one obtains records on the past behavior of the market (the prices charged, the quantities sold, and other data) and infers from them, by a fairly elaborate statistical analysis, what the demand curve must be.

Figure 5–13 is about as close as we can come to a genuine demand curve without elaborate processing of the data. It shows data on the price and consumption of electric power for domestic use in 53 widely scattered American communities. Each dot shows the data for a single community. For example, the dot labeled "Honolulu" shows that in that city the typical cost for consuming 250 kilowatt-hours ("kwh" for short) in a month is $8.52, and that the typical household there consumes 5,084 kwh a year. Each of the other dots shows the cost of electric power, and the average annual usage by a household, for a different community.

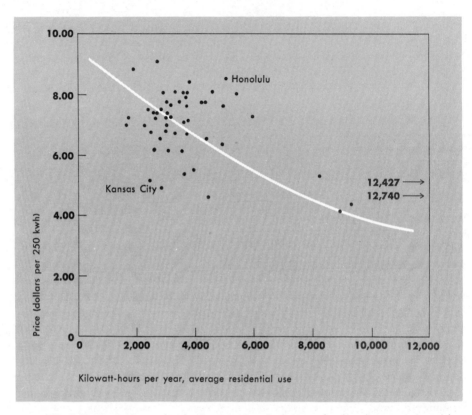

FIG. 5–13   Demand curve for electric power. Even in the case of such a cheap necessity as electric power, consumers tend to use less when the price is high. (Source: *Reports of the Federal Power Commission.*)

The general appearance is far different from the smooth and regular progression of an idealized curve, such as in Fig. 5–12. Of course it is. Any family's use of electric power is influenced by many factors in addition to power rates: the family's income, the number of children, the size of the house, the number of electrical appliances, the prices of competing products such as gas, the climate of the city, and many more. These other factors are so important that we are hardly aware that the price of electric current makes any difference at all to our decisions. Accordingly, the average use of electric power in a city is affected by the proportion of families in each income bracket, the proportion of families of different sizes, the proportions living in houses and apartments of different sizes, the climate, the price of household gas, and many other conditions in addition to the price of electricity. No wonder these dots scatter all over, and no wonder that a good deal of statistical adjustment, to allow for these other factors, is required to bring out clearly the effect of differences in the price of power. Nevertheless, it is evident in this figure that these complicating factors tend to average out, and that there is a general tendency to use more power where it is cheaper. Neither city where the price of 250 kwh was in the neighborhood of $9 used as much as 3,000 kwh per household per year. One city where the price was under $5 used less than 4,000 kwh per year, but that one turns out to be Kansas City, Kansas, where natural gas is exceptionally cheap.

This general tendency to use more power where the price is lower is shown by the curve drawn through the cloud of dots. It shows that *on the average,* consumption falls by about 385 kwh per year for every 1 mill increase in the price of a kwh. Through that is what our theory leads us to expect, it is still a little surprising to see it borne out in the case of a commodity for which the price appears to be such an insignificant element in the purchase decision.

AN OLDER APPROACH: MARGINAL UTILITY

The analysis of consumers' decisions that we have presented is the prevalent one in modern economics. It supplants an older approach that has so much appeal and sufficient validity that it remains indispensable to thinking about consumption. The central assumption of this older approach, which is descended from the utilitarian philosophy of Jeremy Bentham, is that the amount of satisfaction that a consumer obtains from a market basket is a genuine and measurable magnitude called *utility*. The consumer, naturally, chooses the market basket that gives him the most utility for his money.

Translated into terms of our indifference-curve analysis, every indifference curve specifies a family of market baskets each of which confers the same amount of utility as the others. When the consumer strives to attain the highest possible indifference curve, he is, in effect, trying to obtain the most utility that he can afford with his budget.

The distinction between the two approaches arises when we compare various market baskets on different indifference curves. When we were analyzing Fig. 5–5, all we said was that every market basket on indifference curve II is preferred to every market basket on indifference curve III, and that was all we had to say to determine the consumer's decision. But the utility approach says much more. According to it, each basket on indifference curve II yields a certain amount of utility (a certain number of "utils," say) and so does each one on indifference curve III. The difference between the numbers of utils corresponding to the two curves measures how much better indifference curve II is

131

than indifference curve III, a comparison about which the indifference-curve analysis remained stubbornly silent. So the crucial issue is: Can we or can we not say how much better one indifference curve or market basket is than another one? The utilitarians said, "Yes"; the modern economists say, "No."

Surely there is some sense in the utilitarian position. We all know that sometimes we like *A* a little more than *B,* and *B* a great deal more than *C.* Why, then, should economists refuse to pay attention to such differences in the intensity of feelings or preferences? Simply because they have thus far defied all attempts at objectification or measurement. If a consumer chooses *A* when he could afford *B,* we know that he likes *A* more than *B,* but we have no indication of how much more.[10] And since we can explain consumers' decisions without presuming to measure the intensity of preference, we are better off following the more modest course.

But let us waive these scruples for a moment, and accept that utility can be quantified and measured. Then we don't need the technicalities of indifference-curve analysis but can base our theory on two simpler postulates:

1. (Analog of nonsatiation.) The consumer will spend his budget so as to obtain as much utility as possible.

2. (Analog of diminishing marginal substitutability.) Each successive unit of a commodity confers less utility than its predecessor. This is the postulate of diminishing marginal utility.

The first of these postulates is virtually a tautology; the second is classic common sense. Everyone knows that it is practically essential to have one pair of shoes, that a second pair is very useful, a third pair is frequently convenient, and so on. In general, each unit purchased of a commodity meets more urgent needs than its successor. This is all that the postulate says.

These two postulates lead directly to the consumer's demand curves and purchasing decisions. For, imagine a consumer in the process of deciding how much to buy of some commodity that costs $p a unit. He will not buy any of the commodity unless the first unit purchased is more useful to him than the things he would have to go without if he spent $p on it. If the commodity passes this test he will buy one unit, and he will buy a second unit if the additional utility derived from a second unit is greater than the utility he could obtain by spending $p on something else. Continuing, he will keep on buying units of the commodity just as long as the additional utility added by

[10] It might appear that we can measure how much a consumer prefers A to B by comparing the amounts that he is willing to pay for them. But this doesn't work. For example, the fact that a consumer is willing to pay $3 more for A than for B tells us something about his marginal rates of substitution. It tells us that the advantages of A over B are worth as much to him as $3 of unspent money. But unless we know the number of utils that an unspent dollar confers, we cannot convert this observable MRS into an absolute amount of utility. But we have no means of discovering the number of utils conferred by a dollar. All we know is that if the phrase has any meaning at all it is complicated because, for example, it would be meaningless to say that if a consumer's income were increased tenfold he would be ten times as happy as he is now. Money is a rubber yardstick, and cannot be used to measure utility. The same is true of all other yardsticks that have been suggested.

the successive units is at least as great as the utility of $p spent on other commodities. He will stop when he has purchased enough units so that this condition no longer holds.

Naturally, the last unit purchased is the *marginal unit* of the commodity, and the utility derived from it is the *marginal utility*. What we have just seen is that a consumer will continue to buy units of a commodity until its marginal utility is (approximately) the same as the utility that could be obtained by spending the amount that a unit costs on some other commodity. The postulate of diminishing marginal utility assures that this condition will be met sooner or later.

Clearly, the lower the price of a commodity, the more units will be purchased before its marginal utility falls to the point where no more units will be bought. This establishes the consumer's demand curve for the commodity. For if we know the consumer's marginal-utility curve for the commodity and for alternative commodities (the curves showing the marginal utility of each successive unit) we can tell how many units he will buy at each successive price.

This reasoning applies to all commodities, even those that are normally purchased one unit at a time, such as television sets or pairs of shoes. For such commodities the decision is likely to take the form of replacing more or less promptly units that are wearing out, or of having more or fewer of them on hand, but the principles are the same.

To relate this reasoning to our earlier findings, consider the choice between two commodities: X costing $p a unit, and Y costing $q. When the consumer has bought the most satisfactory amount of each, he will be in the following position: If he buys one less unit of X, he will sacrifice the marginal utility derived from that unit—call it $MU(X)$. But he will thereby have $p more to spend on Y, which is enough to buy p/q units of it. By doing so he can obtain $(p/q)MU(Y)$ units of utility from the increased purchases of Y. Since his budget is already well allocated, no such transfer of funds is worthwhile. Therefore the utility gained must be equal to the utility sacrificed, or $MU(X) = (p/q)MU(Y)$. This can be written in the more symmetrical forms

$$\frac{MU(X)}{p} = \frac{MU(Y)}{q} \quad \text{or} \quad \frac{MU(X)}{MU(Y)} = \frac{p}{q}.$$

In words: The marginal utilities of all commodities are proportional to their prices, or the additional utility purchasable for $1 is the same for all commodities. As far as concerns observable behavior this conclusion is in exact agreement with what we found from the indifference-curve analysis. In fact, the ratio $MU(X)/MU(Y)$ is the same numerically (not conceptually) as the $MRS(Y:X)$.

The advantage of assuming quantifiable utilities is that it permits us to go beyond the mere assertion that the consumer will divide his budget so that an additional dollar spent on any commodity buys the same amount of utility. It enables us to estimate the gain in utility that accrues from being able to purchase various commodities at stated prices. This gain is called *consumers' surplus*, and it is very important both in economic theory and in practical economic policy.[11] The concept of consumers' surplus is illustrated in Fig. 5–14. Units of commodity X are plotted horizontally. The height of the rectangle above each unit shows the amount that the consumer would be willing to pay for that unit if he had already bought the preceding units.[12] This "marginal willingness to pay" is the observable counterpart of marginal utility; it is the

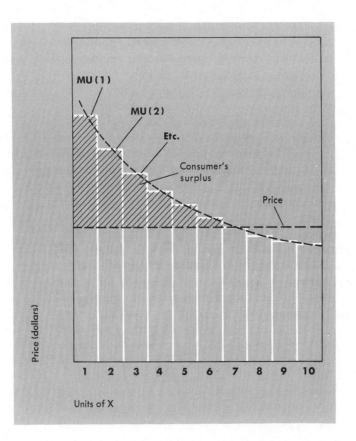

FIG. 5–14 Consumer's surplus. The gain to a consumer from being able to purchase a commodity at a given price is the excess of the marginal utilities of all the units he purchases over that price.

[11] An analog to consumers' surplus, called the *compensating variation,* comes out of the indifference-curve analysis, but it is too technical for us to pursue here. If you are curious, see J. R. Hicks, *Value and Capital* (London: Oxford University Press, 1946), Chap. 2.

[12] There is an embarrassing ambiguity here. The amount that a consumer would be willing to pay for the third or nth unit may very well depend on how much he has already paid for the previous units. The more he has paid for them, the less he may feel able to afford to pay for one more. For example, if shirts are priced "$4 each, three for $11," a consumer may buy three, but if they are "$5 each, three for $13," his budget may permit only two. This is the problem of the "rubber yardstick," or the changing marginal utility of money, in another guise.

consumer's expressed valuation of the utility of that unit of the commodity. The dashed curve through the tops of the rectangles is the consumer's demand curve for the commodity, since he will buy all units of the commodity for which his willingness to pay at least matches the price. At the price shown he would buy seven units.

Let us identify willingness to pay with utility, for want of a better measure. Then the utility of x units to the consumer is the amount he would be willing to pay for them, or $MU(1) + MU(2) + \ldots + MU(x)$, apart from the complication noticed in the last footnote. But if the price is p, all he has to pay is px. The excess of the sum of marginal utilities over px is a pure gain to the consumer, an amount of utility that he enjoys but does not pay for. It is his *consumers' surplus*. Formally, consumers' surplus is the excess of what a consumer would be willing to pay for the amount of a commodity that he buys over what he actually pays. It is represented by the shaded area in the figure. The lower the price of the commodity, the greater the surplus, both because more units will be bought and because the surplus attributable to each unit is greater.

Notice that the consumers' surplus corresponding to any price can be estimated from the demand curve. Just as in Fig. 5–14, it is the area in the warped triangle under the demand curve and above the horizontal line at the level of the price. But, be warned again, this is a defective measure to the extent that the amount a consumer has paid for previous units affects the amount he is willing to pay for additional ones.

In spite of all difficulties of concept and measurement, consumers' surplus is not just a figment of economists' imaginations. Many sellers know about it and try to secure it for themselves. "$4 each, 3 for $11" is not just an obscure way of pricing shirts at $3.67 each; it is also a way to collect $4 each for the first two shirts that a customer buys and thereby to capture 67¢ of his consumers' surplus. All varieties of bulk discounts serve the same purpose.

The policy implications of the consumers'-surplus concept result from the fact that the purpose of economic activity is not really to provide commodities but is fundamentally to provide utility via commodities. We have just seen that the utility of a commodity to a consumer—or its importance to him—is not reflected fully in the amount that he spends on it. If a householder consumes 5,000 kwh of electricity at $2.40 per kwh the utility he derives is not measured adequately by the $120 it costs him and is not necessarily the same as the utility he obtains from a $120 suit. In order to estimate the actual utility derived from any kind of consumption, the consumers' surplus must be added to the actual amount of expenditure. This is hard to do, though, as we have seen, a rough estimate can be derived from a demand curve.

Many government policies influence the quantities of commodities available to consumers or the prices of commodities. The government taxes some commodities, subsidizes others, and produces still others, such as municipal water supplies. All such activities influence the amounts of consumers' surplus as well as of expenditures. A fair appraisal of the effects of changes in these policies ought to take account of their effects on consumers' surplus, among other things. But this is a doctrine of perfection, since there is no fully satisfactory way to estimate consumers' surplus or changes in it.

In summary, the concept of quantifiable utility and its corollaries are potentially powerful tools of analysis. Economists have abandoned them reluctantly in the light of the conceptual difficulties that we have discussed. Nevertheless, these concepts remain highly suggestive, and they are often used in practical work in spite of their well-recognized limitations.

"A GRAIN OF SALT"

The adage "Habit is stronger than reason" applies just as surely to purchase decisions as it does to any other decisions. No housewife out shopping can be constantly cudgeling her brain with questions like "Does my family need these shoelaces more than any other 25 cents item I can think of?" Many families, following longstanding customs, eat fish on Friday but meat the rest of the week, and have Sunday dinner out—and few review this pattern every week in the light of the current prices of fish, meat, and restaurant meals. Yet these customary purchase patterns are not impervious to price changes: the family that eats out pays attention to the right-hand side of the menu, and the fish-once-a-week housewife may respond to a swordfish sale on Tuesday. More fundamentally, though, if prices rise or the pay envelope falls until the customary pattern of purchases costs more than the household can afford, the pattern *has* to be changed.

The theory of consumption sketched in this chapter can best be thought of as a theory of how customary patterns of consumption are formed and altered in the light of how much different things cost and how much the family can afford. To be sure, throughout the chapter we talked of individual purchase decisions, but that was only for simplicity. For our purposes the individual purchase is much less important than the family's general purchase policy. Our concern is not with the amount of meat that Mrs. X will buy next Tuesday, but rather with the amount she will buy on the average—week in and week out—at different levels of meat prices and other data. If our theory is understood in this light, as a description of the kinds of purchase policy that are evolved in the light of experience and stand the test of time, then it may not appear to be such an unrealistic caricature as it seems when taken literally. In this spirit, then, let us evaluate the main conclusions of the chapter.

A typical consumer or family has a limited budget to divide among all the different goods and services it wants and needs. This is not, as we assumed in the text, a precise number (for example, $50 a week for meat and vegetables); rather, it is a general appreciation, acquired through experience, of what the family can afford to spend in the light of its income, its obligations, its expectations, and its habits of saving. Just as the family learns what it can afford to spend by observing the general drift of its assets and debts, so it learns how to divide its budget among different commodities by experience and incessant experimentation. If the payments on the old car were met without trouble, the family is likely to think of a fancier car when the time comes for replacement. If the budget pinches, the family is likely to make a choice between Friday night at the movies and Sunday dinner out, or may make its old bowling shoes last a little longer, or find some other means of retrenchment. In short, although most purchases are an unthinking repetition of habitual patterns, the family is constantly probing for possible changes in these patterns, shifting expenditures from one commodity to another to see whether it can obtain more satisfaction from its expenditures (technically, to see whether it can reach a higher indifference curve).

In reality this probing never stops, but our analysis has shown the nature of the purchase pattern that is being sought: it is the purchase pattern in which the transfer of a dollar from any commodity to any other will neither increase the family's satisfaction appreciably, nor diminish it. In technical language, the pattern sought is one wherein the marginal rate of substitution between any pair of commodities is the same as the ratio of their prices. Though this exact pattern is not likely ever to be attained, obvious discrepancies from it are soon corrected, and the family's actual pattern is normally not far different from this ideal one.

A few implications follow immediately. If a product's price rises, a dollar spent on it will no longer buy as much satisfaction as before. The pattern of expenditures that was ideal before the price change will no longer be appropriate, and families will migrate toward new consumption patterns in which less of this commodity is used. This is the logic behind the demand curves. On the other hand, if a family's income rises, the pressure restraining the consumption of all commodities will be relaxed. The family will be able to afford a higher indifference curve and indeed will move toward one, still maintaining the same marginal rates of substitution between every pair of commodities. This is the logic behind the Engel curves.

IMPLICATIONS OF THE ANALYSIS

We have found that there is an essential logic to consumers' decisions and their consumption patterns, even when our theorizing is taken with the recommended grain of salt. It is by virtue of this logic that consumers' decisions are significant for the economy. In fact, consumers' decisions are the ultimate guides of economic activity, a condition known as *consumers' sovereignty*.

An economy is said to display consumers' sovereignty when its productive activities are responsive to consumers' preferences as reflected in their purchasing choices. Let us see how this works.

We have found that a typical consumer, like our unforgettable Mrs. X, will divide a budget among commodities so that an additional dollar's worth of any one commodity is as desirable as an additional dollar's worth of any other. Suppose, for example, that after Mrs. X had decided on her best consumption bundle (point C of Fig. 5–15) she discovered an additional $1 in her purse. Then it would be practically a matter of indifference whether she spent it to buy one pound of meat or 2½ pounds of vegetables.

Since all consumers trade at the same prices (more or less), the same is true of Mrs. Y, Mrs. Z, and everybody else. So we can say that the whole community is about equally desirous to have an additional pound of meat as to have 2½ additional pounds of vegetables. This is important information for farmers, for businessmen, and for anyone else concerned with arranging the productive efforts of the community. It informs them that if there is an opportunity anywhere for redirecting the use of land and other economic resources so as to increase the production of meat by more than a pound at a sacrifice of no more than 2½ pounds of vegetables, that opportunity ought to be taken. Similarly, if the output of vegetables can be increased by more than 2½ pounds by diverting resources that are being used to produce no more than one pound of meat, that ought to be done. In short, when all consumers face the same prices, those prices indicate the community's relative desires for the different commodities.

We can already see, in a general way, that consumers will be sovereign in an economy in which consumers and producers make their decisions in the light of prices and all use the same prices. For suppose that some farmer can convert a field from pasture to a vegetable plot, reducing his output of meat by 300 pounds and increasing his output of vegetables by 900 pounds. Then, if the prices for which he sells meat and vegetables are the same as those at which Mrs. X buys, his sales of meat will fall by $300, his sales of vegetables will rise by $360, and he will enjoy a net increase of $60 in the value of his output. Then he will convert the land to vegetable production and, indeed, will divide his efforts between meat and vegetable raising so that further increases in vegetable output cost him .4 pounds of meat for each pound of vegetables produced.

Of course, the farmer's wholesale prices are not the same as Mrs. X's retail prices, and the story is more complicated than this. But we already know the essence of it. We acquired the key in our study of production, where we found that under competitive conditions, businessmen will arrange production so that the marginal costs of producing every pair of commodities are proportional to their prices. This means that if some resources are transferred from producing one commodity to another, the decline in output of the commodity that is cut back will have the same money value (and, we now see, the same psychological value) to consumers as the increase in output of the commodity that is expanded. In other words, under competitive conditions, commodities are produced in the proportions that consumers want. A competitive economy obeys consumers' sovereignty.

There is one implication of this analysis that helps tie all its loose threads together. Suppose that there is a general inflation in which the prices of all commodities rise in the same proportion, and suppose that there is some family whose earnings also rise in that proportion. Since the ratios of the prices of different commodities will not change, neither will the marginal rates of substitution among commodities. Since the family will be able to afford, and just afford, the preinflation level of consumption of all commodities (its income having risen in the same proportion as the cost of that expenditure pattern), it is neither tempted nor compelled to change its consumption pattern for financial reasons. In this highly unlikely situation, therefore, the family will continue to consume just what it did before the inflation.

Table 5–1 EXAMPLE OF THE EFFECT OF UNIVERSAL INFLATION ON CONSUMERS' BUDGETS

Commodity	Weekly Consumption	Before Inflation		After Inflation	
		Price	Cost	Price	Cost
Meat	16 pounds	$1.00	$16.00	$1.10	$17.60
Fruit juice	20 pints	.30	6.00	.33	6.60
Bowling	8 strings	.40	3.20	.44	3.52
Expenditure	—	—	25.20	—	27.72
Income	—	—	28.00	—	30.80

An example will make this clearer. Table 5–1 presents data for a family with an income, before inflation, of $28.00 a week, 10 per cent of which it saves, and 90 per cent of which it spends on the three commodities listed, which are all that it consumes. Its preinflation pattern of consumption is shown in the second column. Note that these quantities account for exactly 90 per cent of its income. Note also that at those consumption levels one string of bowling is deemed to be worth just as much as the 1⅓ pints of fruit juice, or the .4 pounds of meat that 40 cents will buy. After the inflation, the family's income and spendable budget have both risen by 10 per cent, but so have all prices. Therefore, the preinflation pattern of consumption will just absorb the amount of income available for consumption. And, since one string of bowling will still be exchangeable for 1⅓ pints of fruit juice (and so forth), there is nothing to be gained by altering the pattern of expenditure. The price changes and the income change cancel each other out.

The importance of this remark is twofold. First, it shows that price changes (especially if they are widespread) and income changes are very much the same kind of thing. Every trade-union leader appreciates this; he knows that as far as his members are concerned, an increase in the consumers' price index is the same thing as a cut in their wage rate. Second, this remark shows that the significant characteristic of a price system is the scheme of relative prices—the ratios of the prices of different commodities. The absolute prices are subsidiary; they are only a convenient vehicle for expressing the relative values of different commodities. (The statement that hamburger costs $1.35 a pound tells nothing to a person who doesn't know the prices of other commodities. Samuel Johnson understood this: when he was told that in the Hebrides one could buy an egg for a farthing, he said "That doesn't prove that eggs are cheap there, but only that money is hard to come by.")

In a whole community of consumers, each allocating his budget so that the relative desirability of commodities is in the same proportion as their prices, these price ratios measure the relative desirability (per unit) of commodities to the community as a whole. This is the essential social message conveyed by prices. It tells how the community's resources should be allocated among the production of different commodities. If consumers are willing to pay as much for a pound of meat as for three pints of fruit juice, and if the resources required to produce two pints of the juice could produce a pound of meat, then consumers could be made better off if the resources were redirected from juice to meat production. Retail prices convey the desirability side of this comparison. Relative production costs, as we saw in earlier chapters, convey the information about the consequences of redirecting resources. The price system as a whole conveys all this information, as well as the motivation for acting on it, and that is why it is an almost indispensable tool for organizing production in a complicated economy. This is a theme to which we shall return often in this book.

SUMMARY AND REVIEW OF CONCEPTS

The main object of the theory of consumption is to explain demand curves, for it is through these that consumers' wants enter into the determination of prices, influence the amounts of different commodities that are produced and supplied, and ultimately contribute to the guidance of the economy.

The significance of a demand curve is derived from the logic of the consumers' decisions that stand behind it—logic revealed most clearly when a consumer has to divide a fixed budget between two commodities. Then the amount of the budget, together with the prices of the commodities, determines a budget line, a line that specifies all combinations of quantities of the two commodities that cost as much as the budget permits. The budget line incorporates all the objective data that influence the consumer's choice.

The subjective data, the consumer's needs and tastes, can be depicted by a set of indifference curves. Each indifference curve shows all combinations of quantities of the commodities that are just as satisfactory as each other. Each possible combination of commodities lies on some indifference curve; in general, if one combination contains more of one commodity than another, and no less of the second, it will be preferred and will lie on a "higher" indifference curve.

The indifference curves, together with the budget line, determine the consumer's choice: he will choose the combination on his budget line where it touches the highest possible indifference curve. The essential psychological properties of the combination chosen can be expressed in a number of different ways. One is to say that when the consumer has that combination, an additional dollar's worth of any commodity is deemed to be just as desirable as an additional dollar's worth of any other. A second way is to use the concept of the marginal rate of substitution: the marginal rate of substitution between any two commodities is the number of units of the first that would just compensate the consumer for the loss of one unit of the second. Graphically, the marginal rate of substitution at any point is the slope of the indifference curve through that point. In terms of this concept, the consumer chooses the point on his budget line at which the marginal rate of substitution between any two commodities is equal to the ratio of their prices.

A change in a consumer's income will result in a change in his consumption budget. Diagrammatically, this is represented by a parallel shift in his budget line. This permits the consumer's response to changes in his budget to be ascertained easily from his indifference-curve diagram. The amounts he consumes of a commodity, plotted against possible budgetary levels, are shown by his Engel curve for that commodity. Engel curves for necessities curl downward, curves for luxuries curl upward, and curves for inferior goods fall when the budget becomes large.

Demand curves also are derived conceptually from indifference-curve diagrams. For this purpose it is convenient to use a diagram in which the purchases of one commodity are shown horizontally and the amount of money left over for other things, *MLO,* is shown vertically. Then an increase in the price of the commodity is represented by a steepening of the budget line. This type of diagram shows that a price increase has a twofold effect. First, it makes the consumer poorer; he can no longer purchase the previous market basket unless his budget is increased. Second, if his budget is increased so that he can afford the old market basket, he will not want it. This will be so because the price is no longer equal to the marginal rate of substitution of *MLO* for the commodity when the old market basket is bought. In normal cases these two effects operate in the same direction: the consumer buys less of the commodity whose price has risen. He does this both because he is poorer and because at the higher price, he prefers a combination where the marginal rate of substitution of *MLO* for the commodity is higher. Pathological cases aside, therefore, the consumer buys less of a commodity the higher its price, as is shown by the usual demand curve.

Since all consumers purchase at the same (or at least similar) prices, all consumers will have the same marginal rate of substitution between every pair of commodities. We are therefore justified in saying that there is a community marginal rate of substitution between every pair of commodities, and that it is equal to the ratio of their prices. But in our study of production we found that competitive businessmen tend to allocate productive resources in such a way that the ratio of the marginal costs of producing every pair of commodities is also equal to the ratio of their prices. Putting these facts together, we see that in competitive equilibrium every productive resource is being used in such a way that if it were shifted to a different commodity it would not produce goods that consumers valued more highly than the ones it currently produces; every resource is being used as consumers want it to be. An economic system that allocates resources in this way is said to obey consumers' sovereignty.

If we can assume that utility can be quantified, most of these conclusions can be reached more easily, and we can go beyond them. We can then explain consumers' purchasing decisions by the theorem that the consumer will divide his budget so that an additional dollar spent on any commodity will buy the same amount of utility as a dollar spent on any other commodity. We can also estimate the utility of a commodity to a consumer by estimating the consumers' surplus he derives from it—the amount he would be willing to pay for it minus the amount he actually has to pay. Each supramarginal unit consumed of the commodity contributes somewhat to consumers' surplus; the marginal unit does not. A rough estimate can be made by measuring the area of an appropriate triangle under the consumers' demand curve. The consumers' surplus should be added to the amount spent on a commodity to measure its importance to the consumer.

But, unfortunately, utility is not measurable, and the concept, though suggestive, cannot stand up to scientific criticism.

Monopoly and Oligopoly

CHAPTER SIX

In this chapter we shall descend from the high plane of generality and abstraction that we have been inhabiting. Thus far we have studied the behavior of competitive markets and their participants. Competitive markets are the simplest to understand, the most predictable, and the most conducive to efficient economic performance, and for these reasons hold a central place in economic analysis. But they are not the only kind of market or even, in modern industrial economies, the most prevalent. To understand the operation of real economies, we must therefore study the behavior of other types of market, too.

THE GENESIS
OF MONOPOLY AND OLIGOPOLY

The hallmark of a competitive market is that every participant in it is a price taker. That is, everyone in it takes it for granted that he cannot affect the prices at which he buys or sells, so does the best he can in the light of those prices. For this situation to hold there must be a large number of suppliers in the market, tolerably equal in size, so that no one firm can have an appreciable effect on the price or aggregate supply of the commodity, and so that no one firm's actions significantly influence the fortunes of any other firm. It must also be true that consumers do not care much, if at all, which firm they buy from, so that they respond readily to small differences in the prices charged by different firms if any should arise. Some examples of competitive markets are women's clothing in manufacturing, coal in mining,

143

and wheat in agriculture. In all those industries the firms are numerous and small, and the products of one firm are virtually indistinguishable from those of any other.

But modern methods of mass production and mass marketing tend to be incompatible with competition,[1] and it is easy to see why this is so. Consider, first, modern methods of production. They tend to require large amounts of fixed capital equipment and to be characterized by *decreasing long-run costs*. That is to say, a large plant operating at an efficient volume of output will have lower average costs than a small plant operating at its most efficient level of output.

When these technological conditions obtain, even an industry that starts out competitive will soon degenerate into some other market form, because the firms in it will tend to grow in order to reduce their costs of production by operating larger, more efficient plants. But they will not all grow synchronously. Historical accidents will guarantee that some of the firms will build large, modern plants before the others, and these will be under strong pressure to cut their prices in order to attain sales volumes at which the large plants can operate efficiently and cover their enhanced fixed cost. Furthermore, by virtue of their increased efficiency, the large firms will be able to operate profitably at prices *below* the average costs of their smaller competitors. This will produce an unstable situation. One by one, the smaller firms will be driven out of the market, forced to bequeath their erstwhile customers to the larger firms—which therefore will grow larger still. Eventually only a few firms will remain, all of them large enough to reap the full advantages of economies of scale.

When this state of affairs is reached, true competition cannot survive. The exact outcome depends on many factors, including especially the proportion of the market that is served by a firm large enough to be fully efficient. In Chapter 3 (Table 3–6) we saw that frequently there is room for only two or three fully efficient firms, even in a large national market. Now, General Electric and Westinghouse cannot pretend that they are participants in a competitive market; both know that between the two of them they control the price and volume of output of many of the products they sell, and this knowledge cannot help but affect their behavior. They constitute an oligopoly (see Chapter 2). To repeat our definition:

> An oligopoly is a market in which there are a few firms, each of which recognizes that its actions have a significant impact on the price and supply of the commodity.

[1] There is an unfortunate divergence between the technical meaning of the word "competition" and common usage. Participants in competitive markets do not "compete" with each other in the common meaning of the term; they merely respond to impersonal market forces. Participants in markets of other forms often do "compete" vigorously (each firm keeps a sharp eye on its rivals' prices and products, makes sure that its own prices are in line, and strives to offer a product with more sales appeal than the rival goods have), but they are not competitive according to the technical meaning of the word, which is reserved strictly for price competition. We, of course, shall always use the words "competition" and "competitive" in their technical senses, but shall have to use the verb "compete" in both meanings, for there is no adequate synonym. These things understood, there is not much risk of confusion.

The process of consolidation that we have just described can go even further if economies of scale continue to accrue (that is, if the long-run average-cost curve continues to decline), until a single firm is so large that it supplies the entire market, or at least the great bulk of it. In that case only one firm will remain, and a monopoly will be established.

A monopoly is a market in which all or virtually all of the commodity is provided by a single seller.

Besides, as we shall see, oligopolists have strong incentives to merge their firms into a monopoly, which from their point of view is the more profitable market form. This is the origin of the trust-building movement of the late nineteenth century.[2] Trusts and other forms of monopoly are now illegal in this country and most others, except in special circumstances. Nevertheless, the eternal vigilance of the Antitrust Division of the Department of Justice is required to prevent monopolies from reemerging in various surreptitious forms.

An extreme form of economies of scale is a so-called *natural monopoly,* exemplified by local electric-power companies, telephone companies, and other public utilities. There the technical advantages of supply by one large firm are so commanding that a single firm is licensed by the government to serve the entire market. In return for this exclusive license, or franchise, the firm submits to control by regulatory authorities that endeavor to assure adequate service at reasonable prices on the part of firms that are insulated from any competitive pressures. The regulatory agencies, in effect, try to prevent the monopolies from behaving like monopolies. We shall shortly see why this is important.

To summarize briefly: the advantages of mass production, or economies of scale, engender oligopoly and, in extreme form, monopoly; the advantages of mass marketing reinforce, and in many cases replace, the effects of economies of scale.

Mass Marketing

Mass marketing is a phenomenon quite alien to competition, and of relatively recent origin. The discovery is generally attributed to the National Biscuit Company, which launched a product called "Uneeda Biscuits" about 70 years ago and thereby consigned to a nostalgic past the old cracker barrel filled with crackers from small, anonymous bakeries. No recent discovery, save only the automobile, has had so deep and pervasive an impact on our way of life.

Mass marketing consists in distinguishing a firm's products from those of its competitors by means of branding and trademarks, and in creating a pref-

[2] A *trust* is a corporate device in which the stockholders of a number of oligopolistic firms assign their shares to an organization that holds them "in trust" and is thus able to control the firms and coordinate their policies. See pp. 56–57 of Richard Caves, *American Industry: Structure, Conduct, Performance,* 2nd ed., in this series.

erence for the brand by advertising. The interplay among mass marketing, mass production, and the formation of oligopoly is very intricate. Mass marketing depends on the identification of a product with its producer.[3] In an oligopoly based on decreasing long-run costs, this identification arises spontaneously: when only a half dozen firms manufacture a product, purchasers come to know which one made each article; the manufacturer's signature is on every item he produces, be it in the form of merely his firm name or in the form of an elaborately concocted trademark. In these circumstances the firm might as well turn the inevitable to advantage, and try to make consumers *want* his particular brand of the commodity.

This opportunity is also almost a necessity because of the economics of large-scale production and the nature of the rivalry among competing oligopolists. Mass production requires an elaborate plant with heavy fixed costs, and so a large volume of sales is imperative. The owner of a large plant cannot afford to entrust his sales volume to the caprices of an anonymous market where even a high-cost, pipsqueak competitor can steal sales from him, or a respectable rival can attract his customers with ease. He must tie his customers to himself as firmly as he can. And this is where mass merchandising helps, because it is one of the most effective expedients available to oligopolists in their struggle to attract each other's customers and hold their own. So oligopoly, which makes mass merchandising possible, also makes it necessary.

But mass merchandising can succeed even when there is no technological basis for oligopoly; it can create oligopoly single-handedly. This comes about through a number of mechanisms, of which the most evident is the existence of economies of scale in advertising. If a firm doubles the number of insertions of an advertisement or advertises in media with double the circulation of media previously used, its advertising costs will approximately double, but the effectiveness of its campaign will more than double. The psychological causes of this phenomenon are obscure, but it seems that repeated exposures to a firm's advertisements reinforce each other. Advertising men say, "Repetition is reputation." It appears that an advertising campaign leaves a residue of feeling of familiarity that makes the customer assured and comfortable when he buys the product, and uncertain and dubious when he confronts an unadvertised article. And customers sometimes believe that if a firm spends a great deal on advertising, it cannot afford to offer an inferior product. But be this as it may, single or rare exposures to a firm's advertisements do not predispose the consumer to purchase; frequent exposures in large-circulation media do. This gives marked advantages to the large firms that can afford large advertising campaigns. It conduces to oligopoly.

Moreover, success in selling is self-reinforcing. When prospective purchasers see people all around them using a particular brand, they presume that

[3] The contrasting anonymity of producers in a competitive industry is illustrated by women's dresses. If a woman likes the looks and price of a dress, she buys it, and she rarely knows or cares which company manufactured it except in the case of *haute couture*.

it gives satisfactory, and perhaps even superior, service. This is the *demonstration effect*. Because of it, each sale makes the next one a bit easier. It is a boon to the large firms whose products are visible everywhere, helping them grow, whereas the smaller, less well-known firms find it difficult to attract the consumer's attention to their brands. Any disparity in the size of firms tends to increase rather than to shrink.

Finally, large volume is the key that unlocks the channels of distribution. Some products, such as automobiles and gasoline, are marketed through franchised dealers and chains of brand outlets (respectively). For such products the volume of sales in each locality served must be large enough to support an outlet of minimum efficient scale. The number of outlets must in turn be great enough to provide convenient service to customers throughout the region in which the product is sold—frequently the entire country (to gain the advantages of national advertising). Multiplying the required level of sales per outlet by a large number of outlets leads to a requirement for selling to a substantial proportion of the entire market, and again, this is the essence of oligopoly.

Large volume is also essential to products distributed through general retailers. The consumer is most likely to buy what he sees; namely, what is on the dealers' shelves. Dealers, in turn, assign their scarce shelfspace to brands that are selling well. Thus, large volume helps generate still larger volume. Here is yet another self-reinforcing mechanism, and all these mechanisms reinforce each other. In short, bigness per se is an advantage to a firm: large firms grow and small ones vanish or are relegated to narrow, specialized segments of the market.[4]

To recap: in many industries the advantages of mass production and mass merchandising conspire to concentrate the market in a few large hands. Since the ultimate in concentration—monopoly—is impeded by legal restraint, it is not surprising that oligopoly has become the characteristic form of market in modern, industrial economies; practically all the famous companies you can name are oligopolists. We must now investigate the performance of these two market forms. Monopoly, being simpler, comes first.

MONOPOLY

Everyone envies the happy monopolist. The competitive firm has to sell at the market price, and squeeze out what profits it can by holding production costs down to their very minimum—but even then is likely to have its profits competed away. The oligopolist has formidable rivals to contend

[4] Magazine publishing is a prime example of these reinforcing mechanisms. The result is a handful of general-circulation giants such as Time, Inc., along with thousands of smaller—though often quite respectable—firms catering to specialized and localized markets. (These smaller firms are called "the competitive fringe.")

with. But the monopolist chooses his own prices and has no serious rivals; indeed, he has practically nothing to worry about except the Antitrust Division, or perhaps a regulatory commission. How should he conduct himself to take advantage of this unparalleled felicity?

The answer is basically a familiar one by now, but we have to introduce a new concept to express it clearly. The essential peculiarity of the monopolist is that his firm's individual demand curve is identical with the demand curve for his product. The monopolist has the privilege of setting the price of his product, but then he can sell only the quantity corresponding to that price on his product's demand curve. If he raises the price, he must be content to sell less; if he wants to sell more, he must lower the price. So his essential decision problem is to find the most profitable price–quantity pair on his demand curve. He does this by the now familiar process of equating his margins—by equating the marginal cost of his product to the increase in his gross sales revenue that would result from selling one more unit. This is the concept we need, the concept of *marginal revenue*.[5]

> Marginal revenue is the increase in the gross value of sales that would result from selling one more unit.

The distinctive feature of a monopoly is that a monopolist's marginal revenue is *not* equal to his price, as is a competitive's firm's. For the monopolist to sell an additional unit he must reduce the price on all units sold, in accordance with the slope of his demand curve.[6] Hence the amount he realizes by selling an additional unit is less than the price he sells it for; reduction in the price of his previous sales has to be subtracted off. For a monopolist, though not for a competitor, then, we must distinguish between price and marginal revenue.

It should be pretty evident why it is most profitable for a monopolist to select the volume of sales at which marginal revenue equals marginal cost. If marginal revenue is greater than marginal cost, selling one more unit will contribute more to his sales revenues than producing it will add to his expenses. It will enhance his profits. On the other hand, if marginal revenue is less than marginal cost, he is losing money on the last unit he produces, and perhaps on others. But when marginal revenue is equal to marginal cost, he cannot increase his profits either by reducing or increasing his levels of output and sales.

From a competitive firm's point of view, the demand curve for his product is too remote to be of interest; no conceivable increase in his level of sales

---

[5] The exact symmetry between marginal revenue and marginal cost should be noted.

[6] There is such a thing as a "discriminating monopolist," one who is in a position to charge different prices for different units of output. This is even better than monopoly simpliciter. The average renowned surgeon is in this happy position, for example, and so are most electric-utility companies and railroads. But we shall not be able to study the behavior of discriminating monopolists.

could have a visible effect on the total sales of the industry or on the market price. But a monopolist realizes that he can depress the price by his own activities, and this makes increases in output less attractive to him than to a competitive firm.

To see the force of all this, suppose that a monopolist can sell 800 units a month at a price of $13 per unit and that his demand curve shows that he has to reduce his price by ⅝ cents in order to sell 801 units a month. Then, with an output of 800 units a month, his total value of sales is 800 × $13 = $10,400; with an output of 801 units a month his total value of sales is 801×($13− $.00625) = $10,407.99. Note that his *marginal revenue* is about $8, which is substantially less than the price of $13 that he is charging.

Whether the monopolist will want to increase his monthly sales from 800 to 801 depends on the comparison of this marginal revenue with his marginal cost. If his marginal cost at an output of 800 a month is *less* than $8 per unit, it will be profitable for him to increase his production. But if his marginal cost is *more* than $8 a unit, even though it is less than his price of $13 a unit, he will want to reduce his output to 799 a month (which would permit him to raise his price about ⅝ cents per unit), or even further. He will be content with sales of 800 a month only if his marginal cost is just about $8 a unit. In general: a monopolist will choose a price–quantity combination on his demand curve at which his marginal revenue is equal to his marginal cost.

This is the salient difference between competition and monopoly: the competitor and the monopolist both produce outputs such that marginal revenue equals marginal cost, but a competitor's marginal revenue is equal to his price, whereas a monopolist's is inevitably less. We shall soon see the consequence of this.

A Graphic Representation of Monopoly

The behavior of a monopolist can be analyzed with the help of a convenient diagram. To help construct it, imagine a monopolist whose cost data are the same as those of the competitive firm discussed in Chapter 3 and shown in Table 3–3. (For convenience, those cost data are reproduced in Table 6–1 and graphed in Figure 6–1.) A monopolist does not confront a market price, but he does have to consider the demand curve for his product, for this shows how many units he can sell at each price that he might select. This curve also is shown in Fig. 6–1.[7]

The worthwhileness of an additional sale per month to a monopolist does not depend upon its price but upon the marginal revenue that it yields, and

---

[7] The formula for the demand curve in the graph is $p = 18 - (x/160)$. That formula shows the price, p, at which consumers will purchase any given monthly volume, x. Try $x = 1,200$. You should get $p = \$10.50$ for the price at which 1,200 units a month will be bought.

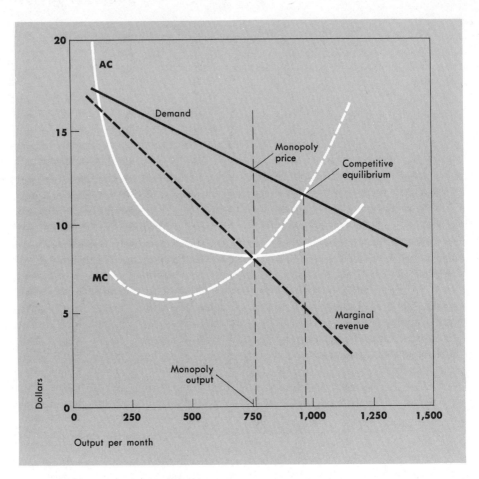

FIG. 6–1 Short-run equilibrium of a monopolist. The price is higher than it would be for a competitor, and the quantity is smaller.

Table 6–1   COST AND REVENUE DATA FOR A MONOPOLIST

Monthly Output (Units)	Average Cost ($ per unit)	Marginal Cost ($ per unit)	Price ($ per unit)	Marginal Revenue ($ per unit)
100	19.00	—	17.375	16.74375
200	13.00	7.00	16.750	15.49375
300	10.67	6.00	16.125	14.24375
400	9.50	6.00	15.500	12.99375
500	8.80	6.00	14.875	11.74375
600	8.42	6.50	14.250	10.49375
700	8.21	7.00	13.625	9.24375
800	8.19	8.00	13.000	7.99375
900	8.33	9.50	12.375	6.74375
1000	8.65	11.50	11.750	5.49375
1100	9.14	14.00	11.125	4.24375

we already know that this will be less than the price. The marginal revenue corresponding to each level of sales is also shown in the figure.[8]

The marginal-revenue and marginal-cost curves intersect at an output of 800 units a month. (The average-cost curve is irrelevant for the moment.) By our previous reasoning, this is the most profitable output for the monopolist, so that he should charge the corresponding price on the demand curve, or $13. If he should charge a higher price (sell fewer units) he would be declining to produce some units that would add more to his revenue than to his costs, because for them, marginal revenue would exceed marginal cost. If he should charge a lower price, he would be selling some units that cost him more than their contribution to his sales revenue. Only $13 is just right.

How about his profit at this most profitable level of output? Profit arises from the excess of price over average cost. It so happens, in this instance, that the average and marginal costs are almost equal at the most profitable level of output. (We shall see shortly why the data were chosen to work out that way.) Therefore, marginal revenue is equal to average cost, and since price is necessarily greater than marginal revenue, there is a positive profit—the monopolist's profit.

But, we should emphasize, the data didn't *have* to work out that way. The most profitable level of output, determined by the intersection of the marginal-cost and-revenue curves, might have occurred in the rising portion of the average-cost curve. In that case, marginal cost would have been greater than average cost, and price, being greater than marginal revenue (= marginal cost), would have been greater still. Finally, the most profitable level of output might have occurred in the falling portion of the average-cost curve. Then marginal

---

[8] The marginal revenue resulting from an additional sale at any level is a consequence of the demand curve in the following way. At any level of sales the total revenue, call it $TR(x)$, equals quantity time price, or $xp(x)$, where we write $p(x)$ for p to remind ourselves that p depends on x. Thus:

$$TR(x) = xp(x) = x \left(18 - \frac{x}{160} \right).$$

Then, by the definition of marginal revenue:

$$MR(x) = TR(x + 1) - TR(x)$$

$$= (x + 1)\left(18 - \frac{x + 1}{160} \right)$$

$$- x\left(18 - \frac{x}{160} \right)$$

$$= 18 - \frac{x + 1}{160} - x\,\frac{x + 1}{160} + x\,\frac{x}{160}$$

$$= 18 - \frac{2x + 1}{160}.$$

(Compute the marginal revenue for $x = 800$. It should be $7.99375.) $MR(x)$ is the marginal-revenue curve shown in the diagram.

cost and marginal revenue would be less than average cost. But the price, which exceeds the marginal revenue, could still be greater than the average cost, leaving a positive profit.

In the short run, then, the monopolist with a given fixed plant operates at the level of output at which marginal revenue and marginal cost are equal. His long-run adjustments are then very much like those of a competitive firm. Having attained the most profitable level of output in the short run, the monopolist will enlarge, reduce, or modify his plant if by doing so he can reduce the average cost of his current level of output. In the long run, therefore, he will have the plant in which his current output can be produced as cheaply as possible.

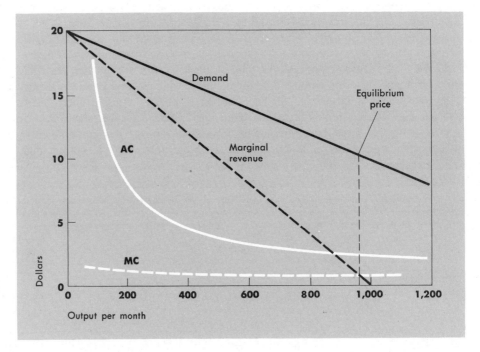

FIG. 6–2 Long-run equilibrium of a monopolist with decreasing long-run costs. Price is inevitably higher than marginal cost.

If the monopolist's technology is one with constant long-run costs, then, just as in a competitive industry, when he has the most appropriate plant for his current output, he will also be using that plant at its most efficient level: the bottom of its average-cost curve. This is the situation depicted in Fig. 6–1, which accordingly shows the long-run equilibrium of a monopolist with constant long-run costs. By contrast with the competitive case, in which profit is competed away in the long run, a substantial margin of profit remains for the monopolist.

We know, however, that monopoly typically tends to arise in a different sort of industry, one characterized by decreasing long-run costs. The situation shown in Fig. 6–2 is therefore much more characteristic of monopolies. In that figure, the curve labeled *AC* is a long-run average-cost curve—that is, a curve showing the average cost for each level of output when produced in the plant in which that cost is lowest. (Note that it declines throughout its range.) The corresponding marginal-cost curve is also shown; it is always below the average-cost curve. (Why?) This diagram makes it clear that a monopolist cannot be blamed for behaving like a monopolist. Since his marginal cost is always lower than his average cost, if he were to charge a price equal to marginal cost, as a competitor does, he would be losing money. No matter how economists may extoll the virtues of marginal-cost pricing (that is, charging for each unit of a product the addition to costs attributable to it), the monopolist cannot afford to follow that policy.

Demand and marginal-revenue curves are also shown in Fig. 6–2. The long-run equilibrium for this monopolist is to produce about 960 units a month for a marginal cost of 68 cents and a price of $10.40. A regulatory agency might require the monopolist to charge a price equal to average cost, interpreting cost to include a reasonable return on invested capital; and this is often done. In this instance, however, extrapolating the data in Fig. 6–2 shows that such a regulation would result in an output of 1,850 units, a price of $1.50, and a marginal cost of 54 cents. Although the monopolistic restriction of output would be greatly reduced, the principle of marginal-cost pricing would still be violated.

Monopoly and Elasticity of Demand

What makes monopoly possible is the efficiency of large-scale operation; what makes it worthwhile is the slope of the demand curve. For remember: the more nearly horizontal a monopolist's demand curve is, the closer together are his demand and marginal-revenue curves, and the smaller is the discrepancy between price and marginal cost. If a monopolist could have an absolutely horizontal demand curve, he would behave just like a competitor. The difference between competitive and monopolistic behavior therefore depends on the slope of the demand curve. Perhaps we had better see in a bit more detail how this slope influences the monopolist.

For this purpose, the most significant characteristic of a demand curve is its *elasticity,* a very natural measure of how responsive demand is to changes in price.

The elasticity of demand for a commodity is the percentage reduction in the volume of sales that would be induced by a 1 per cent increase in price.

To illustrate this concept, let us compute the elasticity of demand for the monopolized product of Table 6–1 when 800 units are being sold. The price is then $13, and a 1 per cent increase would raise it to $13.13. From the formula for the demand curve (footnote 7, above) we can compute that 779 units would be sold if this price were charged. This is a fall of 21 units or 2.6 per cent, which accordingly is the elasticity.

The critical value of elasticity is unity, or one. For if elasticity = 1, then a 1 per cent increase in price will cause a 1 per cent decrease in the volume of sales. These two changes will just about offset each other, leaving the total value of sales unchanged. But with 1 per cent fewer units to be produced, total variable costs would be diminished by such a change. It follows that if a monopolist should find himself producing an output for which the elasticity of demand is unity or lower, he would restrict his output and increase his price. As he does so, his elasticity of demand will increase, generally speaking (but not inevitably). This is illustrated in Table 6–2, which is derived from Table 6–1 by the computation just explained. The monopolist will stop raising his price, as we already know, when he has restricted output to the point where marginal revenue and marginal cost are equal.

Table 6–2 ELASTICITY OF DEMAND DERIVED FROM A LINEAR DEMAND CURVE

Monthly Output (Units)	Price ($ per unit)	Marginal Revenue ($ per unit)	Elasticity
100	17.38	16.744	27.8
200	16.75	15.494	13.4
300	16.12	14.244	8.6
400	15.50	12.994	6.2
500	14.88	11.744	4.8
600	14.25	10.494	3.8
700	13.62	9.244	3.1
800	13.00	7.994	2.6
900	12.38	6.744	2.2
1000	11.75	5.494	1.9
1100	11.12	4.244	1.6
—	—	—	—
1440	9.00	−0.006	1.0

It is shown in the appendix to this chapter that when this equality is attained, the percentage markup of price over marginal cost, from which the monopolist's profit is derived, is equal to the reciprocal of the elasticity of demand. If the elasticity of demand is high, this percentage markup is small; if demand is inelastic, it is large. The profitability of a monopoly depends, therefore, directly on the elasticity of the demand curve.

The Consequences of Monopoly

In effect, the monopolist restricts his output to maintain his price. Some monopolists, recognizing this, do not even bother to set a price openly. De Beers Consolidated, Ltd., the world monopolist of gem-quality diamonds, simply controls the output of its subsidiaries and allows the price to be determined by a kind of auction of this controlled output. They get the desired result without the bother and embarrassment of having to publish an elaborate price schedule.

If by some miracle the industry graphed in Fig. 6–1 could be converted to a competitive industry with the same cost and demand conditions, the principles of Chapter 3 would apply. Each competitor would ignore, correctly, the effect on the price of an expansion of his sales, and output would rise until the marginal cost was as great as the price. If this industry were competitive, therefore, output would rise to 1,000 units a month; the price would fall to $11.60.

The fundamental objection to monopoly is that by holding down production to the level at which marginal cost equals his marginal revenue, the monopolist wastes economic resources. It is important to see why this is so. When the output is 800 units a month, the marginal cost is $8 per unit. This means that an 801st unit could be produced by purchasing and using labor services, raw materials, power, and other ingredients worth, in all, $8. The fact that the monopolist would have to pay $8 for these ingredients indicates that other firms —especially including competitive ones—are willing to pay that much for them; otherwise the price would be different. This indeed is the true meaning of prices: what one man *has to* pay for something is what another one *would be willing* to pay for it.

Now, why would a competitive firm be willing to pay $8 for these resources? Because it could use them to produce something worth $8 to its customers, thereby adding $8 to its total sales. (Remember that in a competitive industry price equals marginal cost, so that a product that adds $x to costs will sell for $x.) We have encountered again the notion of opportunity costs—the idea that the real cost of anything is the value of the things that could have been produced with the resources it consumes. The opportunity cost of the monopolist's unproduced 801st unit, for which customers are willing to pay about $12.99, is only $8, and herein lies the waste. Since the customers would be willing to pay $12.99 for the unavailable 801st unit, they clearly prefer it to the $8 worth of alternatives that are produced in its stead. By declining to produce the 801st unit, the monopolist has compelled the economy to use certain resources to produce something worth only $8 when he could have used those resources to produce something worth $12.99. The monopolist has barred some resources from their most productive employment.

We can look at this same distortion in another way: by pegging the price at $13, the monopolist has put a false signal into the price system. From the standpoint of his customers, the opportunity cost of his product is $13 because that is the value of the other things they have to forgo in order to obtain a unit of it; from the standpoint of the economy the opportunity cost is $8. Consumers therefore unduly restrict their use of the monopolized product. Perhaps they use an inferior substitute for it that costs $11 to produce, thereby consuming $11 worth of resources for a purpose that could be served better by $8 worth. Consumers are misled, from the point of view of making the best use of the resources available to the economy, into buying too little of the monopolized product, and too much of others.

There is also a moral objection to monopoly that most economists, including me, prefer to shy away from. It is often said that monopolists are in a position to "exploit" their customers, that it is *wrong* for a monopolist to charge $13 for a commodity that costs him $8 to produce. The economist would prefer to leave questions of right and wrong out of transactions between consenting adults, simply because there is no clear way to resolve them. Is it wrong for a monopolist to charge $13 for something that has cost him $8? After all, the customer pays the price willingly. And, besides, competitive firms do the same thing, in the short run, until excess profits are competed away. The difference is that in the competitive case the excess profit is a vital signal that induces an increase in the production of the commodity in question, whereas the monopolist inhibits the constructive competitive response. So the social damage comes back to the same thing, monopolistic restriction of output.

Take an extreme case: suppose someone monopolized the water supply in a desert community. He could charge an exorbitant price and impose desperate hardship. But the hardship would result from the fact that he profited by distributing too little water. The harm would lie again in the monopolistic restriction. This is the feature that the economist objects to. The monopolist makes his customers willing to pay too much for his commodity by distributing too little of it. He does impose hardship in extreme cases, inconvenience in others, but always by distorting the use of economic resources.

For the above reasons, unregulated monopoly is generally considered to be intolerable. But in the public-service industries,[9] especially, the economies of scale are so striking that it seems almost inconceivable to have several firms serving a single area or route. Consequently, in these industries it is usual to permit a monopoly subject to government supervision. Unfortunately, we cannot discuss in detail here the problems of regulating a public-service monopoly; it would be instructive to do so.[10] Suffice it to say that they all arise from the extraordinary difficulty of making sound economic decisions without the guidance of market prices. (A regulatory commission has, in effect, to set the price schedule of the industry it supervises. This alone is hard enough, since, as we have seen, marginal costs are not an adequate guide. But on top of that, once this has been accomplished, the commission usually finds that the quality of service that it expected will not be provided at the set prices without incessant supervision, because of the absence of competitive pressures.)

[9] Telephone and telegraph, electric power, gas, railroad and air transport, pipelines, urban transit, and the like.

[10] Some of the difficulties are considered in Caves, *American Industry*, pp. 68–73.

OLIGOPOLY

Some idea of the prevalence of oligopoly can be gleaned from Table 6–3. The table shows the percentage of shipments made by the largest four and the largest eight companies, and some other data, in each of the eleven census-classification industries that shipped more than $3 billion worth of products in 1963. The most concentrated of these industries is automobiles and parts; there the largest eight of 1,655 firms shipped 83 per cent of the total product. The least concentrated was newspapers, but even there the largest eight firms accounted for more than one-fifth of sales. The most concentrated major industries in the Census Bureau listing are cigarettes and aluminum production, in both of which seven firms produce the entire output. The least concentrated major industries with national markets are dresses and special tools and dies. Both of them have upwards of 4,500 firms, of which the largest eight produce 9 per cent of industry output. Clearly the norm for manufacturing industries is to have a handful of large firms dominating the market, that is, oligopoly.

Table 6–3 CONCENTRATION RATIOS FOR MANUFACTURING INDUS-
TRIES THAT SHIPPED $3 BILLION OR MORE IN 1963

Industry	Value of Shipments ($billion)	Number of Firms	Percentage Shipped by	
			Largest Four Firms	Largest Eight Firms
Motor vehicles and parts	12.3	1655	79	83
Aircraft	3.5	82	59	83
Aircraft engines and parts	4.1	194	56	77
Blast furnaces and steel mills	7.5	162	50	69
Organic chemicals	4.8	343	51	63
Petroleum refining	16.5	266	34	56
Cotton-weaving mills	3.1	229	30	46
Radio, TV, communications equipment	7.1	1001	29	45
Paper mills	3.8	186	26	42
Pharmaceuticals	3.3	944	22	38
Newspapers	4.5	7982	15	22

Source: Senate Committee on the Judiciary, Concentration Ratios in Manufacturing Industry, 1963, 89th Cong., 2d sess.

Oligopoly is not a compromise between competition and monopoly; it is fundamentally different. Competition and monopoly have this in common: that each firm confronts impersonal and anonymous market forces. A competitive firm knows that nothing it does will have a noticeable effect on the profitability or behavior of any other firm, and that no other firm can affect its profits significantly. A monopolist deals with numerous customers, no one of whom has an appreciable influence on his sales or profits. But an oligopolist stands in a different relationship both with his competitors and with his customers.

157

With respect to the oligopolist's competitors: there are only a few of them, and so whenever he changes his price, alters his product, or does anything else of that sort, the move is noticed and the impact is felt by the other firms in the market. Because they may be induced to retaliate in some manner, the oligopolist must weigh carefully the pros and cons of his moves. The inescapable fact is that the profits of an oligopolist depend not only on what he does, but on what each of his rivals does, and vice versa. We shall shortly explore the consequences of this interdependency.

With respect to his customers: the oligopolist, being one of but a few suppliers, lacks the anonymity of the true competitor. (We have already noted some of the far-reaching implications that follow from this.) Indeed, the identification of the oligopolist with his product is so important that it pays to distinguish two variants of this market structure: *differentiated* and *undifferentiated* oligopoly.

In a differentiated oligopoly the products of different firms are distinguished clearly and purchasers have definite preferences among them. In undifferentiated oligopoly, purchasers have no strong preferences among producers.

The oligopolist prefers differentiated to undifferentiated oligopoly. To the extent that he succeeds in differentiating his product, his customers regard competing brands as inferior substitutes, and he attains the position of a weak monopolist with some inelasticity in his demand curve to exploit. Well-differentiated brands (for example, Cadillacs, Parker pens) can sell for more money than can comparable competing products. So the oligopolist strives to differentiate, and for this purpose has two devices: advertising (which we have already discussed) and *product variation* (by which the oligopolist endeavors to incorporate "selling features" into his product, in order to make it better, or at least different).

The development of selling features that appeal to customers is one of the main bases for the claim of the merchandising profession that it makes a positive social contribution—a claim that is difficult to appraise. Some very sardonic remarks used to be made about high tail fins on automobiles (though they did make it possible for a driver to see the rear of his own car for once), but the same critics had almost nothing derogatory to say about the introduction of automatic shifting (which gave mechanics nightmares and reduced gasoline efficiency by more than 10 per cent). Fundamentally, it would seem that the critics had no basis for judging that one of these changes was "progress," the other not; consumers accepted both gladly.[11] What we are driving at is that these and all such changes are very costly: it has been estimated that the frequent model changes in the automobile industry cost about $1 billion a year.[12] Are the improvements worth it? You have to judge yourself.

[11] It so happened, of course, that one of these changes became permanent and the other proved evanescent. Perhaps this provides a basis for belated appraisal.

[12] See also Caves, *American Industry*, 3rd ed., p. 107.

Products differ in the extent to which they can be differentiated. It happens to be extraordinarily difficult to devise really substantial technical improvements that competing brands cannot easily imitate (though there are occasional exceptions). Therefore, product differences exist mostly in the mind of the customer, and it is much easier to insinuate them into the minds of untrained consumers than into the minds of hard-bitten purchasing agents, who tend to concentrate on price and serviceability. The essential contrast can be visualized by comparing the tactics to be used in selling an automobile fleet to the purchasing agent of a large firm with those most effective in selling a single car to his wife. The result is that differentiated oligopoly is most characteristic of products sold to ultimate consumers, whereas undifferentiated oligopoly is common in industrial products.

From all this it should be clear that an oligopolist's concerns and methods are very different from those of an anonymous competitor. An oligopolist's primary concern is with his sales strategy. His firm stands or falls with his success in attracting sales without changing price, a situation that is quite alien to all other market forms. His situation is complicated by the fact that his competitors will not stand idly by while he does his best: they will ape his innovations, make some of their own, and match his advertising campaigns with theirs. We must now turn back to the strategic interrelationships among oligopolists.

Oligopolistic Strategy

To recap: whether his product is differentiated or not, an oligopolist has a handful of competitors to worry about. What each of them does affects him, as what he does affects each of them. This mutual interdependence sets up a very complicated relationship.

Such a situation, in which there are several participants with conflicting interests, each of whom has significant influence on the attainments of the others as well as on his own outcome, is known as a *game of strategy*—or, for short, as a *game*. (Chess and other board exercises are one sort of game; oligopoly—like international diplomacy, labor management negotiations, and so on—is a game of quite another sort, but subject to analysis by remarkably similar methods.) The crucial feature of any game is that each participant bases his decisions on what he expects the others to do, and therefore on what he thinks the others expect him to do, and indeed on what he thinks the others think he expects them to do, and so on. Can anything useful be said about such complicated situations? Well, sometimes.

Consider this case—about the simplest game conceivable. Firms A and B make virtually identical products. Each spends $1 million a year to keep its customers from deserting to the other. Actually, they could reduce their advertising budgets to $200,000 without hurting their sales, and each would be $800,000 better off. But if A cut his advertising budget unilaterally, he would lose sales to B on which he made a profit of $1,200,000 a year. The result of this unilateral action would be, then, to reduce A's profit by $400,000 and

159

to increase B's by $1,200,000. Firm B is exactly symmetrically situated. These data are summarized in Table 6–4, called the *payoff matrix* of this game. For example, it is shown there that if A cuts his advertising expenditures to $200,000 while B continues at the current level, then A's profits will be $400,000 less than at present while B's will be $1,200,000 greater.

Table 6–4 PAYOFF MATRIX FOR ADVERTISING GAME

(Entries show A's gain/B's gain in $1,000, compared with status quo)

Firm B's Advertising Budget	Firm A's Advertising Budget	
	$1,000,000	$200,000
$1,000,000	0/0	— 400/1200
$ 200,000	1200/ — 400	800/800

A's decision is very, very easy, and B's is the same. For there are only two possibilities permitted, and both point in the same direction. If B maintains his current budget, then A will lose $400,000 by cutting his. If B cuts his budget, then A is $400,000 better off if he retains his than if he cuts. In short, A should retain the high level of expenditure, whatever B does, and B should behave the same, and this is in spite of the fact that both would be better off if they could mutually agree to cut back. (The analogy with armaments races is striking.) [13]

The game we just played was especially simple because although the two firms' profits were interconnected, their decisions were not; the best decision for each remained the same irrespective of what the other did. But another simple example will illustrate that this needn't always be the case. Again there is a pair of oligopolists who are required by industry custom to announce simultaneously their prices for the next season. They cannot communicate with each other beforehand, either because of mutual antipathy or for fear of the Antitrust Division. Demand is strong and inelastic, so that if both announce price increases, both will enjoy profit increases of $100,000 for the season. If, however, only one increases his price, he will lose sales to the other and his profits will decline by $50,000, whereas the firm that stands pat will gain $50,000. The situation is summarized in Table 6–5.

Clearly, both firms are best off if both increase prices. But suppose you were firm A: would you do it? Remember that you would thereby run the risk of losing $50,000 if your opponent stood pat. There are two circumstances under which you would not increase your price: (1) if you were a conservative

[13] Let us emphasize again that this is the very simplest, and therefore the least-interesting, game situation known. For a lively introduction to more interesting games see J. D. Williams, *The Compleat Strategyst* (New York: McGraw-Hill Book Company, 1954).

Even this simple game, known as "the prisoners' dilemma," has its paradoxical side, as we saw, and has a surprising variety of applications to economics and sociology. It is analyzed further in R. D. Luce and H. Raiffa, *Games and Decisions* (New York: John Wiley & Sons, Inc., 1957), pp. 94–99.

manager for whom the hope of gaining $100,000 wasn't worth the risk and worry of possibly losing $50,000; and (2) if you believed that firm *B* was under conservative management and would not assume the risks of a price increase. Indeed, there is a third circumstance that leads to the same decision, and that suggests how subtly one has to reason when money is at stake. It is (3) if you believed that firm *B* believed that you were a conservative firm and would therefore not raise your price.[14] So it is far from certain that the firms would make mutually advantageous decisions if they were not allowed to communicate.

Table 6–5   PAYOFF MATRIX FOR PRICE-CHANGE GAME

(Entries show *A's* gain/*B's* gain in $1,000, compared with status quo)

Firm B's Choice	Firm A's Choice	
	Increase price	Maintain price
Increase price	100/100	50/ — 50
Maintain price	— 50/50	0/0

These two trivial games suggest one ingredient of life in an oligopoly: the strategic interplay among the rivals. In practice, the games oligopolists play are far more complicated. Each firm may have to contend with the actions of several confreres rather than only one, and each will have a range of alternatives with respect to prices, product design, merchandising policy, and many other things, instead of only a single dichotomy. On top of that, the inevitable uncertainties of business make it impossible to write down a sure-fire matrix, as we have done.

But the crucial complication that we have neglected is that every decision an oligopolist makes has two effects. One is the direct, intended consequence that is recorded in the payoff matrix. The other is the information or impression that is conveyed to the other oligopolists in the market. The price-change example shows how important this second aspect is; it is important therein for each firm to impress upon its rival that it is willing to take a chance. Communication is relevant in the advertising example, too, though less obviously. Thus, firm *A* in that example might well cut its advertising budget and sustain its $400,000 loss in the hope of communicating to firm *B* that it is prepared to cooperate if that firm cuts its budget.[15]

---

[14] Notice that this opinion on firm *B's* part is likely to be self-confirming, even if erroneous. You can follow out these lines of reasoning much further if you want to. But things can be even more confusing if there is no mutually advantageous pair of decisions—and there need not be any.

[15] We don't know of any instance where this has actually happened in the field of advertising. A few years ago, though, there was an instructive episode in the automobile industry. The manufacturers managed to cut back on horsepower ratings by such *tacit bargaining*. The improvement—and it was an improvement from everybody's point of view, teen-agers excepted—did not last because the "agreement" was unenforceable. The manufacturers in relatively weak market positions broke the industry discipline in the hope of making some inroads, and the market leaders were forced to follow.

The communications aspect of oligopolistic strategy is used in many ways. An important one is that a prominent firm will teach its rivals not to cut price by responding promptly to every price cut by a slightly deeper one. It also complicates oligopolistic behavior by making every move ambiguous.[16] If one oligopolist reduces his price, the others must conjecture whether he is trying to tell them that the time is ripe for reducing the industry's price structure, or whether he is aggressively trying to increase his market share. Even the best-intentioned price cut, if misinterpreted, may touch off a price war, and an oligopolist thinks at least twice before running this risk. Oligopolists often try to avoid this risk by making surrepetitious price cuts, either quietly granting discounts from list prices, or not charging for quality improvements. But such subterfuges do little more than delay retaliation, since customers have proved to be very poor at keeping them secret.

Two implications follow. In the first place, the convenient distinction between short-run and long-run decisions is obscured in oligopoly, since every move, by changing the rivals' assessment of the firm's intentions and situation, has long-run consequences. In the second place, since the risks and uncertainties of every move are greatly enhanced, oligopolists become reluctant to initiate *any* changes. Oligopoly is a peculiarly sticky and rigid form of market.

Oligopolies in Practice

We have seen that oligopoly is almost inevitable in industries that rely on modern technology, but that it is an unresponsive form of market in which firms cannot react readily to changes in market conditions, or even pursue their mutual advantage. Obviously it is far from an ideal state of affairs—but then, social institutions do have ways of adapting themselves to such challenges, and oligopoly is no exception.

The ideal way out, for the oligopolists, is to cooperate with each other. In the late nineteenth century, when oligopoly first became important, it showed strong tendencies to break down into monopoly. The original oligopolists in steel, tobacco, oil refining, tin-can manufacture, and many other industries merged into trusts and cartels to reap the advantages (to them) of monopoly. The antitrust movement on the part of the government, however, soon either impeded this trend or forced it underground. Oligopolists then turned to semiformal consultations, such as the "Judge Gary Dinners" in the steel industry,[17] but these too were disallowed by the courts.

Beaten by the bench, and anxious to avoid further scrutiny and unfavorable publicity, oligopolists were forced to rely on more circumspect methods of cooperation. These depended heavily on the tacit bargaining mentioned above, and on the observance and enforcement of unwritten behavioral conventions.

---

[16] Just like bidding in bridge. In bridge, elaborate conventions have been introduced to clarify the meaning of bids. We shall see that something very similar occurs in oligopoly.

[17] See Walter Adams, ed., *The Structure of American Industry* (New York: The Macmillan Company, 1961), Chap. 5.

The most ubiquitous of these conventions was that price competition was disallowed—and to this day oligopolists contest bitterly with each other by advertising, by product variation, by expense-account entertainment, by industrial espionage, and by every other expedient that ingenuity can invent, but they do not cut prices.[18] Price cutting is a weapon that is too readily available, and too destructive to all concerned.

This makes the price changes that are inevitable from time to time a very delicate matter. By far the most common way to handle the matter is through the convention of price leadership: one prominent firm, often but not always the largest in the industry, is accepted as the one with the responsibility for initiating price changes for all to follow. Although this prevents misunderstandings, the price leader remains, as it were, a king who rules on sufferance. He may lead, but if the move is not generally advantageous, perhaps no one will follow. And sometimes his price leadership is contested—particularly when a price reduction seems more urgent to his followers than it does to him. The continued maintenance of the leader's reign depends heavily on general acquiescence in the current distribution of market shares; when some of the firms vie vigorously to improve their positions in the market, or struggle desperately to survive, the peace is likely to be fragile. In short, an oligopoly with an established price leader is not the same as a monopoly—the leader's freedom of action is much more circumscribed.

No one really knows how oligopolists decide on a new schedule of prices when the need for a change has been recognized. There has been much testimony on this subject, before congressional committees and on other occasions, and what the oligopolists say is always much the same: they compute their prices by estimating long-run average costs and adding a markup that will allow them a reasonable profit on their invested capital. This "rule" is too vague to mean much. It does not say what volume of sales is to be used in estimating average costs, nor how one decides on a "reasonable profit," nor how the price structure is to be preserved when the price that is appropriate for one firm is either excessive or insufficient for others. In fact, the rule is perverse; it implies that prices should be raised when sales are slack, to cover fixed costs. Close questioning, not surprisingly, discloses that the "rule" has to be interpreted "in the light of competitive conditions," and that there are numerous exceptions to it. What this all probably means is that the formula gives a first approximation to prices, which are then adjusted in conformity to strategic considerations that are too varied and subtle to be explained to congressmen and the lay public.

A plausible hypothesis, though one very hard to confirm, is that the price leaders act like monopolists on behalf of the entire industry. That is, they recog-

---

[18] A famous example of this behavioral convention in practice occurred in 1956, when Chevrolet and Ford were vigorously contending for market leadership. When the prices for the 1957 model year were announced, Ford discovered that its prices were 3 per cent below those of Chevrolet. Ford promptly raised its prices. Evidently both firms realized that price competition could do nothing but harm to both, rivalry or no rivalry.

nize the industry demand curve and the cost curves of the average firm, and attempt to set a price that will afford such a firm the largest possible profits. In following this policy the price setter is not being altruistic to his competitors; his task is to propose a price schedule that will be followed. He must take into account the fact that one that favors himself unduly is likely to lead to disruptive retaliation, especially if he is either a low-cost firm (such as General Motors) or a high-cost one (such as U.S. Steel). Even the interests of the competitive fringe must be considered for they, too, can upset the delicate balance of power.

The Cost of Oligopoly

Oligopoly is so prevalent in the United States and other advanced economies that it is important to form a judgment about how much difference it makes or, in other words, how much more the economy would produce if its markets were truly competitive. This cannot be done with any precision; the difference between oligopoly and competition is too radical and pervasive for all its ramifications to be evaluated. But a shrewd, crude estimate can be made with the aid of a little ingenuity and the concepts that we have been developing.

The economic loss caused by a monopoly or oligopoly depends upon two things: the amount by which the price of the commodity is raised above the competitive level, and the amount by which the output of the commodity is reduced. Furthermore, these two factors are related by the elasticity of demand. Assume, for example, that the elasticity of demand is 2, which is on the high side for a realistic estimate of the elasticities prevalent in oligopolistic industries in the United States.[19] Then if an oligopoly resulted in prices 1 per cent higher than they otherwise would be, the amount produced and sold would fall by 2 per cent. (Remember that the elasticity of demand is the percentage reduction in the amount demanded that results from a 1 per cent increase in price.) In fact, it appears that American oligopolies result in prices about 15 per cent above the competitive level, as a rough upper estimate. So we can estimate that the output of oligopolized industries is no more than $2 \times 15 = 30$ per cent lower than it would be if those industries were competitive.

This is an impressive figure but, as we shall see, it is far greater than the actual economic loss. The reason is that the oligopolistic industries, by producing 30 per cent less output than they would without restriction, release to the competitive industries 30 per cent of the resources they would use if they were competitive. Those resources are not wasted, but we know that the products of resources are less highly valued when they are used in competitive industries than when they are used in oligopolistic or monopolistic industries. That is where the waste lies, in the extra value that the resources could have produced but for oligopolistic restriction of output.

[19] For this and other estimates of the impact of oligopoly see David Schwartzman, "The Effect of Monopoly on Price," *Journal of Political Economy*, 67 (August, 1959), 352–62.

We can even estimate this loss in value by looking at Fig. 6–3, which shows the demand curve for an oligopolized product whose price has been forced up from 100 to 115 monetary units, decreasing the quantity sold from 100 to 70 physical units. The figure shows that consumers would have been willing to pay, on the average, 107½ for the unproduced commodities if they had been available. Translating into percentage terms, the 30 per cent of output that remains unproduced are worth, on the average, 7½ per cent more than the competitive price. The loss in the value of output is therefore 7½ × 30 = 2.2 per cent of the value that would have been sold under competitive conditions. So, chiefly because released resources are used in competitive industries, the economic loss caused by oligopoly is very much less than it appears at first.

Several things must be said about this estimate, aside from reiterating its obvious crudeness. It includes only the loss caused by oligopolistic restriction of output. It does not include the costs of oligopolistic competition—advertising, model changes, and so on. For some (but not many) oligopolistic industries advertising budgets run as high as 10 per cent of gross sales. Further-

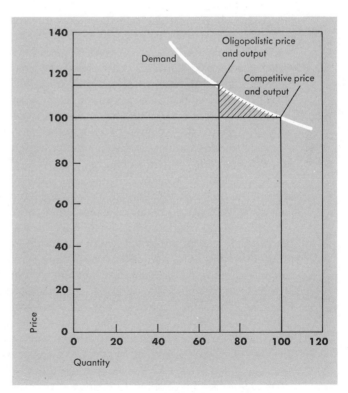

FIG. 6–3 Economic loss from oligopolistic restriction. The shaded area under the demand curve measures the economic loss.

more, oligopoly raises long-run average costs as well as prices. For example, wages are noticeably higher in oligopolistic industries than in competitive ones, largely because employers are relieved of the fierce competitive pressure to keep costs down and unions claim a share of the oligopolistic gains for their members. So the 15 per cent excess of prices over the competitive level (which is equal to long-run average costs) rather understates the amount of price distortion and, at the same time, the value of the resources released to competitive industries is rather overstated. Weighing these various considerations, the cost of oligopoly and monopoly to the economy appears to be in the range of from 5 to 7 per cent of the value of output of the oligopolized industries. Since these industries account for roughly a quarter of the value produced in the economy, the overall burden is something like 1–2 per cent of the value of economic output.

So oligopoly, for all its visibility, turns out to be a surprisingly minor source of economic inefficiency. One wonders why oligopolists use their undoubted powers so abstemiously. We saw one of the reasons above: the oligopolist cannot move very adroitly to exploit his theoretical powers because he cannot count on much cooperation from his colleagues. But he faces other impediments that we have not mentioned so far. The ultimate moderator of prices, even in competitive industries, is the introduction of new capacity both by existing firms and by new entrants to the industry. When the price of a product is favorable, the oligopolists themselves are sorely tempted to expand their capacities and sales. Once new facilities are installed, they are even more tempted to shade their prices in order to keep the new plant busy. Cartels (illegal in this country), which form the highest refinement of oligopoly, contend with these temptations by regulating the sales volumes of their members along with the prices they charge. Lacking the powers of cartels, the ordinary oligopoly finds it hard to maintain unduly profitable prices in the face of the expanding capacity of its members.

At the same time, there is the ever present threat of new entrants, both foreign and domestic. We have seen that oligopoly typically depends on economies of scale, both in production and marketing. The need to enter such an industry at large and hazardous scale impedes entry. But it does not annihilate the possibility, and sometimes, when conditions are attractive enough, it matures. The invasion of computer manufacturing by General Electric and Xerox, and the invasion of the American automobile market by many foreign manufacturers are typical examples of the incidents that oligopolists are most anxious to avoid. To avoid attracting formidable new competitors, oligopolists often strive to maintain prices that are profitable for them but insufficiently profitable to attract outsiders—so-called entry forestalling prices. All these considerations severely limit the powers of oligopolists: their own difficulties in maintaining rivalrous cooperation and the unremitting threat of new competitors keep them from departing very sharply from competitive price levels.

SUMMARY: AN APPRAISAL OF MARKETS

In this chapter we have considered two common alternatives to competition: monopoly and oligopoly. Monopoly, we noticed, causes economic waste (and perhaps some injustice, the ill effects of which fortunately can be moderated by regulation). Oligopolists, caught between economic necessities and legal restrictions, are not able to perform efficiently from either their point of view or the economy's. Nevertheless these market forms are needed to take advantage of modern technology.

The purpose of all markets is to transmit information. The firms themselves are organized to do the substantive work of the economy: to produce, store, transport, and deliver all the goods and services required by consumers. But what to produce, where to deliver it, and so on—those are decisions that can be made wisely only if consumers are informed of the relative costs of producing various commodities and if firms are informed of the relative prices that consumers are willing to pay. It is the entire purpose of markets to transmit this information, and they can quite properly be judged by the accuracy and promptness with which they do so.

Competition transmits economic information faithfully. Each firm, under the impetus of profit seeking, produces to the point where marginal cost equals price. The prices paid by consumers then measure the costs of the resources required to produce the goods they buy. If the price of any competitive good is so high that consumers are induced to substitute other products for it, the resources are released to produce those other products. Knowing the value of the goods that must be forgone to produce the things he buys—knowing, that is, the opportunity costs of his purchases—the consumer, by allocating his personal budget, can guide the producers to allocate the national resource budget in the way that satisfies him best.

The short-run adjustment will conduce to the best disposition of resources, including available plant and it will simultaneously point out the industries where plant expansion is needed most. For profits will be greatest where short-run marginal costs most exceed average costs, and those excesses will indicate precisely the industries wherein more and/or larger plants will be of greatest economic benefit in reducing marginal costs toward long-run average costs. In more concrete terms, a large excess of marginal costs over average costs indicates that labor and raw materials are being expended to overcome deficiencies in the available plant.

Monopoly and oligopoly, in their different ways, block the transmission of the sort of information we have been discussing. In neither is the price of the product likely to be equal to its marginal cost: the monopolist does not wish it so, the oligopolist is too rigid to keep it so. And in neither does the level of profits automatically signal and induce the appropriate level of investment. **167**

We saw that in competitive markets new investment takes place until extraordinary profits are competed away, but this is not an outcome that holds much appeal for monopolists or oligopolists. Though they invest, they stop far short of that, and the entrenched positions of the established firms deter investment on the part of newcomers.

Regulation of monopoly is a partial cure for its defects. But the judgment of government authorities, especially when contested by the powerful companies they are charged with regulating, is a poor substitute for a sensitive market mechanism. Regulation brings prices into better accord with costs than they otherwise might be, but it also introduces rigidities that have something in common with those characteristic of oligopolies. Antitrust measures tend to produce oligopoly rather than competition.

Oligopolies suffer from being peculiarly rigid and unresponsive to market conditions. They also are practically compelled to dissipate economic resources in advertising [20] and in meretricious variations in product characteristics. And there is yet another objectionable side to oligopoly. Oligopoly induces advertising, and the function of advertising is to make consumers want the products advertised. But if the purpose of economic effort is to satisfy consumers' desires, what can be said in favor of a market form that makes consumers desire what the firms produce? What can we say for a form that makes people want to smoke in spite of the pleas of physicians? The answers to these and other critical questions like them deserve your attention. Unfortunately, we cannot explore them here.[21]

No effective means for regulating oligopolies have been devised—and it would be unreasonable to expect oligopolists to behave otherwise than they do; the system of rewards and punishments will tolerate nothing else of them.

The prevalence of monopoly and oligopoly is a serious defect in the free-market system of organizing economic activity. This system works best in its original environment of small-scale producers, and is less well adapted to controlling and guiding the industrial giants who have developed to take advantage of mass production and mass merchandising. Nevertheless, the measurable costs of oligopoly are surprisingly small.

APPENDIX: MARGINAL REVENUE, ELASTICITY, AND MONOPOLIST'S PROFITS

We shall develop the algebraic relationship between elasticity of demand and monopolist's profits, using the same general notation as in the appendix to Chapter 3. Let p be the price at which x units can be sold, and

---

[20] The total bill for advertising has been estimated at around $12 billion a year, amounting to about 5 per cent of the value of the products advertised.

[21] For a trenchant development of this theme, see J. Kenneth Galbraith, *The Affluent Society* (Boston: Houghton Mifflin Company, 1958).

$p - \Delta p$ be the price at which $x + 1$ units can be sold. Then the total revenue when x units are sold is xp, and the total revenue when $x + 1$ units are sold is $(x + 1)$ $(p - \Delta p)$. Marginal revenue when x units are sold is therefore by definition

$$MR(x) = (x + 1)\ (p - \Delta p) - xp$$
$$= p - x\Delta p - \Delta p$$
$$= p(1 - \frac{x}{p}\Delta p) - \Delta p.$$

The second term is negligible quantity in comparison with the first and will be ignored. If we write $\Delta x = 1$, for the sake of symmetry, we then have

$$MR(x) = p\left(1 - \frac{x\Delta p}{p\Delta x}\right).$$

Let us denote the elasticity by the Greek letter *eta*, η. It is defined as *the ratio of the percentage change in the quantity demanded to the percentage change in price,* or

$$\eta = \frac{p\Delta x}{x\Delta p}$$

—which is the reciprocal of the fraction in the formula for marginal revenue. Hence marginal revenue, price, and elasticity are connected by the relationship

$$MR(x) = p\left(1 - \frac{1}{\eta}\right).$$

Solving this equation for $1/\eta$, we obtain

$$\frac{1}{\eta} = \frac{p - MR}{p} = \frac{p - MC}{p}$$

—as stated in the text.

Economic Efficiency

CHAPTER SEVEN

We come now to the crux of our discussion: the social function of prices and markets. In the preceding chapters we have taken up many details of economic organization—supply curves, the behavior of production costs, the logic of consumers' choices, and so on—details that are essential for understanding the operation of an economy that depends on market guidance and incentives. But now the time has come to take a broader point of view, to see what these economic decisions and activities are supposed to contribute to a society, to consider how economic performance can be evaluated, and finally to appraise the performance of a system that depends on prices and markets for most of its decisions. These will be the tasks of the present chapter and the next one.

SOME ASPECTS OF SOCIAL DECISIONS

In this chapter we shall regard the economy as part of the social decision-making apparatus of the country and devote most of our attention to considering how it *ought* to perform. A vast number of social decisions are made through the operation of the economic system, many of them important, such as how many men will be employed and at what wages, how many million tons of steel will be produced, and even how long skirts will be. At the same time many important decisions are made by other means, chiefly the political system. We can gain a great deal of insight into the nature of the economic system by asking the questions: Why do we have these two parallel systems of

170

decision making, and what determines the kind of decision that is made by each? Why do we not decide virtually everything through the semiautomatic operation of the economic system (which would be an extreme application of the doctrine of laissez faire) or alternatively through the political-governmental apparatus (which would be an extreme version of centralized planning)?

A partial explanation of the existence of the two systems can be seen by noting that they share a common disadvantage: both the economic system and the political system place a great deal of power in the hands of people whom other people do not trust. We all have heard about the cupidity and narrow vision of the businessmen who make the most important decisions in the economic system. They are motivated by the pursuit of profit, and even after having studied the principles of decision making that follow from this motivation, as we have done in the earlier chapters, it is not easy to see how such decisions can be in the general interest. We shall return to this question.

On the other hand, distrust of politicians and fear of governmental power are deeply embedded in American traditions. The Constitution, with its three counterbalancing branches of government and its three semiindependent levels of government, is a monument to our suspicion of politicians and of governmental authority.

Dividing the power of decision between these two systems serves, at the least, to diminish the power in the hands of either, and to set up still another kind of check and balance. This is an important virtue, and our sensitivity to it becomes evident whenever there is a threat to the balance of power between the two systems. But it does not explain what kinds of decision are remanded to each of the two systems. To find this explanation we have to look into the nature of social decisions and their consequences.

Any decision is a choice among alternatives. Social decisions can be distinguished from others, which we can call technical decisions, on the basis of the nature of their consequences and the criteria used to evaluate them. A technical decision is one whose alternatives can be rated objectively according to the degree to which they attain some single, well-defined goal. For example, if a river is to be dammed as cheaply as possible, the selection of the site at which construction cost is lowest is a technical decision, and it can be left to the engineers. On the other hand, a social decision is one whose alternatives affect the attainment of a number of different goals, so that the choice among alternatives depends on the relative importance of those goals. Such decisions are not purely matters of engineering or technology because there is no objective way to decide which of several alternatives is best. For example, if the cheapest site for the dam is also the one most destructive of scenery, then a judgment has to be made as to how great an increase in construction cost would be justified in order to preserve certain scenic features. You might say that such a judgment is too important to be left to the engineers. At any rate it cannot be made objectively nor, usually, will different people agree on it. So, as a matter of definition, we shall say that whenever a decision affects a number of different social goals, it is a social decision. Every decision that affects a number of people is a social decision, since the well-being of every individual is a distinguishable social goal. Economic decisions are a subclass of social decisions, those that concern the direction of economic activity.

The key difficulty in reaching a social decision lies in weighing the importance of the diverse consequences of the different alternatives. No alternative is unambiguously "best." One is better from one point of view; a different one is better from another viewpoint. Even a single individual finds it hard to make up his mind in such circumstances; when several or many individuals are involved difficulties multiply. Both the political and the economic system are social devices for assembling individual preferences and judgments and arriving at social decisions.

In the end a social decision depends upon how many people feel strongly about the different aspects of the different alternatives, and how strongly they feel about them. Generally speaking, the strength of feeling about a choice is one of the hardest of all human perceptions to express with any degree of precision and one of the easiest to dissemble. But in one circumstance it is easy to express, and that is where the economic system becomes effective.

The clue is to notice that "strength of preference among consequences" is just a nontechnical way of saying "marginal rate of substitution among them." Imagine a choice between alternatives, one of which is superior in some respects, the second in other respects. The choice, even though made by means of the political system, is basically economic; the advantages of the selected alternative will be bought, in effect, at the cost of the advantages of the rejected one. Thus the choice depends on how willing people in the aggregate are to substitute one set of advantages for the other, and this is the marginal rate of substitution.

Now if people can be made to disclose their marginal rates of substitution between the different advantages, the social choice will be greatly facilitated, for then it will be clear which alternatives offers advantages that are judged to be worth accepting on balance. This can be done for many—but not all—questions of resource allocation, and the economic system is the social device for eliciting these marginal rates of substitution, or preferences.

Let us illustrate. One comparatively simple social decision is how to divide a society's supply of animal hides among shoe manufacture, attaché cases, ladies' handbags, and other uses. It is an easy decision precisely because it is easy for individuals to express how urgently they want these different commodities. The relative prices that people are willing to pay for them disclose the marginal rates of substitution and thereby tell whether a pound of hides will be more useful socially in one application or the other.[1] In fact, the division of

[1] You may deny this at first glance, holding that five pair of shoes for impoverished children are more important socially than an additional attaché case for a corporation lawyer, though they may cost the same. That is a legitimate subjective evaluation of disparate social consequences. But on

the supply of hides will be socially optimal when it is such that people are willing to pay the same amount for the product of an additional or marginal pound whether that pound is used for shoes, attaché cases, or whatnot.

On the other hand, tanneries are an important source of water pollution. A tannery discharges about two tons of highly polluted water for every hide processed. This fact induces a much more difficult social decision problem: the greater the amount of leather produced in a community, the more pollution everyone in the neighborhood has to live with or the more taxes everyone must pay for its elimination, whether he uses the leather products or not.[2] The ordinary citizen doesn't know how much pollution tanning causes,[3] and even if he did know he would have no effective way to express the strength of his preference (or marginal rate of substitution) between tannery products and clean water.[4] This complicates the social decision vastly. In the leather-allocation example, society had only to respond to the clearly expressed preferences of its members. In the leather versus pollution case it has both to ascertain the preferences and respond to them; this is much harder.[5]

The two kinds of social decision that have just been illustrated can be characterized as those concerning private goods, on the one hand, and those concerned with public goods or externalities, on the other. The distinguishing property of a decision about private goods is that its impact on each individual can be decided separately (for example, the individual might choose for himself how much to buy or otherwise acquire), so that he can be made to reveal how anxious he is to have that kind of good in comparison to other private goods that might be supplied. Clearly, this type of social decision can benefit from social arrangements that take advantage of the available information. The economic system is, fundamentally, the network of those arrangements.

---

second glance you will see that the shoeing of children and the equipage of lawyers are not consequences of the allocation of leather but of something else: the distribution of income. Leather could be redirected from attaché cases to children's shoes by social fiat. The result would be to depress the price of shoes and induce impoverished mothers to buy more of them. But then they would buy less of other things that they consider to be at least as essential (mittens or dental care). The analysis that we are embarking on will show that social conditions would not be improved merely by reallocating leather.

If a society wishes to provide more liberally for its children and less liberally for its lawyers, it must do so by redirecting income, not leather. The socially desirable usage of leather is the one in which people are willing to pay the same amount for a pound of leather in all its forms, as stated in the text, given the distribution of income.

[2] There is now some tendency to charge tanneries (and, indirectly, their customers) for the costs of treating their effluents. To the extent that this is feasible and is implemented it eliminates the illustrative issue discussed in the text by transferring the decision to the economic system.

[3] In contrast, he does know how much leather and other resources any particular leather good requires; the prices tell him that.

[4] He could, of course, join a demonstration to protest the extent of pollution or the insufficiency of the supply of leather goods. This is activity in the political system and, typically of such activity, does not convey the information requisite for decision making, which is (in this instance) how much leather people in the aggregate would be willing to forgo in order to attain a specified increase in water quality.

[5] The density of parenthetical footnotes in this passage is regrettable. It reflects the intricacy of the considerations under discussion.

Decisions about public goods or externalities have consequences that we all share willy-nilly, or can avoid only with considerable difficulty, just as we all have to live with the same river or else move away. There is no way in which individuals can be confronted with the alternatives in a realistic context and thereby be induced to disclose their preferences with any precision. Those decisions have to be made by political processes.

These are the grounds, then, on which social decisions are remanded to the political system or the economic system, as the case may be. Decisions about private goods, for which individuals can express their preferences intelligibly, are decided economically. Decisions about public goods (including such important matters as war, justice, and education) are made politically.[6] Simply because better information is available in the economic sector, the decisions made there tend to be more sensitive and responsive than political ones, and there is some effort to transfer decisions to it wherever possible. For example, the decision about how much leather goods to produce can be made more wisely if the users of those goods are charged for the pollution produced on their behalf than if it is made by governmental fiat. Our present concern is to pull together our strands of knowledge about how the economic system reaches its decisions. But first we must make clear the standards by which the quality of those decisions can be judged.

SOME CRITERIA FOR ECONOMIC PERFORMANCE

We got a little ahead of our story in the last section, for example when we alleged that it would be advantageous for an economy to divide its supply of hides so that consumers would be willing to pay the same amount for a pound of hides no matter which final product it was used for. By what criteria would this be advantageous, and why would that particular allocation meet the criteria? These are the questions that we must look into further.

Our starting point is that the main purpose of economic activity is to provide consumers with the goods and services that they want. This is not a simple purpose from any point of view, technical, administrative, or social. Often one consumer can be satisfied more only by satisfying some other consumer less, and then conflicts of interest arise of the sort that we discussed in the last section and shall discuss again. But often, also, it is possible to increase some consumer's satisfactions without detracting from those of anyone else, and this would be a clear social gain. So our first criterion for the performance of an economy is that it should be efficient in a very straightforward sense: that it not forgo any opportunity to increase the satisfaction of any consumer when this can be done at no cost to anyone else. This is known as the *Pareto criterion,* after Vilfredo Pareto who first perceived its importance.

[6] Decisions about income distribution are shared between the two sectors in a peculiar manner. We shall come to that.

It is not easy to satisfy the Pareto criterion, and no economy does it perfectly. Consumers are numerous and diverse; causes are often remote from consequences. The men who allocate hides are not likely to know the mothers and lawyers who will use the products. Still, if the economy is to be efficient, they have to make their decision in such a way that no consumer could be better pleased and none worse pleased by some alternative. To do this, clearly, elaborate provisions have to be made for communicating information to and fro, and the broad, basic criterion has to be spelled out in sufficient detail so that it can be applied in making specific decisions. These are among the most important tasks of any economic system.

To understand these tasks it is useful to break the criterion into four more specific components: efficiency in distribution, efficiency in production, consumer sovereignty, and aggregative efficiency. These will be defined in the next few paragraphs and analyzed in the remainder of the chapter.

Efficiency in distribution is achieved when the goods produced in the economy are distributed to the consumers who want them. If things work out so that Mrs. Jones, who likes coffee, gets tea, and Mrs. O'Grady, who loves tea, gets coffee, the economy is not performing well in this respect. Any restriction on a consumer's scope for individual choice is almost sure to reduce this kind of efficiency. Examples are frequent. In wartime rationing, sugar was allotted to diabetics and gasoline to nondrivers, and they were not permitted to exchange with each other. As part of our antipoverty program a poor family may receive food stamps, though it feels in more urgent need of warm clothing. There are reasons, perhaps sufficient, for such anomalies, but they do result in an inefficient distribution of such commodities as are available.

Efficiency in production means that as much should be produced of every desirable good as the available resources and technical knowledge permit, in the light of the output of all the other desirable goods. A failure in this regard occurs whenever it is technically possible to increase the output of some commodity without reducing the output of any other. An obvious implication is that the economy should avoid methods of production that use more of any resource than is technically necessary, given the quantity of output desired and the usage of other resources. There are other, less-obvious, implications that we shall come to.

Consumer sovereignty means that the goods produced should be the ones that the consumers want. When Henry Ford proclaimed that his customers could have any color car they liked, provided it was black, he was violating the standard of consumer sovereignty.[7] Rationing systems and centrally planned economies are likely to do badly by this standard. Under such arrange-

---

[7] This is probably an unfair example. With the methods of production and production control available in the days of the Model T it would have been far more expensive (that is, would have required many more resources) to attempt to match consumers' color preferences than to produce a uniform color. All that consumer sovereignty required of Henry Ford was that he satisfy his customers' preferences as well as possible with the resources that he used, and he may have done that.

ments the economy will produce the commodities that the planners ordain, and it is very likely that consumers would prefer some other set of commodities that could be produced with the same resources. The planners would have no effective way of knowing what consumers would like to have produced.

Aggregative efficiency requires that all the resources available to the economy be used. Unemployment of either men or machines is a failure in this regard. It is even more wasteful to let usable resources stand idle than to employ them inefficiently.

These, in brief, are the requirements for an efficiently operating economy. We shall now look into them a little more closely, in the order listed, to perceive their implications for specific economic decisions.

EFFICIENCY IN DISTRIBUTION

An efficiently operating economy should distribute its products among consumers so that no one is forced to take one commodity when he prefers a different one that is also available. In other words, after the commodities have been allocated among consumers, there should not remain any way to reallocate them that would make some consumers better off without harming any other consumers.

This aspect of economic efficiency centers around the familiar concept of consumers' marginal rates of substitution. Think of any two commodities and suppose that there are two consumers in the economy who have different marginal rates of substitution between them. Then these two commodities could be reallocated so as to make both of those consumers better off without affecting anyone else. When any such easy opportunity for improving well-being remains, the current division of commodities among consumers cannot be fully efficient.

The argument behind these assertions is an extension of the reasoning of Chapter 5. Suppose that two members of the economy, Mrs. White and Mrs. Gray, have different marginal rates of substitution between some two commodities—say bread and wine. To be specific, suppose that Mrs. White's *MRS* (bread : wine) is 2 and that Mrs. Gray's is 3. Then Mrs. White would remain on the same indifference curve if she exchanged two loaves of bread for one pint of wine, or one pint of wine for two loaves of bread. And therefore she would move to a higher indifference curve if she exchanged one pint of her wine for 2½ loaves of Mrs. Gray's bread.

Mrs. Gray would also benefit from that exchange. She remains on the same indifference curve if she exchanges three loaves of bread for one pint of wine, and gains if she receives a pint of wine in return for only 2½ loaves. Therefore, an allocation of bread and wine to consumers is not fully efficient if it leaves a Mrs. White and a Mrs. Gray in the situation described, where a mutually advantageous opportunity for exchange still remains. Such an opportunity will remain if there is any pair of consumers who have different marginal rates of substitution between any pair of commodities, as we have just seen. We conclude, therefore, that efficient distribution of commodities requires that all consumers have the same marginal rate of substitution between every pair of commodities.

Notice that if all consumers buy their commodities at the same prices, their marginal rates of substitution will be equated automatically. For we saw in our study of consumption that each consumer chooses his quantities of different commodities so that his marginal rate of substitution between every pair of commodities is equal to the ratio of their prices. The allocation of commodities by consumer choice on free markets, accordingly, achieves this kind of efficiency; it is very hard to attain otherwise.

EFFICIENCY IN PRODUCTION

The second main task of an economy is to produce the maximum possible output. Of course, the output of any single commodity can always be increased by shifting to it resources and efforts that are being used to produce other commodities—but that is not what this criterion means. It means that as much of each commodity should be produced as is possible without reducing the output of any other commodity. This is no mean feat in a varied and complicated economy, but the problem exists when there are as few as two commodities clamoring for the available resources, and it can be seen most clearly in that context.

To set forth the problem in its starkest form, let us think of Robinson Crusoe alone on his island. And let us from the first understand that Robinson Crusoe is only a piece of pedagogical scaffolding; the name is a code for any society, no matter how populous, that has well-defined, uniform objectives. (It happens that there are no such societies, except for Crusoe himself, but working out the economic principles for a one-man society is a large first step toward working out the principles for real societies. That is why we study Crusoe.)

The problem we give Crusoe can be stated very briefly. Everything he wants is available on his island in abundant supply, save only bread and wine. These he must produce if he wants them, and he does. All that he needs to produce bread and wine is land, of which he has, say, 100 acres. He can plant all 100 to wheat, but will then have no wine. Or he can plant all to vines and have no bread. Or, what is likely to be most sensible, he can divide the land between the two crops in any proportion he chooses, and have some of each.

Now think back to our study of consumption. For all that has been said so far, Crusoe, dividing his land between two crops, is in exactly the same position as a consumer dividing his budget between two commodities. The same principles would seem to apply, and we shall see that, with a slight modification, they do. The need for modification rises because Crusoe is also a producer, so that the principles of production, discussed in Chapters 3 and 4, must also apply to him. The crucial difference between consumers' and producers' choices is that when a consumer spends an additional dollar on a commodity, he receives an additional dollar's worth, but when a producer spends an additional dollar on a factor of production, he obtains a smaller increase in output than before, because of diminishing marginal productivity. Crusoe, too, must face this problem, but not in the familiar form because, being an isolate, he has no dollars-and-cents costs.

It is not hard to see that, in a sense, we have gotten down to the bare fundamentals—to the real phenomena that stand behind dollars and cents. Now we have to specify in some detail Crusoe's problem as a producer. This is done in Table 7–1, where it is assumed that Crusoe's 100 acres are divided into six classes of land. Some of this land is level and best suited for wheat (types V and VI). Some is hilly and best adapted to wines (types I and II). And there are graduations in between, as shown. These are all the production data we need.

Now we can see the decisions that Crusoe has to make. Essentially, they are two:

1. He must decide how much of each commodity to produce. But he cannot do this in a vacuum; he must take account of the fact that the more he produces of one, the less he can have of the other. This decision is a strictly economic one. It depends on his preferences and relates, indeed, to our third aspect of efficiency, consumers' sovereignty.
2. Whichever combination of outputs he selects, he must decide which land to use for each crop. This is a strictly technological problem. Preferences have nothing to do with it; it depends only on allocating the different classes of land so as to obtain the largest possible crops overall.[8]

These two decisions are closely intertwined. For one thing, if the technological decision is made unwisely, Crusoe the consumer will have to be content with a smaller total output than is really necessary. Besides, as we shall see, the analysis of the technological decision provides information about the marginal costs of wheat and wine that is useful in making the economic decision. The technological decision is our present concern.

Technical Decisions: Production-Possibility Frontier

The technical conditions of production, specified in Table 7–1, determine the range of choice open to Crusoe, the range within which he must finally make his economic decision. At one extreme, if he devotes all his land to wheat, he can produce 1,125 bushels, as shown in the next-to-last column. This same possibility is shown in Fig. 7–1, as the right-hand end of the

---

[8] An important exception to this assertion will be discussed below.

broken-line curve drawn there. Now suppose that Crusoe would like to have 100 gallons of wine. Then he faces his first, and most critical, technological decision: which type of land to use. He might be tempted at first to use land of type II, which has the largest output of wine per acre. But that would be wrong. To produce 100 gallons of wine on type II land would require 2½ acres, enough to grow 15 bushels of wheat. But on type I land, 100 gallons of wine require 3⅓ acres on which only 10 bushels of wheat can be grown. Clearly he has to sacrifice fewer bushels of wheat for his 100 gallons of wine if he uses type I land than if he uses type II.

The general principle here at work is one of the most important and pervasive principles of production economics, known as the principle of *comparative advantage*. It applies whenever a decision can be made about which factors to use in producing a given commodity, and it provides us with this very common-sensical rule: *Always use the factors that are least productive in alternative applications in comparison with their productivity for the commodity desired.*

Table 7–1 ROBINSON CRUSOE'S PRODUCTION POSSIBILITIES

Class of Land (1)	Acres (2)	Output per Acre		Output Ratio	Potential Output	
		Wheat (bushels) (3)	Wine (gallons) (4)	Wheat–Wine (5)	Wheat (bushels) (6)	Wine (gallons) (7)
I	10	3	30	0.10	30	300
II	10	6	40	0.15	60	400
III	20	9	30	0.30	180	600
IV	25	12	20	0.60	300	500
V	25	15	10	1.50	375	250
VI	10	18	5	3.60	180	50
Total	100				1,125	2,100

Note: By world standards this is very poor land and especially unfitted for wine production.

Let us make the required comparison for type I and type II land. The marginal productivity [9] of type I land is three bushels per acre when used to produce wheat, and 30 gallons per acre when used for wine. Thus, its marginal productivity for wheat is one-tenth of its marginal productivity when used for wine (see column five of the table). The same comparison for type II land shows that its wheat productivity is about one-seventh of its wine productivity (ignoring units of measurement, which cancel out). So type I land is relatively less productive of wheat than type II land, and should be used for producing the 100 gallons of wine. In that way, less wheat will have to be sacrificed to obtain the wine than would be possible with any other choice.

The comparative-advantage rule is just another version of the opportunity-

[9] And also average productivity, as it happens.

cost principle. The opportunity cost of a gallon of wine is the amount of wheat that has to be forgone in order to produce it. The comparative-advantage rule tells us to produce the wine in such a way that this sacrifice of wheat, or opportunity cost, is as small as possible. This establishes that when the production of wine begins, it should begin on type I land, where the number of bushels of wheat sacrificed·per gallon of wine produced is lowest. When all the type I land has been committed to wine (that is, when more than 300 gallons of wine are desired), resort must be had to type II land, which has the next highest comparative advantage in wheat. And so on down the list, which has been arranged in order of comparative advantage in wine production.

Figure 7–1 has been constructed in accordance with this principle. It shows the combinations of wheat and wine output that result when the first 300 gallons of wine (or fraction thereof) are produced on type I land, the next 400 gallons (or fraction thereof) on type II land, and so on. Accordingly, it shows the greatest output of wine that can be had in conjunction with any given output of wheat and, conversely, the greatest output of wheat attainable with any given output of wine. It shows, in short, the complete menu of choice.

To drive things home: suppose that the principle of comparative advantage were violated—what then? Suppose, say, that 950 gallons of wine were desired and that they were grown on land of the even-numbered types. Then 585 bushels of wheat would be grown on the land of odd-numbered types, resulting in the output shown by point X in Fig. 7–1. Clearly that is an inefficient allocation, since point E shows that 960 bushels of wheat can be had in conjunction with 950 gallons of wine with a proper allocation of the land.

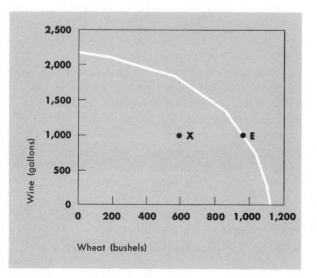

FIG. 7–1 Crusoe's production-possibility frontier. The broken line shows the most he can get of either commodity, given the quantity of the other.

The broken-line curve in Fig. 7–1 is known as the *production-possibility frontier*.

> The production-possibility frontier shows the greatest amount of one commodity that can be produced in conjunction with any prescribed amounts of all the other commodities in the economy.

This production-possibility frontier is obviously of the greatest importance to Robinson Crusoe. It tells him what he can afford, just as the ordinary budget line tells the consumer what he can afford. In exactly the same way, the vastly more complicated production-possibility frontier of a real economy is of the greatest importance to the members of that economy. It prescribes the complete range of goods and services open to the members of that economy.

Two geometrical characteristics of the production-possibility frontier are noteworthy. First, it curves downward as we move to the right; in technical language, it is concave.[10] This is a direct consequence of the principle of comparative advantage. Starting at the left-hand end (no wheat produced), the first land to be converted to wheat will have a comparative advantage in wheat—that is, will require the smallest reduction in wine output per bushel of wheat produced. When all of this land has been converted, then land where the sacrifice in wine is somewhat higher will have to be used, making the curve steeper. And so it will go.

The second noteworthy property of the production-possibility frontier is that its slope at any output point has an evident economic meaning. It is the number of gallons of wine that must be forgone in order to obtain one more bushel of wheat. This ratio is known as the *marginal rate of transformation* of wine into wheat.

> The marginal rate of transformation of wine into wheat at any point of the production-possibility frontier, denoted MRT (wine : wheat), is the number of units of wine that have to be given up in order to produce one additional unit of wheat.

The name is a happy one, though it suggests that there is some mystical alchemy for transforming wine into wheat. Wine can indeed be transformed into wheat in an economy—not, to be sure, after it is fermented, but before the

---

[10] The production-possibility frontier in Fig. 7–1 is made up of six line segments because we distinguished six qualities of land. If we had assumed that there were a great many different types of land, the line segments would have been vastly more numerous and shorter, so that the frontier would be indistinguishable from a smooth curve. The curve would remain concave, however, looking generally like an isoquant turned upside down.

There is no way to say for sure whether the production-possibility frontiers of real economies are more like smooth curves or more like broken-line curves. Economists use both versions, depending on which is the more convenient for a particular problem. The smooth frontier is the traditional version, dating back to Ricardo's day, but the broken-line type is currently enjoying a vogue because the associated mathematics, called *linear programming*, has proved remarkably fruitful in business and economic applications.

vines are planted, by the unmystical economic method of redirecting resources from wine to wheat production.

On Crusoe's island, efficiency in production demands that he cultivate his land so as to produce at a point on the production-possibility frontier, and Crusoe will do so if he is any farmer at all. To do otherwise would mean sacrificing some consumption to no advantage. In a real economy the fundamental problem of resource allocation is the same, but the problem of implementation is unimaginably more complicated. Crusoe's island economy is ridiculously simple: there are only two commodities, only six factors of production (six qualities of land), and each commodity requires only one factor of production. In a real economy there are millions of products and millions of factors. Each product requires several factors of production, perhaps hundreds, and the factors can be employed in numerous ways in accordance with that product's production function.

Nevertheless, certain fundamentals still apply. There is a production-possibility frontier. That is to say, there is a certain maximum amount of any commodity (say, frozen apple pies) that can be produced by the available resources in conjunction with given amounts of all other commodities. No one knows exactly what it is, but it is there. That being so, we can conceive of all the maximal combinations of goods and services that the economy can produce, and these constitute its production-possibility frontier. Efficiency in production requires that the economy actually produce a combination that is on or close to the frontier; to do otherwise would be to produce less and have less of some commodities than is necessary, to no purpose. This frontier is concave, just as Crusoe's was, and for the same reason. The resources used to produce any commodity in an efficient economy will be those whose use entails the smallest sacrifice possible of other commodities. As the output of any commodity is increased, resources less well adapted to it will have to be drawn in, and the sacrifice of other commodities will increase. This produces the concavity of the production-possibility frontier. It also accounts for the shapes of the cost curves studied in Chapter 3.

Furthermore, there is a marginal rate of transformation between every pair of commodities, telling the amount by which the production of one of them can be increased by applying the resources released by a unit reduction in the output of the other. It is easy to see that there is a marginal rate of transformation between frozen apple pies and canned applesauce, but is the same thing true in general? Can wool be "transformed" into wedding rings? Indeed it can. The resource reallocation might go as follows: some wool spinners might be shifted to spinning rayon so that the rayon industry can substitute spinners for chemists (spinning more carefully fiber made under lower standards of quality control), thus releasing the chemists needed to supervise the refining of more gold. Even longer chains of substitutions may be required. But however that may be, all commodities draw on a common pool of resources, so that the resources released by reducing the output of any commodity become available, generally indirectly, for increasing the output of any other. The production-possibility frontier describes the possibilities for all such shifts; the marginal rates of transformation measure how many units of any commodity have to be forgone in order to secure a unit increase in the output of any other, all other outputs remaining the same.

To that extent, a real economy is just a magnified version of Crusoe's. But the magnification brings its difficulties. All Crusoe had to do to find and achieve his production-possibility frontier was to compute and obey the comparative advantages of his different qualities of land. No such simple calculation avails in a real economy. No one controls the allocation of all the resources; the data on all the ramified possibilities of substitution and reallocation do not exist anywhere. Yet a real economy, like Crusoe's, should strive to produce outputs somewhere close to its production-possibility frontier. In the next chapter we shall see, as perhaps you already suspect, that in a market-guided economy the relative prices of any pair of commodities is a pretty good estimate of their marginal rate of transformation. That is, the resources required to make one automobile are sufficient to produce about 5,000 ball point pens. This is the essential clue used in such an economy. For if a way were discovered to make 10,000 pens with those same resources, or resources of equal value, it would be profitable to employ it and it would be employed. This suggests that the quest for producing at lowest cost keeps a market-guided economy close to its production-possibility frontier. We shall see more explicitly how this works in the next chapter.

Is the use of markets and prices the only way that a complex economy can achieve productive efficiency, that is to say, produce outputs close to its production-possibility frontier? In principle it is not. We can conceive of accumulating an enormous data bank containing all the production functions in the economy (most of them currently unknown) and a census of all the resources available. With these data at hand it would be a purely mathematical problem to compute the greatest amount of frozen apple pies that could be produced in conjunction with given amounts of all other commodities, or any other point on the production-possibility frontier. Of course, this purely mathematical problem would be many orders of magnitude more difficult than any computation that has yet been attempted, but it is conceivable in principle. If the data were precise and this computation were performed, the result would be a plan of operation that would undoubtedly be more efficient than that achieved by any real economy because the price-and-market system and all others fall substantially short of perfection.[11]

---

[11] A mathematical comment may be illuminating. If the calculation described in the text were carried out, it would yield certain pseudo-prices (called "Lagrange multipliers" by mathematicians) which would have the same significance as real prices. The ratio of the pseudo-prices of any two commodities would be the marginal rate of transformation between them, and these pseudo-prices could be used to guide detailed decisions to implement the plan, just as real prices are used. So it appears that prices are not the result of a particular social structure but are inherent in the logic of efficiency. In some of the socialist economies there is an effort to use the pseudo-prices that result from a small-scale version of this calculation for guidance in economic decision making.

But, though thinkable in principle, this method for achieving productive efficiency is too formidable to be contemplated in practice now or in the future because the resources required to acquire, communicate, store, digest, and manipulate all those data would be an appreciable subtraction from the resources available for other uses. No economy much more complex than Crusoe's has ever been operated on such centralized, mechanistic principles. The most centralized system yet attempted is probably that of the USSR. They control centrally a couple of thousand basic commodities, and make most of their detailed decisions in a decentralized way under the guidance of an atrophied kind of price system. There are signs that this compromise system costs them heavily in terms of productive efficiency—shortages, queues, complaints about the assortment of output—though obviously the extent of inefficiency cannot be measured, since no controlled experiments can be run. In the American economy the most wasteful industries appear to be those where, for one reason or another, the price system does not operate. An outstanding example of waste of resources at present is the medical-care industry and, particularly, the provision of hospital services.

On balance it appears that in practice most decisions about production have to be made locally, where the pertinent technical information and experience reside, and that the efficiency of those decisions depends upon having guidance prices that reflect marginal rates of transformation.

Having emphasized the importance of prices as a practical implement in the search for productive efficiency, that is, for an output close to the production-possibility frontier, we have to remember that they are not always available, even in a predominantly price-and-market economy. In particular, as we have already noted, there are no prices for externalities and public goods: for clean air, uncongested streets, educated neighbors, quiet undisturbed by the whine of jets, and so on. There are no prices for these things, and market-guided decision making does not take them into account. They have to be dealt with through political decisions.

Such problems are not a consequence of any special social structure; they can arise even on Crusoe's island. Crusoe might be allergic to chaff, or he might have a strong preference for a view of vineyards to one of wheat fields. Then, if it should happen that his hut is surrounded by type VI land, which has a comparative advantage in wheat production, he still might be wise to plant that nearby land to vineyards and be pushed below his production-possibility frontier.

The inefficiency of so doing, however, would be apparent, not real. By introducing environmental considerations we have, in effect, added two new commodities into his economic calculus: chaff-free air and scenic amenity. There are marginal rates of transformation between them and the previous two commodities, and those have to be taken into account in achieving full-fledged productive efficiency. The only trouble is that, whereas Crusoe can make the necessary calculation in his head, there is no way for a price system to do so.

The principle of productive efficiency still obtains, but it cannot be implemented by the usual economic arrangements.

CONSUMER SOVEREIGNTY

Consumer sovereignty exists in an economy when that economy is responsive to consumers' desires; that is to say, when that economy does not devote resources to producing any good if those resources could have been used to produce something that consumers would have preferred. This is the standard that monopolies violate. It entails that producers should somehow know which commodities consumers want most, and that consumers, on their part, should know enough about the conditions of production, so that they can formulate realistic demands.

On Crusoe's island, where producer and consumer are one, the problem is trivially simple, and yet we can learn something from it. We have already seen how Crusoe can attain any of the points on his production-possibility frontier. Now we ask which point he should select.

Once Crusoe has determined his production-possibility frontier, he behaves like a consumer except that he has a production-possibility frontier instead of a budget line. This is shown in Fig. 7–2, where a few of Crusoe's indifference curves between wheat and wine are superimposed on the graph of the production-possibility frontier. He selects point P, where the frontier touches the highest possible indifference curve. All other points on the frontier are on lower indifference curves (that is, they are less desirable). He does not have to be content with any point below the frontier, and he cannot attain any point above it. Point P is the best output combination he can attain, as evaluated by Crusoe's own preferences and desires.

The essential fact to notice in Fig. 7–2 is that at the optimum point the frontier is tangent to the relevant indifference curve (that is, their slopes are equal). The slope of the indifference curve, we know, is the marginal rate of substitution between the two commodities; the slope of the production-possibility frontier is their marginal rate of transformation. Hence the optimal output for a one-consumer economy occurs at the point where the economy's marginal rate of transformation between any two commodities is equal to the consumer's marginal rate of substitution between them.

That solves the problem for Robinson Crusoe—but not, unfortunately, for any economy with more than one member. Any economy, no matter how populous, has a production-possibility frontier and attains it when operating efficiently. What a populous economy lacks is a well-defined set of indifference curves, such as the ones we used to resolve Crusoe's final choice in Fig. 7–2. This difficulty obtrudes itself even when there are only two members in the economy.

To see our way into this problem, let us provide Crusoe with a companion,

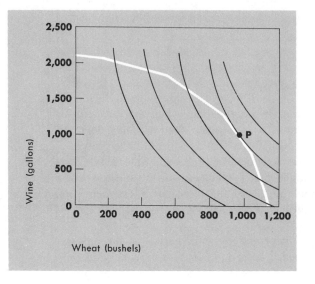

Wine (gallons)

Wheat (bushels)

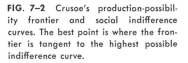

FIG. 7–2 Crusoe's production-possibility frontier and social indifference curves. The best point is where the frontier is tangent to the highest possible indifference curve.

not Man Friday but a doughty equal named Smith. Then Crusoe and Smith have to agree on a point on the production-possibility frontier, and on a division between them of the amounts of the two crops corresponding to that point. These are two distinct decisions involving different social issues. We shall deal with them separately, taking up first the question of how to divide the crops corresponding to any selected point on the production-possibility frontier.

To this end, suppose that an output point such as point P in Fig. 7–2 has been selected. A thousand gallons of wine plus 945 bushels of wheat are available to be shared between Crusoe and Smith. The only principle that we have to go on is that the wheat and wine should be shared in such a way that Crusoe and Smith have the same marginal rate of substitution between the two commodities as we found when discussing efficiency in distribution. But this principle is not sufficient to determine the division of the crops; it can be satisfied in too many different ways. A famous diagram, called a *box diagram,* will help us to visualize the problem and its social implications.

The box diagram is based on the indifference-curve diagrams introduced in Chapter 5. Figure 7–3 shows a few of Crusoe's indifference curves between wheat and wine. The only new feature is that the indifference curves are enclosed in a box whose dimensions are the total amounts of the commodities to be divided. Each point in the box therefore shows the quantities assigned to Crusoe, in the conventional way, and also the quantities left over to be assigned to Smith. According to point $A,$ for example, Crusoe gets 480 bushels of wheat and 400 gallons of wine. Smith gets the remainder: 465 bushels of wheat and 600 gallons of wine, as can be read off the two new axes in the diagram. Crusoe's indifference curves, as shown, indicate how he rates different possible divisions of the two crops. He prefers B to A and A to C. Smith's preferences among divisions cannot be told from Fig. 7–3, but we can take care of that by adding some of Smith's indifference curves to the diagram. This is done in Fig. 7–4 where Smith's indifference curves are shown by dashes. Smith's curves may look somewhat peculiar in that diagram, but if you turn the page upside down you will see that they form a perfectly normal indifference-curve diagram referred to Smith's 0–0 point. Now we can see that Smith's ranking of divisions A, B, and C is just the opposite of Crusoe's.

The divisions that correspond to points at which one of Smith's indifference curves is tangent to one of Crusoe's are of special importance. To emphasize

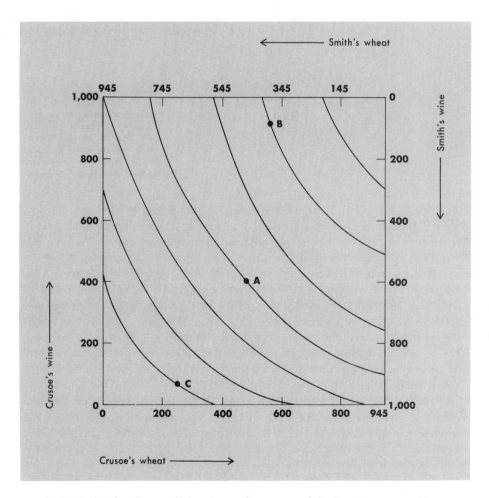

FIG. 7–3 A box diagram. Each point specifies one way of dividing given amounts of two commodities between two consumers.

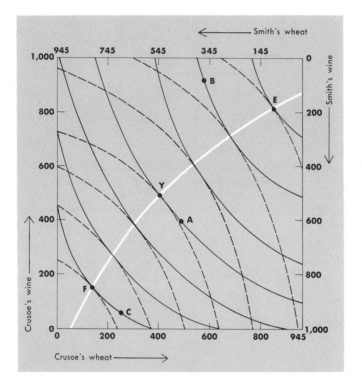

FIG. 7–4 Box diagram with two sets of indifference curves. The indifference curves show the preferences of both consumers. Every point at which two indifference curves are tangent represents an efficient distribution of the commodities between the consumers.

them, the curve *FYE*, called the *contract curve*, is drawn through all such points. For, consider any point (such as point *A*) not on the contract curve: like every other point, it lies on one of Crusoe's indifference curves. As we move along that indifference curve toward the contract curve at *Y*, we pass through a succession of points representing divisions that are equally satisfactory from Crusoe's point of view, but are increasingly good according to Smith's scale of preferences. But at *Y* we reach the highest indifference curve for Smith that intersects the given indifference curve for Crusoe. We cannot find any reallocation taking *Y* as a point of departure that benefits Smith without harming Crusoe—and this is the fundamental characteristic of the contract curve. Any division *off* the contract curve can be improved from the viewpoints of both Crusoe and Smith; no division *on* it can be.

There is nothing surprising about all this when we remember that the slope of an indifference curve is the graphic representation of the consumer's marginal rate of substitution between the commodities. On the contract curve, where Smith's and Crusoe's indifference curves are tangent, the two men have the same marginal rate of substitution between the commodities, and we have already found this to be a condition for an efficient distribution of the commodities between them. The trouble is that there are so many such points; *FYE* is full of them.

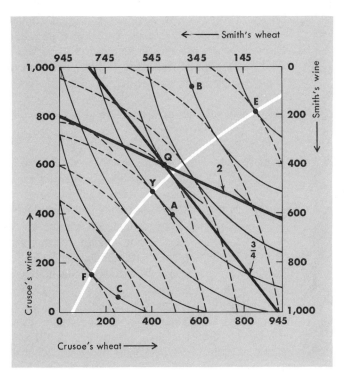

FIG. 7–5 Box diagram with trading lines. The trading lines show the ratios in which the commodities are traded. The only feasible one is tangent to one indifference curve from each set at the same point.

So the situation is this: the principle of equating marginal rates of substitution tells us to divide the wheat and wine between Crusoe and Smith according to some point on the contract curve, but it doesn't tell us which point. However, a glance at the box diagram shows what is involved in a choice among points on the contract curve. As we move along the curve from *F* toward *E,* we move through successively higher indifference curves for Crusoe, and lower ones for Smith. In other words, as we move in that direction, Crusoe gets richer at Smith's expense. The choice we are now considering is the choice of income distribution, one of the most serious and contentious questions in any society. Indeed, Crusoe and Smith are likely to argue vehemently about which point to choose on *FYE*.

The Pareto criterion gives no guidance for decisions about the distribution of income because its entire content is that no decision should be adopted if there is some alternative that gives some member of the society more satisfaction without reducing the satisfaction of any other. But any movement along the contract curve that increases Crusoe's satisfaction will reduce Smith's, and vice versa. So we cannot say anything about that at present and shall return to the issue of income distribution in the last chapter.

To get on with the problem of choosing the best point on the production-possibility frontier, we assume that Crusoe and Smith have agreed on some

189

rule for dividing the product, whatever point might be selected. The rule might be, for example, that Crusoe will receive initially the crops grown on land of odd-numbered types and Smith the crops on even-numbered types of land. This initial distribution is not likely to be on the contract curve. If so, the two will agree on a price for wine in terms of wheat and will trade in accordance with that price.

It is worth checking that the suggested procedure will lead them to a definite point on the contract curve. Suppose they should decide to produce 1,000 gallons of wine and 945 bushels of wheat. The use of land and the initial shares of output that would result from this decision are shown in Table 7–2. Crusoe's land would produce 465 bushels of wheat and 600 gallons of wine, Smith's would produce the rest. The resulting distribution of commodities is point Q in Fig. 7–5. It is not on the contract curve.

Now the two have to agree on a price for wine and trade. Suppose, for example, that they decide that a gallon of wine should cost 2 bushels of wheat. At this price Crusoe (or Smith) could trade x gallons of his wine for $2x$ bushels of wheat or y bushels of wheat for $\frac{1}{2}y$ gallons of wine. These possibilities are shown by the line labeled "2" in Fig. 7–5. Crusoe would want to trade about 200 gallons of wine for 400 bushels of wheat, for that is where the trading line reaches the highest possible indifference curve for him. Contrariwise, by turning over the book you will see that Smith would want to trade about 160 gallons of wine for 320 bushels of wheat. Now they cannot both sell wine to each other. Clearly this price is too high, and they will not agree on it.

The other line shown depicts the possibilities of trade at a price of 0.75 bushels of wheat per gallon of wine. This trading line has the important property that it reaches the highest indifference curve for Crusoe and the highest one for Smith at the same point, both, of course, on the contract curve. (Why?)

Table 7–2 ALLOCATION OF LAND AND PRODUCTS BETWEEN CRUSOE AND SMITH

		Acres Used for		Output	
		Wheat	Wine	Wheat	Wine
Crusoe's share					
Land type	I	0	10	0	300
	III	10	10	90	300
	V	15	0	375	0
Crusoe's total				465	600
Smith's share					
Land type	II	0	10	0	400
	IV	25	0	300	0
	VI	10	0	180	0
Smith's total				480	400
Total Product				945	1,000

At that price Crusoe will want to sell about 40 gallons of wine for 30 bushels of wheat and Smith will be agreeable. They will end up at the point where that trading line crosses the contract curve.

This small calculation illustrates a number of points. Primarily it shows how the choice of a point on the production-possibility frontier together with a rule for dividing the product determines a point on the contract curve and, in effect, a distribution of income. Secondly, it shows that implicit in that decision (given the rule of division) is a communal marginal rate of substitution between wheat and wine. Since Crusoe and Smith have the same marginal rate of substitution of wine for wheat at every point on the contract curve, though this rate is likely to be different at different points, the output decision plus the rule of division determine an *MRS* (wine : wheat) common to both, or all, members of the society. The particular rule of income distribution chosen is not important for this argument, though it is very important to Crusoe, Smith, and anyone else whose income is affected. Just as long as it permits a final allocation on the contract curve, which is required for efficiency in distribution, our conclusions will be valid. These conclusions apply also to larger societies, although they are not as transparent when more commodities and people are involved.

This apparent digression has really brought us a long way along the road to discovering the best point on the production-possibility frontier. Another graph will be helpful in finishing the job. In Fig. 7–6 the same production-possibility frontier is reproduced, with a slight change. We now drop the assumption that there are only six classes of land, in favor of the more realistic view that there is a very large number. Then the production-possibility frontier will consist of a very large number of very short segments and will take on the appearance of a smooth curve, as shown. It will still be concave, for the principle of comparative advantage still applies. Each point on the frontier signifies certain outputs of the two commodities to which there corresponds a certain division between the claimants and, as we just saw, a certain communal marginal rate of substitution between wine and wheat. The marginal rate of substitution is represented graphically by a slope—specifically, by the common slope of the indifference curves on which the participants find themselves at that point. This slope at point *P* is indicated by the short line-segment drawn through that point.

Notice, now, that this slope is not the same as that of the production-possibility frontier at point *P*—that is, the marginal rate of transformation there. Therefore, point *P* cannot be a good choice. For the slope of the communal *MRS* line, as we may call it, shows the number of gallons of wine that either member of the community would require to recompense him for a one-bushel reduction in his quota of wheat, in accordance with his indifference curve. The slope of the production-possibility curve shows the number of gallons of wine that can be obtained by reducing the output of wheat by one bushel. As shown, the increase in wine output is more than sufficient to compensate either

191

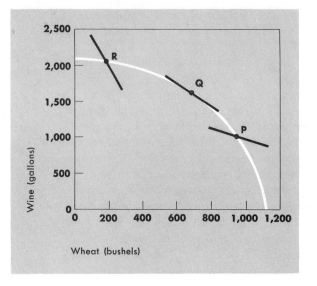

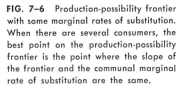

FIG. 7–6 Production-possibility frontier with some marginal rates of substitution. When there are several consumers, the best point on the production-possibility frontier is the point where the slope of the frontier and the communal marginal rate of substitution are the same.

member for a bushel reduction in his wheat allotment. So one member could be made better off, and the other not harmed, if a production point were selected at which one bushel less of wheat was grown and *MRT* (wine : wheat) more gallons of wine. Point *P* is not a good selection on the production-possibility frontier.

But now consider point *Q,* where it happens that the communal marginal rate of substitution is equal to the marginal rate of transformation. There, a small diminution in wheat output will not permit a large enough increase in wine production to promote either member to a higher indifference curve. Similarly, the sacrifice in wine output required to obtain an additional bushel of wheat is not large enough to compensate either member for a bushel reduction in his wheat allotment. If point *Q* is selected, there is no way to increase the well-being of either member without decreasing that of the other. Thus point *Q* may well be a good production point.

Must there necessarily be a point such as *Q,* where the marginal rate of transformation is equal to the communal marginal rate of substitution? We would need an elaborate analysis to answer this question rigorously, including a detailed specification of the rules of income distribution, but it seems very plausible that there should be such a point if communal behavior is at all like individual behavior. At a point such as *R,* wine is very plentiful in proportion to wheat. At such a production point for the community most consumers, if not all, will be alloted a great deal of wine in proportion to wheat and, in accordance with their individual indifference curves, such consumers will have high *MRS* (wine : wheat). Since the communal marginal rate of substitution reflects individual ones, it will be likely to be high also, as illustrated by the steep communal *MRS* line. Note that at that same point the production-possibility frontier is quite flat, indicating a low *MRT* (wine : wheat).

At point *P,* where wheat is plentiful in proportion to wine, the situation is just the opposite. It seems reasonable to believe that the two slopes, one representing preferences and the other production possibilities, will come together at some point intermediate between *R* and *P*. There the marginal rate of substitution and the marginal rate of transformation will be equal. Any such point will have the essential property that no reallocation of resources between the commodities will enable either consumer to reach a higher indifference curve.

At this point the requirements of consumer sovereignty are fulfilled. The consumers—all two of them—are as well satisfied as physical circumstances permit, in the sense that there is no way to move one of them to a higher indifference curve without moving another to a lower indifference curve. The importance of the distribution of income in determining the output point dictated by consumer sovereignty is worth emphasizing. The distribution of income influenced the communal marginal rate of substitution. The output point responsive to consumer sovereignty is the one at which the marginal rate of transformation is equal to the communal marginal rate of substitution. Of course it follows that consumers do not share their sovereignty equally; the economy is most responsive to the tastes of the richer consumers.

To summarize what we have learned: On Crusoe's island, whatever may be the output of commodities, the requirements of efficiency in distribution insure that all (two) consumers have the same marginal rate of substitution between every pair of commodities. This communal *MRS* will be determined by the point selected on the production-possibility frontier. That same selection will determine the marginal rate of transformation between every pair of commodities. If the communal *MRS* is not equal to the *MRT,* then some consumer could be made better off, without harming any other, by moving to a different point on the production-possibility frontier. That selection will violate the Pareto criterion and, in particular, it will violate the consumer-sovereignty requirement. So we conclude that consumers' sovereignty requires that a point be selected on the production-possibility frontier at which the marginal rate of transformation between every pair of commodities is equal to the communal marginal rate of substitution between them.

That is true, and relatively easy to see, for Crusoe's island. But by a more complicated version of exactly the same reasoning it can be seen to hold for any economy, no matter how many commodities, resources, or consumers there may be. If there is a price system in a real economy, the relative prices of commodities will reveal the marginal rates of substitution among them, and the relative marginal costs of production (which will be equal to the prices if the system is not unduly distorted by monopolistic ingredients) will reveal their marginal rates of transformation. So, in a preliminary way, we see that a price system does contain the information needed to obey consumer sovereignty.

AGGREGATIVE EFFICIENCY

The most striking source of waste in an economy is idle resources and unemployed men. When those are present, the economy cannot be on its production-possibility frontier. Yet this source of waste occurs in all economies and is often more serious than the misapplications of resources that we have been discussing so far.

We must not demand perfection. Businessmen and central planners both make mistakes, and when they do idle resources, among other things, are likely to result. Reallocations of resources take time. Much visible unemployment is simply the interval during which a man looks for the job where he is needed and employers search for the men they need. It has been estimated that the practical minimum level of unemployment in this country, for this reason, is about 3.5 per cent. But the level of unemployment is often greater than can be accounted for on these grounds. The excess is an indication of aggregative inefficiency—failure to employ all the resources available.

In a market-guided economy the causes of aggregative inefficiency are quite distinct from the market-adjusting forces treated in this book, and we can only allude to them.[12] The underlying difficulty is that consumers are not compelled to consume all of the incomes they earn, nor are business firms compelled to invest all of the profits they retain or all of the sums consumers wish to save in plants, equipment, or inventories. So it may come about that the aggregate sum that consumers wish to spend on consumption plus the sum that firms wish to invest in various capital goods and inventories is different from the value of the commodities of all kinds produced in the economy. Things will be produced that no one wishes to buy because too many people are trying to use their incomes to add to their liquid savings. Unwanted goods will accumulate in inventories, and eventually there will be cutbacks in production and therefore idle men and resources.

If more is produced of any commodity than people wish to buy at the going price, the obvious cure, and the one we have already noted, is to reduce the price. This works for disequilibrium in an isolated market. But when a shortage of demand occurs in many markets because of excessive liquid saving, a price reduction in any one of them will only attract demand from other markets where demand is already deficient. Price changes are adequate, and indispensable, for redressing imbalances in relative prices; they do not avail when there is a generalized insufficiency of demand for commodities.

Aggregative inefficiency can be attributed to a disequilibrium in the structure of prices, in a somewhat extended sense. It occurs, as we have seen, when people wish to spend less now in order to have the money to buy more later.

[12] They are discussed at length in two other volumes in this series: J. S. Duesenberry, *Money and Credit: Impact and Control*, 3rd ed. and C. L. Schultze, *National Income Analysis*, 3rd ed.

It represents a high marginal rate of substitution of present commodities for future ones. There is a price that corresponds to this marginal rate of substitution of present for future: the interest rate. So unemployment does indicate that the interest rate is out of equilibrium: that it is too high. But the analysis of the interest rate, its causes and consequences, are well outside the scope of this book.

MAIN CONCEPTS INTRODUCED

PRIVATE GOODS. Goods that can be supplied to consumers and firms individually. Each consumer's welfare and firm's profits are affected only by the amount they consume.

PUBLIC GOODS. Goods that cannot be assigned to individual consumers or firms. The welfares of several (or all) consumers or firms are affected jointly by the total amount of the public goods in the community.

EXTERNALITY or EXTERNAL EFFECT. The direct impact on the welfare of any consumer or firm resulting from the use of a commodity by some other consumer or firm.

PARETO CRITERION. The criterion of economic performance that holds that an economy is operating efficiently if there is no feasible change that will enhance the welfare of some consumer without harming some other consumer.

PRODUCTION POSSIBILITY FRONTIER. A specification of the greatest amount of any commodity that can be produced in conjunction with given amounts of other commodities and a given total utilization of resources.

MARGINAL RATE OF TRANSFORMATION. The marginal rate of transformation of commodity X into commodity Y, denoted $MRT(X:Y)$, is the number of units of X that would have to be forgone in order that the economy could produce one more unit of Y.

COMPARATIVE ADVANTAGE. The comparative advantage of any resource in the production of any commodity is the ratio of its marginal productivity when used to produce that commodity to its marginal productivity when used in other industries. In an efficiently operating economy the comparative advantage of every resource in the production of every commodity for which it is used should be at least as great as that of any other resource that could be used to produce the same commodities.

BOX DIAGRAM, sometimes called EDGEWORTH BOX. A diagram that shows simultaneously the distribution of two commodities between two consumers and the indifference curves of both consumers.

CONTRACT CURVE. The locus in a box diagram of the points at which an indifference curve of one of the consumers is tangent to one of the indifference curves of the other consumer.

The main themes of this chapter will be included in the summary of Chapter 8, with which it is closely connected.

The Operation of the

Price System

CHAPTER EIGHT

The last chapter described, in some detail, how an economy ought to perform. It ought to obey consumer sovereignty, produce efficiently, distribute efficiently, and so on. This chapter is concerned with how a particular kind of economy—one in which private businesses produce and distribute in response to the forces of supply and demand—satisfies these criteria. It deals with this issue on two levels, rather intermixed. One level is theoretical: how a perfectly operating free-enterprise system would operate. The other level is more realistic and critical: it considers to what extent the imperfect system we actually have achieves its theoretically possible attainments.

We shall examine these questions by taking up the main criteria in turn and considering what features of the price system contribute to satisfying that criterion and what aspects of the real world impede perfect performance.

First we shall consider distributional efficiency: the requirement that goods be distributed among consumers in such a way that no pair of consumers could gain by bartering or exchanging with each other. Then we shall turn to productive efficiency: the requirement that the resources used in production should be directed so that it is impossible to produce more of any good without cutting back the output of some other good. Third, we shall take up consumer sovereignty: the requirement that the goods and services produced with the society's resources be as desirable to consumers as any assortment that could be produced.

The other requirements for an ideal economy lie beyond the scope of this volume and will not be treated thoroughly. They include aggregative efficiency—the requirement that all the productive resources available to the society be utilized—and dynamic efficiency—the requirement that adequate provision be made for economic growth. The final requirement that we recognize, equity, will be reserved for the last chapter.

MARKETS AND EFFICIENT DISTRIBUTION

The theory of how markets achieve the efficient distribution of commodities is so straightforward that we presented the mechanism when we first introduced the concept in the last chapter. Briefly: in accordance with the principles of Chapter 5, each consumer divides his budget so that his marginal rate of substitution between every pair of commodities is equal to the ratio of their prices. Two things follow. First, since all consumers confront the same prices there is a common, or communal, marginal rate of substitution between every pair of commodities. Second, the distribution of commodities is automatically efficient, since marginal rates of substitution common to all consumers form the condition for this aspect of efficiency.

That's all there is to the argument, but it rests on two assertions that are open to doubt. First, it assumes that all consumers pay the same prices for the same commodities, which is clearly not always the case. Department stores, discount houses, and mail-order companies often charge different prices for indistinguishable articles. Ghetto grocery stores charge more than supermarkets. And so on. So, indeed, marginal rates of substitution cannot be exactly the same for all consumers.

But it appears that this element of inexactness is not very damaging to efficiency, for several reasons. First, the high prices charged in ghetto stores and other local stores largely cancel themselves out. If all the prices in a neighborhood are inflated in the same proportion, the marginal rates of substitution will be unaffected however onerous this may be for the inhabitants of the neighborhood. Income equity may thereby be impaired but not distributional efficiency.

Second, the fact that department stores, discount houses, and luxury stores all charge different prices does not prevent consumers from equating their margins as long as consumers can choose where to buy. The consumers who buy in higher-priced stores presumably have their reasons; it is sometimes said that articles bought in different stores are, for that very reason, slightly different commodities, just as on some occasions the silver candlesticks must come in a Tiffany box.[1] At any rate, and largely because many consumers can

---

[1] It doesn't pay to push this reasoning too far or else each seller will be a monopolist and there will be no competitive markets. The concept that each seller offers commodities somewhat distinct from those of other sellers ignores the fact that the prices that different sellers charge for the same physical commodity are closely tied together—the similarities among vendors dominate the differences. But there is something to it.

select which store to buy from, the differences among the prices charged for similar commodities are generally small. The actual spread of prices paid by different consumers for similar commodities does not, in short, prevent their marginal rate of substitution for different commodities from being very nearly equalized.

The more significant causes of inefficiencies in distribution lie with the other dubious assumption, that consumers actually divide their budgets so as to make their marginal rates of substitution equal to the ratios of the prices of the commodities they buy. Recall how we supported this assumption, back in Chapter 5. We imagined a consumer in a supermarket deciding how much to buy of different grocery items, and having in mind the consequences of previous decisions of the same sort. In confronting such decisions, an experienced consumer can be expected to divide his (her) budget in such a way that an additional dollar spent on any commodity will yield about as much satisfaction as an additional dollar spent on any other commodity. And such decisions account for a large proportion of consumption expenditures (for example, food purchases account for about a quarter of consumers' expenditures).

But there are many commodities that are not at all like that—commodities such as wedding rings and washing machines that are not bought in variable quantities and that are bought so infrequently that the consumer cannot learn by experience how much he should spend on them to reach a high indifference curve. But all is not lost. Some of these, like wedding rings, are once-in-a-lifetime purchases, and of small importance economically. Besides, the consumer does have a marginal option. Wedding rings, washing machines, and other such commodities are offered in a variety of qualities and sizes. The consumer can choose among these, and will choose so that the marginal increase in quality of the item he buys over the next cheaper one is just worth the additional cost to the best of his judgment. Thus he balances his marginal rate of substitution with respect to quality rather than with respect to quantity.

Besides, with most infrequently purchased commodities (but not wedding rings), the consumer chooses a quantity dimension also. At any moment there will be numerous owners of obsolescent and battered washing machines and TV sets who are contemplating replacing them with shiny, up-to-date successors. They will make the decision by comparing the advantages of newer equipment with the price. Thus, for the people who actually make such purchases, the marginal rate of substitution of the infrequently purchased commodity for other goods is about equal to the ratio of the prices, and for everyone the number of purchases made per year (generally much less than one) will be such that the marginal rate of substitution between more frequent purchases of the durable goods and larger quantities of nondurables will be equal to the ratio of the costs.

None of these considerations, however, mitigate the problem of consumers' inexperience or ignorance concerning infrequently purchased items. If the consumer cannot judge the serviceability of an article he cannot estimate its marginal rate of substitution for other commodities and cannot spend his budget in the way that will place him on the highest possible indifference curve. One small episode will indicate the misallocations that result. Once upon a time a high-volume, economy-oriented department store decided to market its own house-brand of electric iron. It ordered a large shipment from a national manufacturer, put its own nameplate on the irons, and priced them 50 cents below the national brand's price. They did not sell. Apparently consumers, knowing that they could not judge quality, preferred to pay 50 cents more and be sure. So the store raised the price on its brand by $1.00. Then they sold just fine. Again it seemed that consumers were glad to pay an extra 50 cents to obtain what they presumed to be superior quality.

This kind of behavior is not limited to infrequently purchased commodities. Do you buy the cheapest grade of gasoline? If not, have you experimented to make sure that the grade you buy is worth 4 cents a gallon more to you? Most people do not bother or dare.

The adverse consequences of consumers' ignorance are twofold. It interferes, of course, with efficient distribution because it prevents marginal rates of substitution from being equal for all consumers. It also interferes with the operation of consumers' sovereignty by permitting, nay encouraging, firms to produce commodities whose marginal rate of substitution for other commodities is far greater than their price ratios. Resources are wasted in the production of disappointments or illusory satisfactions.

The obvious cure for consumers' ignorance is information: more publications like *Consumer Reports,* more intelligible grade labeling, and more dissemination of the results of testing in governmental and other unbiased laboratories. Producers have uniformly, and naturally, resisted efforts in this direction, and have rested their case largely on the true fact that consumers do not appear to be interested. (An advertisement in *Life* has many times more circulation and authority than an evaluation in *Consumer Reports.*) But here is a case where the economy would operate more efficiently if we violated consumers' sovereignty and forced information upon consumers, in order to reduce the other violations. We might, for example, require franchised television stations that broadcast advertisements for certain commodities to devote some (probably less than equal) time to neutral evaluations of those same commodities.

The inexpertness of consumers appears to be the most serious impediment to the achievement of efficient distribution through competitive markets. The markets themselves do not provide the reliable and unbiased information that consumers need. Nor would it be sensible for the consumers themselves to spend the time and effort needed to become competent judges of the thousands of commodities that they buy. Conscientious retailers can help consumers overcome their deficiency of information, but, as we saw in Chapter 6, the retailer is being supplanted by the advertising agency as a source of information. Fundamentally, there is no cure for consumers' ignorance, though it can be mitigated,

199

for example, by making advertisers and media more responsible for providing truthful and complete information about their wares.

Sometimes society interferes deliberately with distributional efficiency, as here defined. The motivation is to improve efficiency from a broader point of view, by compelling some people to spend their budgets more wisely than they would if left to their own devices. The food-stamp program, which subsidizes certain food purchases by low-income families, is a typical case in point. Subsidized low-income housing is another. In these and other cases the recipients are entitled to buy designated commodities at much lower prices than other people, a clear violation of the principle of distributional efficiency. Thus they are induced to buy commodities that other people value more highly than they do and which, indeed, they do not want very keenly.

The resultant dissatisfaction is more than theoretical. Families slightly above the maximum eligible income complain at being excluded from public-housing projects, while eligible families resent having to live in the projects—they would prefer to have their subsidies in cash to spend as they liked.

In so far as the business of an economy is to please consumers, the case against such interferences is strong. The case for them is partly paternalistic, partly based upon externalities.[2] The paternalistic ground is that the society at large has a special right to oversee the expenditure of relief payments so that the monies will not be squandered and the most deleterious manifestations of poverty will be combatted. It is deemed particularly essential to direct the expenditures toward the adequate nutrition and housing of children. Thus the preferences of society as the guardian of all its children take precedence over the preferences of necessitous consumers. The counterargument is that even poor mothers know best what they and their children need, and that even the poor are entitled to their mite of consumer sovereignty. Both points of view have some merit, but the major burden of proof would seem to lie on those who defend the practice of inducing people to buy what they do not want. This burden would consist in showing that the supervisory approach is effective enough to compensate for the administrative burdens and resentments that it entails. Unfortunately, the various programs for controlling expenditures have never been monitored carefully, and our information about their effects is partial and indecisive.

The externality justification for guiding the expenditure of relief disbursements is that substandard housing, undernourished children, and so on are likely to engender antisocial and disruptive behavior that constitutes a burden on the entire society. Certainly the communities in which such conditions prevail also display other symptoms of social pathology, but the cause-and-effect relationships are obscure. The few attempts that have been made to identify the social externalities of slum housing, for example, have not been conclusive.

[2] And sometimes there are other considerations. A significant aspect of the food-stamp program is that it reinforces the demand for farm products. To the extent that it leads to increased farm output it impairs consumers' sovereignty, as all such programs do to some degree.

On the whole, the case for departing from efficiency in distribution, in the technical sense, is weak. This is one reason why economists very predominantly advocate that all restrictions be removed from welfare and relief payments—as by guaranteed minimum incomes or negative income taxes.

MARKETS AND EFFICIENT PRODUCTION

The second major criterion for an efficient economy is efficiency in production. This criterion has two components. First, each firm or enterprise should produce as much output as is technically possible with the resources it uses. Second, the resources should be distributed among firms in such a way that it would not be possible to increase the output of some commodity or commodities without reducing the output of others by transferring resources from one firm to another. The second is the more subtle aspect, so we shall deal first with the other.

Each firm attempts to hold down its costs, according to the principles of Chapters 3 and 4. When it has succeeded in producing its current output at the lowest possible cost it will also be producing the greatest output attainable with the resources that it uses. In other words, producing a given output at lowest possible cost and producing the greatest possible output with given resources are simply two ways of looking at the very same problem. The proof of this assertion is mathematical in form and spirit. We shall show that if it were possible for a firm to increase its output without increasing its use of resources, then that firm could not be producing its current output as cheaply as possible.

For suppose that a firm could, by some change in technique, increase its output by x units without using any more resources and that if it did so, the marginal cost of its product would be c. Then the firm could do two things simultaneously. First, it could adopt the improved technique, thereby increasing its output by x units without changing the total cost it incurred. Second, it could cut back its rate of production by x units, thereby producing its prechange output at a saving of about cx in cost. Thus, a firm with such a possibility for increasing its output could not have been producing at lowest possible cost and conversely if a firm is producing at lowest possible cost, there is no way for it to increase its output without using more resources.

This establishes that individual firms in their efforts to reduce costs make efficient use of the resources at their disposal. Now we turn to the second component of productive efficiency: the requirement that it be impossible for the economy as a whole to increase the output of any commodity without reducing the output of some other by transferring resources from one firm to another. The issue we are confronting can be stated as follows. Suppose a competitive economy has attained full equilibrium. Every firm is maximizing its profits and is paying the same wage or rental as every other firm for the resources it uses. Would it be possible for an omniscient and omnipotent economic planner to reassign resources from one firm to another in such a way as to increase the economy's output of some commodity without reducing the output of any other? We shall show that this would not be possible, so that businessmen operating under competitive conditions achieve as high a level of production as the most skillful conceivable economic planner.

Our argument depends on two facts (still to be demonstrated): (a) when businessmen individually maximize their profits and pay a common wage or rental for each of the resources they use, then they collectively produce the highest-valued bundle of commodities that can be produced with those resources; and (b) if an economy is producing the bundle of commodities that has the greatest possible aggregate value at given prices, then it is operating at a point on its production-possibility frontier. Taken together these facts show that when businessmen succeed in maximizing their individual profits they will, albeit inadvertently, also succeed in producing a bundle of commodities on the economy's production-possibility frontier, which assures productive efficiency.

Fact (a) follows from the principles deduced in Chapters 3 and 4. First, under the inducement of the market prices, each firm produces the output of greatest possible value with the resources it uses. When firms have done this, no rearrangement of resources within the firms will increase the aggregate value of the output of the economy. Second, we have to consider whether aggregate value could be increased by some reassignment of factors of production from one firm to another. Recall, now, that the wage or rental paid to any factor is equal to the value of its marginal product—that is, to the value of its contribution to the output of the firm that employs it. If a unit of some factor should be transferred from one firm to another, therefore, two things will happen. The value produced by the firm that loses the factor will fall by an amount equal to the wage or rent of the factor. At the same time, the value produced by the firm that gains the factor will increase by the same amount. The two changes will cancel each other out; the aggregate value of output produced by the economy will not increase. So no reallocation of resources can increase the value of output of an economy if (1) each firm is maximizing its profit with reference to some set of prices, and (2) every firm that uses a given resource pays the same wage or rental that every other firm does.

Fact (b) is a consequence of the definition of the production-possibility frontier. If an economy is not on its production-possibility frontier, there will be some rearrangement of its production activities and its use of resources that will increase the output of some commodity without reducing the output of any other. But such a rearrangement would increase the aggregate value of its output. In other words, if an economy is not on its production-possibility frontier, the value of its output can be increased and, inversely, if the value of its output cannot be increased, it must already be on its production-possibility frontier.

This completes the proof.[3] The idea is simply that competitive markets induce businessmen to produce as much *value* as possible with given resources, and that when this has been done, they are also producing as much physical quantity as possible The intimate relationship between monetary values and physical quantities in this derivation deserves particular notice. Businessmen are interested in monetary values—their receipts and costs—whereas society is concerned with physical results—amounts of commodities produced and resources used. Nevertheless competitive markets operate in such a way that businessmen are induced to produce physical quantities on the production-possibility frontier. The transition from monetary values to physical quantities was essential to our reasoning; it is equally essential to the efficient operation of a market-oriented economy.

This rather abstract argument may be clarified by applying it to a simple illustration. We can use the technical data of Robinson Crusoe's island, Table 7–1, for this purpose. But now we imagine that the land (still the only resource needed for production) is owned by numerous landlords and that the wheat and wine are produced by numerous competitive wheat-growing firms and wineries. No one knows or cares to know the island's production-possibility frontier, but each firm knows its own production possibilities—its own production function. The production data are given in the third and fourth columns of Table 7–1.

Now suppose that the price of wine is $.60 a gallon, and of wheat $1 a bushel. A winery could produce $18 worth of its product from an acre of type I land, whereas a wheat grower could produce only $3 worth of wheat. Only wineries can afford to rent that land, and they will have to pay about $18 an acre, since if any acre were placed on the market some winery would be willing to offer $17.95.

At the other extreme, type IV land is worth $18 to a wheat grower and only $3 to a winery. All that land will be rented to wheat growers. By similar calculations we can see that all land of types I, II, and III will be used for wine; land of types V and VI for wheat. Type IV land can produce $12 worth of output per acre when used for either crop and will be divided between them. We already know that this allocation of resources is on the production-possibility frontier. No one particularly aimed at that frontier, but the allocation of resources to the uses in which they produced the greatest value led the economy there automatically.

[3] This demonstration that competitive markets guide an economy toward its production-possibility frontier makes no pretense to rigor. To mention just one defect: we showed that no single transfer of resources could increase the value of the economy's output and implied that no sequence or combination of transfers could do so. This implication, itself, requires proof. The proof would depend on the properties of the isoquant diagrams and the production functions described in Chapter 4.

All really adequate treatments of the relationship between prices and productive efficiency are very difficult. For a somewhat fuller discussion see Robert Dorfman, *The Price System*, in this series, Chap. 5. For a still more extensive discussion, which may be understandable, see R. Dorfman, P. A. Samuelson, and R. M. Solow, *Linear Programming and Economic Analysis*, Chap. 13.

The same mechanism operates in more general and complicated circumstances. Each resource will be employed by a firm in whose hands the value of its product is greatest, and that is enough to assure that society's output will be on the production-possibility frontier—the condition for productive efficiency.

Figure 8–1 shows graphically why maximizing the monetary value of the commodities produced by an economy amounts to reaching a point on the production-possibility frontier. The figure contains the smoothed version of Robinson Crusoe's production-possibility frontier with some lines superimposed, along each of which the value of output is constant at prices of $1 per bushel of wheat and $.60 per gallon of wine.[4] The greatest possible value of output occurs where the production-possibility frontier touches, and is tangent to, the line for combinations of outputs worth $1,650. If we had drawn constant-value lines for any other set of prices, we should have obtained a similar result: the greatest possible value would correspond to some point on the production-possibility frontier.

Our conclusion that competitive markets guide an economy toward an efficient organization of production was based on a highly theoretical argument. Strictly speaking, it applies only to an economy that satisfies all the postulates of the demonstration. These include the assumptions that all markets are competitive, that all firms maximize their profits with reference to the current prices of commodities and resources, that equilibrium is attained throughout the econ-

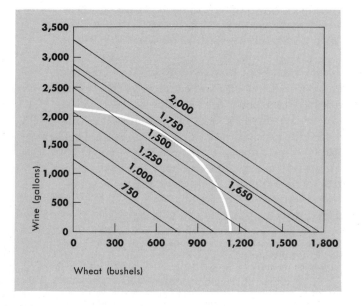

FIG. 8–1 The production-possibility frontier and lines of constant value of output. If there are prices, the best point on the production-possibility frontier maximizes the total value of output.

[4] The formula for these lines is:
1 x bushels of wheat + .60 x gallons of wine = total value of output.

omy, and that there are no external effects of business activity, so that business-men take account of all consequences of production (for example, pollution generation) that affect economic efficiency. The assumptions that equilibrium is attained and that firms make their decisions with reference to current prices impart a timeless and static character to the idealized economy. It is one in which businessmen do not allow for possible future changes, and in which the equilibrium, once attained, persists indefinitely.

All these assumptions are widely at variance with the characteristics of actual economies. In them oligopolistic and monopolistic practices are rife, no firms produce their outputs at theoretically realizable minimum costs, few firms devote themselves single-mindedly to making the greatest possible profits,[5] equi-librium is constantly being sought but never attained, and many external costs and benefits that result from production are ignored by the firms responsible. And, finally, real economies are not static; businessmen devote much of their effort to preparing for the changes they anticipate in prices, demand conditions, and productive technology.

What, then, is the significance of a finding based on such a highly ab-stracted argument? The conclusion that competitive markets lead to productive efficiency under the restrictive conditions that we were forced to assume does not entail that competitive markets have the same effect in an actual, imperfect economy. Still the ideal economy of the theorem is similar enough to actual ones that a number of important things can be learned.

In the first place, our analysis is an antidote to the naive distinction be-tween production for profit and production for usefulness. It shows that under the proper conditions the profit motive is a highly effective incentive for inducing efficient use of a society's resources. To be sure, these proper conditions are highly demanding, are not realized at present, and cannot be realized fully in any practical economy. But the fact remains that production for profit is not inherently antisocial, and there is even some presumption that reliance on independent, profit-maximizing firms is an efficient method of economic organi-zation in a complex economy where global planning and administration are well-nigh impossible.

Second, the theorem provides a frame of reference for the difficult task of appraising the efficiency of an actual economy. An economy that satisfies all the assumptions of the theorem will be perfectly efficient. Any actual economy will violate some of the assumptions, and efficiency will be impaired to an extent that depends both on the severity of the violation and on the sensitivity of the economy to the exact fulfillment of the conditions for perfect efficiency.

In the present state of knowledge, any such appraisal has to be highly judgmental for a number of reasons. In the first place, as we have frequently pointed out, no one knows the production-possibility frontier of any actual

---

[5] Even the concept of the "firm" is a theorist's fiction. Any actual firm is a bureaucracy staffed by individuals who frequently place their own personal goals and convenience above the objectives that economists impute to the "firm."

economy, so that we cannot measure efficiency by the simple device of comparing actual output with the theoretically attainable maximum, which is unknown. Instead we have to rely on indirect methods in which we measure the divergence between conditions in the economy and ideal conditions, and then infer the amount of inefficiency that results from the discrepancies. For example, we have already applied this approach in forming the judgment that the existence of price spreads instead of uniform prices for consumers' goods does not seriously impair efficiency in distribution.

The same approach has been used to measure the economic cost of the price distortions that result from oligopolistic and monopolistic pricing in many markets. Though the details of these studies are controversial, it appears that the price distortions are not very great, and that the impairment of economic efficiency is minor.[6]

The consequences of failure to satisfy the other conditions for perfect economic performance are even harder to measure. It is evident, for example, that no actual business firm succeeds in producing its output at the lowest cost that is theoretically attainable, and that no business firm actually squeezes out the last dollar of profits that it theoretically could. It is impossible in principle to know how much is lost thereby, since if the cheapest method of production for any firm were knowable, that firm would almost surely know it and adopt it. It is a safe inference, however, that production for profit is well designed to hold losses from this source of inefficiency to a practical minimum because of the very strong incentives it affords for doing so. Comparative studies of the performance of market-oriented economies and centrally planned economies indicate that centralized economies are relatively wasteful in this respect.

But the most striking discrepancy between the ideal economy and real ones is the contrast between the timelessness of the ideal economy and the never ceasing change that real economies must adapt to. This contrast renders the level of efficiency attainable in an ideal economy an unrealistic standard of comparison if taken literally Since they are aware of the fact of change, though never of the precise changes in tastes and technology and resource availability that are impending, neither businessmen nor economic planners even attempt to attain perfect efficiency with respect to current conditions. Instead they strive to adjust to the equilibrium that they foresee for the relatively near future. Our theory of the ideal economy shows that competitive firms would make this adjustment efficiently if they were given sufficient time, subject to the reservations already mentioned about the impossibility of fully minimizing costs and the comparatively minor losses caused by competitive imperfections. This is all that can be expected of managers who are not blessed with perfect foresight.

Our theorem about ideal economies, together with these qualitative con-

[6] The leading citation is A. C. Harberger, "Monopoly and Resource Allocation," *American Economic Review*, May, 1954, pp. 77–87. Harberger estimated that monopolistic price distortions reduce the output of the American economy by a fraction of 1 per cent. We presented our own estimate in Chap. 6.

siderations, thus affords a strong presumption that a market-oriented economy is about as efficient in its use of economic resources as can be expected realistically. The motivations assumed in the ideal economy are the same as those present in the real one. The real economy exhibits many hindrances to the ideal responses to those motives that are not present in the theoretical economy, but it appears that the economic losses resulting from those hindrances are either minor or inevitable under any system of economic organization.

Finally, the theorem has important implications for practical economic policy. It prescribes the conditions under which a competitive economy would operate with complete efficiency, and by implication the conditions that diminish efficiency in a real economy. Sound economic policy would strive to bring about as good an approximation to the conditions of an ideal economy as possible. Heedless laissez faire is not enough, for as Adam Smith noticed centuries ago, "People of the same trade seldom meet together, even for merriment and diversion, but the conversation ends in a conspiracy against the public, or in some contrivance to raise prices." [7] It is not true that whatever is good for businessmen is good for the nation, for one good that every businessmen desires is to free himself from the stern discipline of competitive markets, whereas monopolistic behavior violates one of the conditions for perfect economic efficiency. It follows that measures designed to maintain a fair approximation to competitive conditions are an important component of sound economic policy. We have already mentioned the importance of improving consumers' information, for one of the assumptions of the argument is that consumers know how much various commodities will contribute to their satisfaction. In so far as consumers' ignorance contributes to the establishment of monopolies and oligopolies—and we saw in Chapter 6 that it contributes quite a bit—a better-informed public would have a second beneficial effect.

Still another assumption of the ideal economy likely to be violated in a real economy is that businessmen take full account of the external effects of their activities, that is to say of the costs imposed by the congestion, pollution, and the like that result from their operations. We saw in the last chapter that economic markets in the ordinary course of affairs do not bring these costs home to the business firms that create them. For example, a business firm has little incentive to adopt methods of production that reduce the amounts of pollution and noise that it imposes on its neighbors. Such incentives can be provided by imposing taxes that at least roughly approximate the external costs of the operation.

These are but a few of the suggestions provided by the theory for economic policies that would promote more efficient operation of an economy in realistic circumstances.

In short, though the simplified argument bears little correspondence to a real competitive economy in detail, it is sufficiently similar to provide insights into both the attainments and the shortcomings of a real economy.

207

[7] Adam Smith, *Wealth of Nations*, Cannon ed. (New York: Modern Library, Inc.), p. **128.**

MARKETS AND CONSUMERS' SOVEREIGNTY

The third task of an economy is to produce the things that consumers want. No economy is rich enough to provide consumers with everything they want, but what we can demand of an economic system is that it not devote its resources to producing one thing when those same resources could be used to produce something else that consumers want more. A system in which production is responsive to freely adjusting competitive market prices answers this demand. We shall show that when market prices have adjusted so that the quantity supplied of every commodity equals the quantity demanded, the dictates of consumer sovereignty are being obeyed.

We can see this most clearly by observing how markets would operate in a two-commodity world. Suppose now that Crusoe's island has become populated by families, each of which owns some of the land and derives its income by selling the wine and wheat it grows. Each family spends its income by buying wheat and wine at market prices. Even in this simple economy there are supply and demand curves to determine the prices of the two commodities. Let us look first at the supply curve for wheat. The supply of wheat depends on how much land is devoted to it and this, in turn, depends on the ratio of the price of wheat to the price of wine. In order to see how this supply responds to changes in the price of wheat we have, therefore, to assume some definite, fixed price for wine. Suppose that it is 60 cents a gallon. Then the supply curve for wheat can be calculated as follows.

Each acre of land will be used for wheat or wine, depending on which is the more profitable. Suppose that some particular acre can be used to produce y_b bushels of wheat or y_v gallons of wine, and that the price of wheat is p_b a bushel. Then that acre will be used for wheat if and only if $y_b p_b \geqq .60 y_v$ or $y_v/y_b \leqq p_b/.60$. Furthermore, the borderline acres are those for which equality applies in this expression. But the ratio of the yields on the borderline acres is the marginal rate of transformation of wine into wheat and, accordingly, is the slope of the production-possibility frontier at the output corresponding to this price. We can therefore read the supply of wheat corresponding to any price right off the production-possibility frontier (Fig. 8–1). For example, if the price of wheat is $1 a bushel, the marginal rate of transformation of wine into wheat will be $1 : .60 = 1.67$. The production-possibility frontier has this slope when 690 bushels of wheat are produced. Accordingly, 690 bushels are supplied at a price of $1 a bushel. This is one of the points on the supply curve for wheat. Other points can be read off the production-possibility frontier in the same way. The entire supply curve, so derived, is shown in Fig. 8–2.

If we wished to derive a demand curve for wheat analogously from fundamentals, we should have to start our reasoning with the indifference-curve diagrams of the individual consumers and the rules for the distribution of income

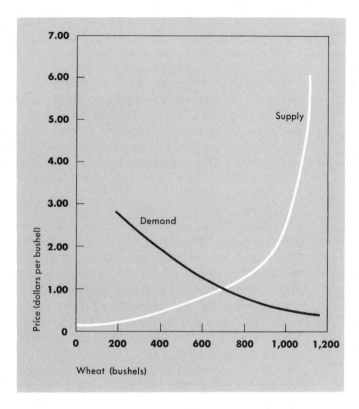

FIG. 8–2 Supply and demand for wheat. These curves are significant, even in a two-commodity economy.

among them. In the absence of these data, a demand curve has been drawn on Fig. 8–2 arbitrarily. The two curves cross at the equilibrium point for the wheat market: a price of $1 a bushel and a quantity of 690 bushels.

The derivation of the supply curve showed that at an output of 690 bushels the marginal rate of transformation of wine into wheat was 1 : 0.60; that is, the reciprocal of the ratio of the prices. At those prices each consumer will divide his budget between wine and wheat so that his marginal rate of substitution of wine for wheat will also be 1 : 0.60. But the demand curve shows that when the consumers have adjusted their budgets so as to attain this marginal rate of substitution, they will be demanding 690 bushels. Thus the output that clears the wheat market also and necessarily equates the marginal rate of transformation to the marginal rate of substitution for each consumer.

In spite of the complications introduced by having many consumers deal indirectly with many producers through purchase and sale on a market, this is very much like the equilibrium attained when Robinson Crusoe was the sole consumer. Then (Fig. 7–2) equilibrium was attained where the production-possibility frontier had the same slope as the highest indifference curve Crusoe could reach. Now equilibrium is attained where the production-possibility fron-

209

tier has the same slope as each consumer's highest attainable indifference curve. In both cases it is physically impossible to produce enough wheat by giving up wine (or enough wine by giving up wheat) to promote any consumer to a higher indifference curve.

The main difference between the two cases is that when Crusoe was alone, the information about the production-possibility frontier and the indifference curve was all contained in a single head. When there are numerous producers and consumers, each producer knows only his own production possibilities, each consumer knows only his own preferences, and they communicate with each other only by their responses to different prices. But this indirect communication is enough to satisfy the consumers as well as the production possibilities permit.

We must not forget about the wine. Given that prices of $1 a bushel for wheat and 60 cents a gallon for wine clear the wheat market, do they do the same for wine? They must, by simple arithmetic. The production-possibility frontier tells us that when 690 bushels of wheat are produced (worth $690), the output of wine will be 1,600 gallons (worth $960, at 60 cents a gallon). Since everything produced in the economy belongs to some member of it, the total income of the economy will be $1,650. Finally, if consumers are willing to spend $690 on wheat, as the demand curve says they are, they will have $960 left over, which is just enough to buy the total output of wine. The prices that clear either market clear the other one also.

This reasoning is perfectly general. It depends on the fact that production and earning income are two aspects of the same activity. The value of everything produced (at any price whatever) is a component of somebody's income, and there is no way to earn income except by participating in production. Hence the total value produced and the total income earned in an economy are the same, and there is always just enough income to buy the entire output. It follows that in an economy that produces 100,000 different commodities, a set of prices that clears the markets for 99,999 of them will leave just enough money over to clear the remaining market.[8]

We find, therefore, that when there are only two commodities there will be some prices that clear the markets for both of them, and that those prices will induce a pattern of production that is obedient to consumers' sovereignty. When there are more commodities life is more complicated, but precisely the

[8] The balance between total incomes and the total value of output is more complicated in real economies than in this one. International trade, in which members of one economy sell to and buy from members of others, introduces new considerations. The operations of governments, which collect taxes and disburse subsidies and benefits, also complicate the balance. But the most serious problem we have ignored is the problem of hoarding: some consumers may choose to spend less than their entire incomes, desiring to put aside some money for later use. When that happens it may be impossible for all markets to clear simultaneously at any set of prices. This is related to aggregative efficiency, which will be discussed briefly below. It is analyzed more fully elsewhere in this series by C. L. Schultze in *National Income Analysis*, 3rd ed., and J. S. Duesenberry in *Money and Credit: Impact and Control*, 3rd ed.

same mechanism is at work. Suppose that bread is one of the commodities in a multicommodity world. We already know how its demand curve is generated. At each price of bread, the prices of other commodities being given, consumers demand the quantity of bread such that the marginal rate of substitution of any other commodity for bread is equal to the ratio of the price of bread to the price of the other commodity. That is to say: if p_b is the price of bread, if MRS is the number of units of some commodity X that a typical consumer is just willing to have substituted for a loaf of bread, and if p_x is the price of commodity X, then at price p_b consumers will demand the amount of bread such that $p_b = MRS \cdot p_x$.

The supply curve reflects a similar balancing of alternatives on the part of producers. At any price of bread, the prices of other commodities (including factors of production) being given, producers will supply the quantity of bread for which the marginal cost is equal to that price. But factors of production will be priced so that the marginal cost is the opportunity cost—that is, the value of the other commodities that could be made with the resources required to produce a loaf of bread. That is to say: if p_b is the price of a loaf, if MRT is the number of units of commodity X that can be made by the resources used in producing a loaf, and if p_x is the price of commodity X, then the quantity of bread that will be supplied at price p_b will satisfy $p_b = MRT \cdot p_x$.

If the price clears the market for bread, so that the quantities demanded and supplied are equal, both of these equalities hold, so that in comparison with any other commodity

$$MRS(X : \text{bread}) = \frac{p_b}{p_x} = MRT(X : \text{bread}).$$

This equation asserts that when markets are in equilibrium, a typical consumer's marginal rate of substitution of any commodity for bread will be equal to the economy's marginal rate of transformation of that commodity for bread. More generally, when all markets are in equilibrium, the consumers' marginal rate of substitution between any pair of commodities will be equal to the marginal rate of transformation between them according to the production-possibility frontier. When this happens, the bundle of commodities that is being produced is the one that accords with consumers' sovereignty, for this is the consumer-sovereignty condition. (A long way back, in Chapter 2, we saw that competitive markets with freely adjusting prices operate to bring about this result.)

The big world is not so very different, after all, from Robinson Crusoe. When market-clearing prices are established for all commodities, each consumer is confronted, in effect, with a miniature version of the allocative choices faced by the whole economy. The consumer has to decide how much to buy of each commodity, and in making this decision the terms on which he can have more of one commodity in exchange for taking less of another (the ratio of their prices) are identical with the terms on which the economy as a whole

211

can produce more of one commodity at the cost of producing less of some other (their marginal rate of transformation). Therefore, the price ratios tell the consumer the economic cost of every commodity he buys, in terms of the commodities that must be forgone in order to produce it, and by the same token the consumer, in making his choices, tells the producers how much of other commodities he is willing to forgo in order to obtain the ones he buys.

Thus the familiar demand and supply curves are the instruments by which a populous economy brings together the facts of life about its production possibilities and the desires of its consumers. No one in a real economy knows its production-possibility frontier, still less the indifference maps of its consumers. No matter. The supply and demand curves convey the information implicitly and guide the economy, by millions of decentralized decisions, to the most appropriate point on its production-possibility frontier.

Or so it would be in a more perfect world. In the real world the operation of consumers' sovereignty is impeded by all the complications we have encountered above and a few others. Consumers' ignorance aggravated by the effects of advertising, failure of markets to reflect externalities or the demand for public goods, price distortions caused by monopoly and oligopoly, the perpetual state of market disequilibrium all interfere with smooth responsiveness to the will of the consumer—but we do not have to review those imperfections.

Probably, the most important novel complication—and it is not very important—is that many purchasing decisions are exempt from the pressure of consumers' budget constraints. This sometimes occurs from efforts to compensate for consumers' ignorance, as when a consumer engages an interior decorator to choose his furniture or relies on a physician to prescribe his medicines. There is good reason to think that doctors often waste resources by prescribing expensive proprietary medicines when generic drugs would be just as effective.

Any situation in which decision is divorced from payment is likely to have similar consequences. Expense-account living is a notorious instance. Insurance claims, especially automobile damage claims, are another class of expenditures that are many millions of dollars greater than they would be if the beneficiaries had to pay the cost. All of these transactions, in which the discipline of consumer budgets is evaded for one peculiar reason or another, lead billions of dollars worth of resources to be used to produce commodities that would not be wanted if they had to be paid for by the consumer. Even so, the waste is small in comparison with the scale of economic activity. These exceptions to the general rule do emphasize the hidden effectiveness of consumers' sovereignty in more normal types of transaction.

Consumers' sovereignty is not absolute. Sometimes we overrule it in order to prevent the production and use of commodities that are deemed harmful or socially undesirable. Examples include restrictions on the use of insecticides, prohibiting the production and sale of narcotics and pornographic material, building codes, safety requirements for automobiles and eyeglasses, licensing requirements for physicians, and many more. All restrict the consumer's freedom of choice. They either prevent him from buying something he may want or compel him to buy something he may not want.

These limitations on the consumer's range of choice are more or less perpetually under fire. The justifications for them vary. Some are intended to avert externalities. This is the justification for the ban on persistent insecticides, for the automobile safety requirements (passengers and third parties are endangered by an unsafe automobile) and perhaps for the prohibitions of narcotics and pornography. Some are designed to combat consumers' ignorance, for example, professional licensing and some safety regulations. If we were willing to rely on consumers' judgments, we should permit them to choose between licensed and unlicensed physicians, safety and shatterable eyeglasses, and the like. Some are sumptuary regulations that discourage antisocial behavior (for example, drug addiction) by suppressing its physical instrumentalities. Whatever the objective, these regulations indicate that the consumer is not in supreme command of his budget and that social goals can take precedence. The pros and cons of such regulations then depend on the validity of the social goals and the efficacy of the regulations, which are not matters for economic analysis.

The exercise of consumers' sovereignty is further circumscribed by producers. Consumers cannot express their demands for things that producers do not offer, and it is not a fair presumption, even in competitive markets, that there will always be some producer for every commodity that can be sold. Books and records go out of print while there are still some demanders. The most dramatic example is women's fashions: the struggle for sovereignty between the women and the fashion designers is renewed every year. 1955 was a vintage year for Chevrolets—perhaps never equaled—but you can't get one today. Any unusual tastes or requirements, and some not so unusual, are likely to go unsatisfied.

This restriction on consumers' choices arises from an inexorable economic conflict: between standardization and variety, a conflict that markets do not resolve automatically. Resources are saved by producing a limited number of varieties of a restricted number of commodities in reasonably large batches that can be sold without long delays. But this same economical policy of standardization limits consumers' choices and may reduce their satisfactions. So a conflict arises, which our theoretical formulation evaded by presuming that the list of commodities dealt in was fixed and that the only economic decision was how much of each to produce and consume. In principle (only) there is a clear economic resolution of the problem of optimal variety: a commodity or variety should be added to the list of those offered if the resource cost of doing so would be counterbalanced by the increase in consumer satisfactions. But markets have no way of indicating the satisfactions that increased variety could afford. Variety is an intangible public good, and the value of public goods is just what market behavior cannot reflect. Competitive markets, in which venturesome competitors can try out new varieties, are probably the best practical response to this problem.

MARKETS AND AGGREGATIVE EFFICIENCY

Aggregative efficiency is the requirement that all resources available to the economy be utilized. It requires a balance between the total demand for commodities and the productive capacity of the economy. In technical language it requires that the total amounts of commodities demanded be somewhere on the production-possibility frontier.

This aspect of efficiency can be violated in two ways. One is insufficient total demand, giving rise to unemployment of men and other resources. The other is excessive total demand, whose symptom and consequence is inflation, which results when people are bidding for more commodities, in total, than can be produced. Figure 8–3, taken from the 1970 report of the Council of Eco-

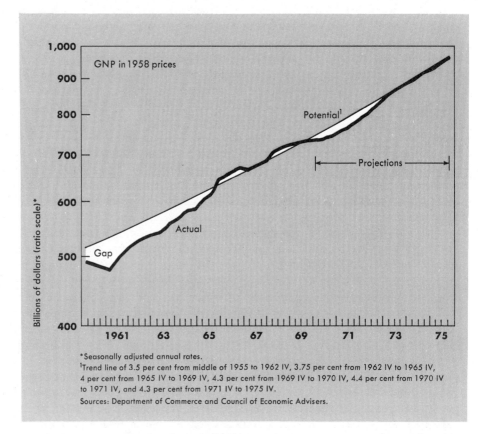

*Seasonally adjusted annual rates.
[1] Trend line of 3.5 per cent from middle of 1955 to 1962 IV, 3.75 per cent from 1962 IV to 1965 IV, 4 per cent from 1965 IV to 1969 IV, 4.3 per cent from 1969 IV to 1970 IV, 4.4 per cent from 1970 IV to 1971 IV, and 4.3 per cent from 1971 IV to 1975 IV.
Sources: Department of Commerce and Council of Economic Advisers.

FIG. 8–3 Gross national product, actual and potential. In practice, actual total output fluctuates around potential, indicating lapses from aggregative efficiency. Source: *Report of the Council of Economic Advisers, 1970* (Washington, D.C.: Government Printing Office, 1970).

nomic Advisors, illustrates the relationship between full utilization of resources and actual utilization in recent (and some future) years. Obviously they are not always identical.

In our analysis of consumers' sovereignty we found that if all income earned were paid out to consumers and if consumers spent their entire incomes, no discrepancy could arise between actual and potential output. When individual markets were in equilibrium, everything produced would be demanded and full utilization would be assured. The same would be true if firms withheld some of their earnings from consumers, as they actually do, and used all of the withheld earnings to buy investment goods. It would also be true if governments abstracted some earnings in the form of taxes, as they do, and bought goods and services whose value was equal to the proceeds. In all these cases the total value of the goods produced would be equal to the total value of the goods demanded, and prices could adjust so that the market was in equilibrium for every good, every service, and every productive resource. When the markets for productive resources are in equilibrium, there is neither underemployment nor overemployment and aggregative efficiency is attained.

So the efficiency of market price adjustments in bringing about aggregative efficiency depends upon the willingness of purchasers to spend all their incomes, and only their incomes, on consumer and investment goods and services. But there is nothing in the market adjustment mechanisms to assure this willingness; nearly all the "ifs" in the last paragraph are violated to a greater or lesser extent. Some consumers spend more than their available incomes by borrowing, some spend less by saving; on balance they save about 7 per cent of their available incomes. This deficiency in consumer demand is compensated for by business firms and governments, which borrow consumers' savings and use the proceeds to pay for investments and government operations. But there is nothing to guarantee that the businessmen and governments will take up precisely the slack left by the consumers, and the figure shows that they normally do not do so. When total demand and total supply are out of kilter, price adjustments in the individual commodity markets cannot bring about full equilibrium; the discrepancy must show up somewhere.

This is not to say that there is no mechanism that tends to bring total demand into balance with total available supply. The same chart that shows that they are not always equal shows that they are closely related. The mechanism is the financial markets, which, through the interest rate and other devices, tend to encourage investment expenditures when savings are relatively plentiful and to inhibit them at other times. These markets have so many peculiarities that distinguish them from other markets that they require special treatment and study. That study is the task of monetary theory and national income analysis.[9]

_____

[9] We refer again to Duesenberry, *Money and Credit* and Schultze, *National Income Analysis* in this series.

MARKETS AND DYNAMIC EFFICIENCY

How an economy grows and develops is more important in the long run than how much it produces at any instant or how efficiently it distributes its product.[10] The division of expenditures among consumption, investment, and government operations, which was mentioned in the last section, clearly has a great deal to do with the pace of economic growth, though it is far from the whole story. This division is, however, the aspect of economic development that is most clearly related to the operations of markets and to the problems of resource allocation, and we shall concentrate on it.

Investment on behalf of the future takes many forms. The most obvious is the installation of plant and equipment to replace the stock that is wearing out and to provide the means for pushing out the production-possibility frontier, in short providing more man-made physical resources to be used in future production. Part of expenditure on education also increases the future productive potential of the economy, by increasing the supply of skilled labor and trained management. This is called investment in "human capital." Moreover, resources devoted to the discovery and development of improved processes and products enhance the productive ability of the economy. So knowledge of all sorts, though intangible, is a kind of future-oriented economic product—perhaps the most important kind.[11]

Decisions have to be made about how much to produce of every kind of physical capital, human capital, and informational capital. In a market economy these decisions are made by numerous individuals choosing their educational plans and by numerous firms making their long-run capital commitments largely as described in Chapter 3. The government also invests and affects economic growth through its education and research programs and through various measures that influence private investment.

We have not yet presented any criterion, call it a criterion of dynamic efficiency, for guiding and appraising this kind of decision. The fundamental question is how much of a society's economic effort should be devoted to various provisions for the future at the expense of currently consumable and enjoyable output. Even a Robinson Crusoe confronts this question: he has to decide how much time and effort to divert from tilling this year's crop to clearing new fields in preparation for a larger crop next year. Crusoe can answer this question by means of the now familiar diagram of a two-commodity production-possibility

---

[10] If country A has twice the national income of country B, but country B grows faster by 3 per cent a year, then country B will overtake in about 23 years.

[11] It is very hard to measure either the amount of increase of economically applicable knowledge or its consequences. One authoritative attempt found that during the first half of the twentieth century about one-third of the increase in the output of the American economy was attributable to the increases in the labor force and the capital stock; two-thirds were attributable to technical progress! These estimates have been disputed, but all estimates confirm the importance of this intangible ingredient.

frontier, as shown in Fig. 8–4.[12] The two commodities now are this year's crop and next year's crop; otherwise everything is the same as when we considered the choice between two different commodities simultaneously available. In particular, Crusoe chooses point Q, where the production-possibility frontier touches the highest attainable indifference curve. This selection determines both the division of his effort and the crops in the two years.

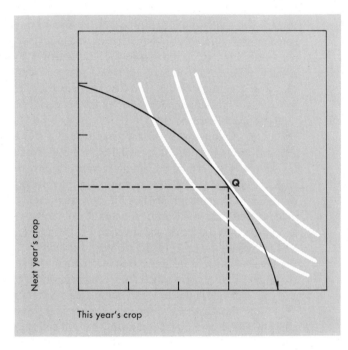

FIG. 8–4 Crusoe's time-preference diagram. Crusoe decides on next year's crop by equating his rate of time preference to the rate of interest.

Next year's crop

This year's crop

In the two-commodity case the choice of a point on the production-possibility frontier also determined the relative prices of the two commodities. Something similar applies here. Suppose that departing from point Q a reduction of one bushel in this year's crop would permit an increase of 1.2 bushels next year. Then we can say two things. From the point of view of production we can say that the *rate of interest* is 20 per cent per year, for an investment of one bushel will be returned with 20 per cent interest next year. From the point of view of Crusoe's preferences or indifference curves, his *rate of time preference* is also 20 per cent per year, for he has chosen to sacrifice a marginal bushel this year in expectation of a 20 per cent return. Crusoe's best choice is the point where the rate of interest (determined by productivity considerations) is equal to his psychological rate of time preference. This is a point of tangency

[12] Even Crusoe might want to take more than two years into account. This would complicate the art work but not affect the basic reasoning.

between the production-possibility frontier and an indifference curve, where both have the same slope.

What is true for an individual is at least suggestive for a great society. But things are far different in a complex economy where firms and the government do most of the investing and households do most of the saving. (Notice that Crusoe did both.) Besides, on Crusoe's island the sole consumer's income increased as fast as the national income (they were the same), whereas no such close tie exists in a real economy, and it is at least conceivable that some consumers will feel very differently from others about sacrificing current for future consumption. On top of that, Crusoe did not have any progeny, but one of the responsibilities of a real society is to provide for future generations. So the proper division of income between current consumption and provision for the future is much clearer for Crusoe than for a real economy, where separated saving and investment decisions must be coordinated and many individual interests must be reconciled.

One notion we can carry over from Crusoe's island. Notice that he chose a point on his production-possibility frontier. Analogously, a real society should invest so as to attain the greatest rate of growth of output that is consistent with the selected level of consumption—to do otherwise would be to sacrifice current enjoyments to no benefit. We shall see below how market operations achieve this. Beyond that, consumer sovereignty implies that each consumer should be free to decide the division of his income between current consumption and provision for the future. These decisions in the aggregate will determine the level of current consumption. Of course, these decisions should be made in the knowledge of how much future consumption a current sacrifice will procure. We shall consider later to what extent free markets provide this information.

But the case for consumers' sovereignty is less compelling in the consumption-saving context than in the allocation of budgets among consumer goods, because the interests of the long future are involved. For example, it is often maintained that the current generation is not entitled to squander the world's irreplaceable supplies of petroleum or to leave behind substantial traces of indestructable poisons in the waters and atmosphere.[13] Individual decisions cannot be expected to take such long-range consequences into account. So it can be held that social decisions should supplant individual decisions with long-lasting consequences. In fact, governments do a great deal of saving on society's behalf and also influence private saving through a variety of channels. Consumers' sovereignty does not reign supreme in the saving–investment sphere.

We are still left with the question of how the social choices should be made. To this there is no general answer. Like the other great questions that markets are not competent to answer, it depends on weighing conflicting, justi-

[13] We should not assume too much responsibility for the future. Would it be sensible for India to give up DDT and reduce its already inadequate food output when the next generation is very likely to know how to eliminate DDT as conveniently as we now purify drinking water?

fiable values through the political process. That is about as close as we can come to setting forth a criterion for dynamic efficiency.

The pertinent private decisions are households' decisions to save and firms' decisions to invest. Unlike Crusoe, households do not know the rate of interest determined by the economy's production-possibility frontier, and firms do not know consumers' rates of time preference determined by their indifference curves. These decisions are coordinated through the financial markets.

Instead of a production-possibility frontier, an individual household confronts a financial market with opportunities to borrow and lend at a market rate of interest. The terms on which it can exchange present for future consumption can be represented by a budget line with a slope equal to one plus the rate of interest at which the household can lend. (Compare with the principles of consumer's choice in Chapter 5.) The higher the rate of interest, the steeper the budget line and the more the consumer will be induced to save, theoretically. In practice, consumers' saving does not seem to be very sensitive to the rate of interest. It appears that the typical consumer's indifference curves between current and deferred consumption go around a sharp corner at the accustomed level of consumption.[14]

Firms' investment decisions are more responsive to the market rate of interest. The firm does not know the production-possibility frontier either, but it does know its own production possibilities and compares them with the rate of interest at which it can borrow, as we saw in Chapter 3. According to that analysis, a firm will tend to expand its plant to the point where the fixed costs of further expansion are greater than the reduction in variable costs that the further expansion will permit, and these fixed costs increase when interest rates do. From the social point of view, the firm compares the value of the resources that would be required now to make the investment with the value of the resources that will be saved in the future if the investment is made. If the future savings in variable costs exceed the current cost by enough to cover interest on the cost, then the investment is undertaken. This is just like Crusoe's decision, with two modifications: several future years are taken into account instead of only one, by means of the sinking-fund formula, and Crusoe's curved indifference curves are replaced by straight lines whose slope indicates the market rate of interest. (These straight lines are the appropriate indifference curves for the firm.)

Now if the market rate of interest adjusts so that the amount that firms wish to invest (demand for loans) is equal to the amount that consumers wish to save (supply of savings), then the productivity of investments (in terms of the resources that they save) will be equal to consumers' rates of time preference, both being equal to the market rate of interest. The answer to the saving–investment question will be very similar to that found, much more simply, by

[14] If you draw the diagram with indifference curves showing sharp curvature at some level of consumption, you will see that this implies low responsiveness to changes in the interest rate.

Crusoe. Although our dynamic criterion is not very well defined, that would be optimal in a sense because under these conditions it would be impossible to save more for the future without forcing someone to sacrifice more current consumption than he is willing to do for the anticipated future increase.

But, in truth, financial markets and investment decisions are not that simple. That is why two other books in this series are devoted to their special characteristics and implications. Some of the complications can be listed very briefly. Financial markets are very imperfect; the interest rates used by consumers in reaching their decisions are quite different from those paid by firms, and different firms have access to different interest rates. So the market rate of interest seen by an individual firm need not coincide with the slope of the production-possibility frontier, and consumers, seeing still a different rate of interest, choose levels of saving where their indifference curves have still different slopes.

The gap between the actual rate of interest determined by the production-possibility frontier and consumers' rates of time preference is widened by the fact that consumers' saving is not closely linked to firms' investing. There is an intervening step: the consumer or his banker must be willing to lend the money saved to the prospective investor, or an investor must be found to borrow the money that the consumer has saved. We saw in the last section that aggregative disequilibrium results if, as is possible, borrowing and saving cannot be matched by market adjustments of the rate of interest. Finally, our discussion has ignored the fact that the results of making an investment are generally not assured and often highly conjectural.[15] This throws an additional wedge between the interest rate at which consumers are willing to save and the one at which firms are willing to invest.

For these and a few other reasons, a real economy cannot attain the nice adjustment of willingness to save to the productivity of investment that the omniscient Crusoe can achieve. Actual financial markets attain at best a crude approximation to dynamic efficiency. They do, however, induce firms to make efficient use of whatever funds they decide to invest. This is because firms will use their investable funds to make the specific investments that promise the highest possible profits in the future. Just as in the static case this striving for high profits is equivalent to aiming for a point on the production-possibility frontier.

THE SOCIAL VALUE OF ECONOMIC EFFICIENCY

We have considered five dimensions of economic efficiency: efficient distribution, efficient production, consumers' sovereignty, aggregative efficiency, and dynamic efficiency. In each case we saw that, as a matter of theory, competitive markets possess the principal characteristics for attaining that kind of

[15] This is acutely true of investments in human capital and informational capital, that is, research.

efficiency, but that in practice the many complications of real economic life prevent perfect attainment. The main practical implication of these analyses was the necessity for various sorts of governmental supervision and correction to bring actual economic conditions into better conformity with the requirements of efficiently functioning markets.

Radical reconstruction was not indicated at any point. Economic efficiency cannot be ordained, and it is too complicated to be planned centrally. We saw repeatedly in the analyses of the various aspects of efficiency how subtle and demanding the diverse requirements are, and how ingeniously decentralized markets respond to those requirements. Indeed, the mechanisms by which competitive markets induce efficient economic behavior have been the central topic of the whole book.

But there is a prevalent school of thought, the New Left economics, that demands a radical reconstruction of our economic system. According to this school, efficiency is not enough, and perhaps not even very important. Efficiency is a false god, a juggernaut, to which the economy sacrifices men and for which it spurns human values and moral standards. Well, that's a position, and anyone who thinks that we buy efficiency at too high a price in ultimate values is entitled to think so. At least, he is so entitled after he has given sober consideration to the actual costs of efficiency and the actual costs of abandoning a highly efficient economic system. It does appear that most New Left writing forensically overstates the former costs and scarcely alludes to the latter.

The Old (Marxist) Left predicted that the advance of capitalism would lead to the immiserization of the working class. Things did not work out that way. Now the New Left shifts the ground to a more subtle level, where empirical verification and refutation are harder. It concedes that capitalism, or market orientation, enriches the working class materially (albeit less so than the workers really deserve), but holds that it simultaneously impoverishes them spiritually and morally. It converts the worker into an alienated, mindless adjunct of a machine, it engulfs him in ugliness, it deprives him of his independence of mind, his sense of community, and his human nobility.

Such evidence as there is against these serious moral charges is waved aside as spurious appearances. To be sure, the working day becomes shorter and shorter, the workingman sits on a bulldozer instead of wielding a pickax, levels of education rise constantly, and there is unprecedented access to a wide variety of recreational, entertainment, and cultural activities. All these appearances of human advancement are false, or at best paltry bribes to cajole the workingmen into submitting to their debasement. I hardly exaggerate or travesty —that is really how the argument goes. And that is how it must go, because it is very hard to argue against economic efficiency. Whatever else may be said, efficiency means more of the material means for human enjoyment in return for less labor.

But must we accept all the notorious inequality, crassness, and vulgarity of a market-oriented economy as the price of efficiency? Or alternatively, can't

221

we be reasonably efficient without despoiling our planet and dehumanizing our society? The answer has to be in three parts at least.

Despoiling our planet is not efficient, by any standards. Nor is it inherent in market-oriented economic organization. But also, a market-oriented economy does not avoid it without some outside guidance. We have discussed this problem at several points under the rubric of "externalities" and have seen that social intervention is required. By appropriate, and not very revolutionary, social controls a pleasant and healthful physical environment can be obtained. In each specific instance, the advisability of social controls on economic activity has to be weighed carefully by the political process because they are inexorably costly, they inevitably entail substantial reductions in the amounts of goods and services available for private use. Not even a businessman would despoil his environment unless he thereby saved economic resources of some sort, resources that he will have to use if he is compelled to protect the environment. A wealthy society—one with a large and efficient economy—can afford that cost; a poor economy may not be able to.

The result is that, despite much calamitous writing, the environments of rich economies are superior in many respects to those of poor communities. They are freer of disease carriers and more amply supplied with many amenities. Wealth creates many environmental problems, but it also provides the wherewithal for coping.

Dehumanizing society is a more profound and elusive charge. It begs at least two questions. First, is a society with a market-oriented economy peculiarly inhuman? History records that humane societies (whatever that may mean) have been very rare—and it is suggestive that the ones we know of have never been very large. Second, is the market-oriented form of economic organization responsible for contemporary lapses from humaneness, or do they rather result from a rapid growth of population coupled with an abrupt agglomeration of people into metropolises of much more than human scale?

Everyone agrees that an impoverished society reduces its workers to insensitive drudges, as depicted in "The Man with the Hoe," or "The Potato Eaters." The essential first step towards a humane society is to move to a comfortable distance away from the subsistence level of efficiency. Historically this step has been taken only by market-oriented economies or by centralized socialist ones that are open to the same strictures as well as to several additional ones. The critics have not proposed any alternative systems of economic organization that seem likely to maintain the requisite level of efficiency.

All this argumentation boils down to a single point: an agreeable environment and a humane society are both luxury goods that a society can afford only when it has ample resources left after meeting the subsistence needs of its population. The market-oriented economy contributes to these goals by providing the required amplitude of means. Any other system of economic organization that contributes to these goals would have to attain a comparable level of productive efficiency.

222

This entire book has been devoted to explaining how and why a market-oriented economy attains an adequate level of efficiency. Any acceptable alternative would have to withstand a comparable analysis. To be sure, efficiency is not enough. But it is the foundation from which other, ultimate goals can be reached. That is why the analysis of efficiency is the central theme of this book.

SUMMARY

Our society utilizes two main systems for reaching economic decisions: the economic system and the political system. The economic system works best for decisions that concern the production and allocation of private goods, for the prices that people are willing to pay are sensitive indicators of how urgently people desire such goods, and costs of production are good measures of the marginal rates of transformation between different goods. But people cannot express their desires for public goods by individual purchase decisions, and market prices ignore externalities. Therefore the political process is used for decisions about the provision of public goods and of goods with significant externalities.

The Pareto criterion is the fundamental criterion of economic efficiency. It holds that an economy is functioning with perfect economic efficiency when there is no possible change in its operations that will benefit any consumer without harming some other consumer. The Pareto criterion can be analyzed into three essentially static subcriteria and two subcriteria with dynamic aspects. The static subcriteria are:

1. Efficient distribution of commodities—distributing the available output of commodities so as to satisfy consumers as well as possible. This requires that all consumers share the same marginal rate of substitution between every pair of commodities, for then no exchange of commodities among consumers could benefit any consumer without harming some other. It is attained when households allocate their consumption budgets wisely among purchases, on markets where all consumers confront the same prices.

2. Efficient production of commodities—producing as much of each good as is possible without impairing the output of any other good. This requires that the value of the marginal product of every resource be the same in every industry and firm that employs it, for then no reallocation of resources among firms could increase the total value of the economy's output or could increase the output of any commodity without reducing the output of some other. Symbolically, we write that if factor X is used to produce commodities A and B, then

$$p_A MP(X \text{ used for } A) = p_B MP(X \text{ used for } B)$$

where p_A, p_B are the prices of the two commodities and $MP(X \text{ used for } A)$, $MP(X \text{ used for } B)$ are the marginal products of X when used to produce the two commodities. In different words, the requirement is that each resource be used in the employment for which it has the greatest comparative advantage or in which its marginal productivity is greatest in comparison with its marginal productivity in alternative employments. This condition is attained when all firms participate in competitive markets and endeavor to produce the most profitable level of output at lowest possible cost.

3. Consumer sovereignty—producing the attainable bundle of commodities that consumers desire the most. This condition holds when the marginal rate of transformation between every pair of commodities equals the ratio of their prices, which in turn equals the marginal rate of substitution between them, common to all consumers. Symbolically:

$$MRT(A:B) = \frac{p_B}{p_A} = MRS(A:B).$$

The two criteria with dynamic aspects are:

1. Aggregative efficiency—using all the resources available to the economy. This requires that the amounts that households want to spend on consumption and that firms wish to spend on investment add up to the total value of commodities produced. In theory, households and firms responding to changes in the rate of interest could achieve this condition, but in practice, various measures of governmental economic policy seem to be necessary.

2. Dynamic efficiency—devoting the amount of resources to provision for the future that will permit the output of the economy to grow at the most desirable rate. This is a very difficult criterion either to formulate or to attain.

The combinations of goods and services among which an economy must choose are described by its production-possibility frontier, which shows the greatest amount of each commodity that can be produced in conjunction with specified quantities of every other commodity. It is wasteful for an economy to produce an output that is not on its frontier, and the frontier can always be reached by following the principle of comparative advantage. This principle holds that when there is a choice among the factors to be used to produce any commodity, that factor should be chosen whose productivity when used for that commodity is greatest in proportion to its productivity in alternative employments. Firms that trade in competitive markets obey this principle automatically.

The marginal rate of transformation between two commodities is the number of units of one that have to be sacrificed if sufficient resources are transferred to increase the output of the other by one unit. This concept enables us to specify the point on the production possibility frontier at which consumers' sovereignty is obeyed, as was done above in summarizing the third criterion of economic efficiency. The location of this point depends on the shape of the production-possibility frontier, the indifference curves of individual consumers, and the distribution of income among consumers.

The relevance of the distribution of income can be seen from the box diagram for the allocation among consumers of the output corresponding to a point on the production-possibility frontier. Efficient distribution requires that the allocation correspond to one of the points on the contract curve in the box diagram, since that curve contains all points where the consumers have a common marginal rate of substitution. Each point on the contract curve represents a different distribution of income, and the common marginal rate of substitution is likely to be different at the different points.

Each point on the production-possibility frontier not only represents a different output of commodities, but corresponds to different marginal rates of transformation between commodities, and therefore to a different set of prices. Since the distribution of income changes when prices change, following the dictates of consumers' sovereignty can be intricate; two data are changing at the same time. There is, however, a point on the frontier with the essential property that if prices corresponding to the marginal rates of transformation there are charged, then the demand for every commodity will be equal to the supply at that point. At such a point (there may be several) the output, the prices consistent with efficient production, and the distribution of income are all in conformity, and all three static criteria of efficiency are satisfied.

In any economy with competitive markets, the price mechanism guides the economy to the consumer sovereignty point on the production possibility frontier. It does this by inducing conformity to two basic formulas. One is

$$MRT \ (A \text{ for } B) = \frac{p_B}{p_A} = MRS(A \text{ for } B).$$

—which was given above. The other is the relation among product prices, factor prices, and marginal productivity. If X is any factor of production used to produce commodity A, if w_x is its wage or rate of hire, and if $MP(X$ used for $A)$ is the marginal product of X when used to produce A, then competition establishes that

$$\text{MP}(X \text{ used for } A) = \frac{w_x}{p_A}.$$

This equation, in conjunction with the preceding one, assures efficiency in production. These two equations are worth remembering since they summarize the gist of the argument for the efficiency of competitive pricing.

Much as the price system can do, it has inherent limitations. It depends on the operation of competitive markets, which tend to break down in the presence of economies of scale. Its responsiveness to consumers' sovereignty makes it vulnerable to consumers' mistakes, which are likely to be serious with respect to certain highly technical or infrequently purchased commodities. By its very nature, it is inapplicable to decisions about public goods—goods concerning which individual consumers cannot make independent consumption decisions. It disregards external effects—the effects of one man's consumption or productive activities on another man's welfare. Its efficiency is substantially reduced in the presence of uncertainty and when markets are not fully in equilibrium. Because of these shortcomings, many important goods and services cannot be provided by private firms operating through markets, and many markets have to be restricted and controlled. Nevertheless, when the conditions required for the effective operation of markets are fairly well fulfilled, markets are the most effective as well as the most democratic mode of economic organization that has yet been developed.

The criteria of economic efficiency and their implications apply to non-monetary as well as to price economies, so our study of a simple two-commodity example showed. Together they characterize perfect economic efficiency—more efficiency than we have a right to expect of any functioning, complicated economy. If you think about them for a moment, you will see that they are very similar and rather peculiar. All of them are unanimity tests. Each says that an economy is falling short of perfect efficiency in one respect or another if all members of the economy agree that the results it is producing are less desirable than some other result that could also be attained. If the members of the economy disagree—if only a tiny minority dissents from the general opinion—our criteria say nothing. In principle, then, an economy may score high marks on all these tests while displeasing, or even oppressing, the great majority of its members. In other words, these criteria of efficiency are strictly economic tests of performance; they have nothing to do with social justice, improving the quality of life, or any consideration other than minimizing unambiguous waste—that is, avoiding any choice when another is possible that is better from everyone's point of view. In particular, they are of no help in appraising the desirability of any distribution of social income among the members of a society, although the distribution of income is one of the most important consequences of a functioning economy.

The criteria have been very carefully constructed over the generations with unanimity in mind. One of the hallmarks of a scientific statement is that it can gain the assent of all reasonable men who understand it. The four criteria and their logical implications are scientific by this standard, but at the cost of remaining mute about all the important issues of economic and social policy about which reasonable and informed men can disagree. However, these criteria do take us close to the limits of scientific economics, and it is remarkable that so much can be said within the stringent limitation of universal agreement.

The Distribution of Income

CHAPTER NINE

The two most significant consequences of an economy are the total output of consumable commodities that it produces and the distribution of income—or the distribution of rights to these commodities —that it generates. For the most part we have been dealing with the first of these, although questions about the second have arisen repeatedly, especially in the later chapters. Now it is time to turn to the distribution of income.

The distribution of income embraces the oldest issues in economics, as well as the most divisive and complicated ones. The questions can be posed on many levels. First, there is the purely factual level: What is the distribution of income in any society, that is how many people, and what kind of people, receive any given amount of income? A good deal is known about this, and we shall summarize some of the more salient facts about the American economy below. Second, there is the prescriptive level: What ought the distribution of income to be? This question contains a good deal of ethical content and therefore does not admit of any answer that is likely to gain universal acceptance. It is the kind of question that has to be resolved, if at all, by weighing the pros and cons of different possibilities and by compromising the claims of different segments of the community. Finally, there is the explanatory level: What are the economic and social forces that make the distribution of income what it is? This is the most interesting level of all because it enables us to understand the first level and contains the clues for implementing any answers to the second level.

In this chapter we shall first present some of the facts to be explained, and then discuss some explanations and some of the considera-

227

tions that have to be faced in deciding what the distribution of income ought to be.

THE CONTEMPORARY DISTRIBUTION OF INCOME

There are two principal ways to describe the distribution of income in a community. The most fundamental is a table or chart that shows the proportions of persons who receive incomes of various amounts or within various ranges. Such a table or chart is called a personal income distribution. (See Fig. 9–1.) This method shows the ultimate result of the income-distribution process but does not throw any light on the causes behind it. The other method shows the magnitude or importance of various sources of income in the total. This is known as a functional income distribution. The categories and data in Tables 9–1 and 9–2 are typical.

The functional income distribution throws some light on the forces that

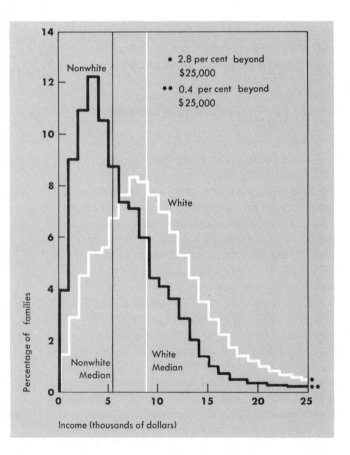

FIG. 9–1 Personal income distributions of white and nonwhite families, 1968. The nonwhites are far more concentrated at the low end of the scale. Source: U.S. Bureau of the Census, *Current Population Reports*, Series P-60, No. 66 (December 23, 1969).

generate the personal income distribution. The income of any household is derived by contributing some factors of production to the economy. Its amount therefore depends on the nature of the factors that it contributes and on the rewards that factors of that type receive. The functional income distribution shows how factors of different broad categories share the income pie, in the aggregate. For this purpose the percentage distribution in Table 9–2 is more revealing than the absolute amounts in Table 9–1.

Table 9–1 FUNCTIONAL INCOME DISTRIBUTION, U.S., SELECTED YEARS

(Billions of dollars)

	1940	1950	1960	1965	1969
Labor income					
Wages and salaries	49.8	146.7	270.8	358.9	509.0
Other (supplements)	0.7	3.8	12.0	18.7	27.6
Proprietor's income					
Business and professional	8.6	24.0	24.2	42.4	50.5
Farming	4.5	13.5	12.0	14.8	16.4
Dividends	4.0	8.8	13.4	19.8	24.7
Interest	5.4	9.2	23.4	38.7	59.7
Rental income	2.9	9.4	15.8	19.0	22.0
Transfer payments	3.1	15.1	28.5	39.9	65.1
TOTAL	79.0	230.5	410.3	552.3	774.9
Less: Personal contributions for social insurance	—	2.9	9.3	13.4	26.0
Personal income, officially reported	79.0	227.6	401.0	538.9	748.9

Source: Economic Report of the President, February 1971, pp. 216–17.

Several tendencies should be noticed in Table 9–2. In the first place, wages and salaries are far and away the most important component of income, accounting for very roughly two-thirds of the total. This ratio seems to be one of the great constants of economic behavior—it has held up, again very roughly, for a long period of time in the United States and applies to the other advanced economies as well, in spite of great changes and differences in economic organization and social structure. A number of explanations for this rough constancy have been advanced, but none is really satisfactory. Whether there is some inherent constancy about labor's share of total income, and if so why, is still an open question.

Since World War II most of the other components have shown marked trends. Proprietary income, whether from unincorporated business, professional practice, or farming has fallen sharply as a proportion of the total. The importance of transfer payments, which is the technical name for Social Security benefits, welfare payments, pension receipts, and the like, is increasing steadily. The transfer payments should be regarded as a social device that rectifies the personal distribution of income resulting from all the preceding components.

229

Table 9–2 FUNCTIONAL INCOME DISTRIBUTION IN PERCENTAGE FORM,
UNITED STATES, SELECTED YEARS

	1940	1950	1960	1965	1969
Total personal income	100	100	100	100	100
Labor income					
Wages and salaries	63.1	63.6	66.0	65.0	65.7
Other	0.9	1.6	2.9	3.4	3.6
Proprietors' income					
Business and professional	10.9	10.4	8.3	7.7	6.5
Farming	5.7	5.9	2.9	2.7	2.1
Dividends	5.1	3.8	3.3	3.6	3.2
Interest	6.8	4.0	5.7	7.0	7.7
Rents	3.7	4.1	3.9	3.4	2.8
Transfers	3.9	6.6	6.9	7.2	8.4

Source: Computed from Table 9–1.

The functional income distribution shows, broadly, the importance of different types or sources of income. The personal income distribution, which emerges from it and from the distribution of wealth, shows how well the families in the society are faring economically. The most straightforward method of presenting the personal income distribution is a chart such as Fig. 9–1, which shows the percentage of families that receive income in different ranges, in this case $1,000 ranges. This chart contains the fundamental data on how claims to the national output were distributed among families in 1968 (a typical year in this respect,) and is worth considering closely. We shall discuss the curve for white families more thoroughly, since about 90 per cent of the families were white.

At the low end about 1½ per cent of white families received less than $1,000. Most of these were genuinely impoverished, but a good (but unknown) number were families with much higher normal incomes who suffered business losses or other financial reverses in that year. Some, indeed, were well-off by any reasonable standards. If we accept $3,500 as a reasonable estimate of the poverty line, about 12 per cent of white families were impoverished. At the high extreme, about 3 per cent of white families had incomes over $25,000. A more detailed chart would show that about one white family in 300 received more than $50,000. The very rich and even the well-to-do are rare.

Reverting to the norm, the average income for white families (not shown on the chart) was $10,000. This is an arithmetical result that is a little hard to interpret. The median is more meaningful; the median is the income that was exceeded by half the population. The median income for whites was $8,900. Even more revealing is the "interquartile range," the range of incomes that were received by the central 50 per cent of the population. This was $5,800 to $12,700.

These data characterize the norms and extremes of the income distribution for whites, and serve as a standard of comparison for the incomes of the nonwhites. Every indicator for the nonwhites is comparatively depressed and depressing. Thirty-one per cent were below the $3,500 poverty line, the median income was $5,400, only 60 per cent of the white median, the interquartile range was $3,100 to $8,700, indicating that less than a quarter of the nonwhites received as much as the white median.

Although this chart of the size distribution of incomes contains the basic information about the level and spread of incomes, it is not very convenient for all purposes and, in particular, it does not show very clearly the extent of inequality in the distribution of income. For this purpose, it is usual to present the same data in a different way, known as a Lorenz curve. Figure 9–2 shows the same income distributions in the form of a Lorenz curve. It shows the percentage of total income received by different percentages of income receivers, arranged in order of size of income. For example, the dashed lines in Fig. 9–2 show that the 60 per cent of white families with lowest incomes in 1968 received 36 per cent of the total income received by white families. The other points are interpreted similarly.

If income were perfectly equally distributed, any x percent of families would receive x per cent of aggregate income. The Lorenz curve would then lie along the diagonal line in the diagram, which is the "line of perfect equality."

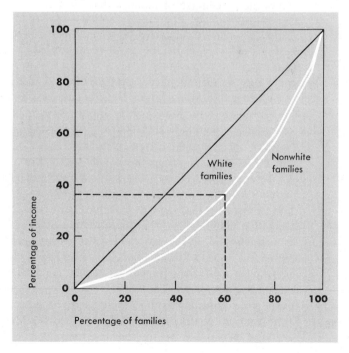

FIG. 9–2 Lorenz curves of white and nonwhite income distributions, 1968. The degree of inequality is shown by the sag beneath the line of equal distribution.

At the other extreme, in an economy in which all members were slaves who received no income, except for one lord who received everything, the Lorenz curve would coincide with the bottom and right-hand edges of the box. This is the curve of complete inequality.

The Lorenz curve suppresses information about the absolute level of incomes in order to emphasize the degree of inequality. In Fig. 9–2 it is no longer evident that the incomes of white families are substantially greater than those of nonwhites, but it is revealed that the incomes of nonwhite families are more unequally distributed than those of whites. In addition to the nonwhite–white inequality shown in Fig. 9–1, there is an important degree of inequality among the nonwhites themselves. The reason, undoubtedly, is the paucity of the non-white middle class. A comparatively few well-off nonwhites receive a larger proportion of the aggregate income of their race than is true for any comparable segment of the white population.

Lorenz curves are useful also for international comparisons. In Fig. 9–3 the income distribution of American nonfarm families is compared with a similar distribution for Czechoslovakia. This illustration was chosen for a number of reasons. The Czech economy is very different from the American one. Like the American economy, it is highly industrialized, but it is much smaller and poorer and is organized according to centrally directed Communist principles. What is of particular interest is that the Czechs claim that they have attained the most egalitarian income distribution of any industrialized country in the world. Their income distribution is seen in the figure to be far more egalitarian than the American one. The poorest 60 per cent of Czechs receive 46 per cent of aggregate income, as compared with only 36 per cent for the same proportion of Americans. The Czechs appear to be about half as far from the line of perfect equality as the Americans.

Since perfect equality is an unattainable ideal, perhaps the Czech distribution could be regarded as a practical goal to be striven for. Before accepting this aspiration level, though, it is important to note that the Czechs seem to be paying dearly for their high degree of egalitarianism. What is the evidence of this? For one thing, the Czech economy is remarkably inefficient and unprogressive. Historically, Czechoslovakia was much more advanced economically than her neighbor Austria, but in recent decades Austria has outstripped her. The income distribution cannot be made to carry all the blame for this. Among the other adverse circumstances that have afflicted Czechoslovakia are recurrent political turmoil and some unwise planning decisions, perhaps dictated by the broader interests of the Soviet bloc. But there are indications that the distribution of income has played its part. For example, there are chronic shortages of skilled workmen and trained managers. At the same time, the schools that train people for these positions have difficulty in finding applicants. The inducements to acquire the skills that the economy needs are evidently insufficient. Older workers, similarly, often do not wish to be promoted to more demanding and responsible jobs where they are needed, for lack of adequate incentive.

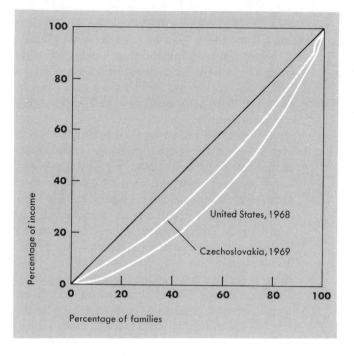

FIG. 9–3 Lorenz curves for non-farm families in Czechoslovakia and the United States. Income is much more equally distributed in Czechoslovakia. Source: For the United States, *Current Population Reports* (December 23, 1969). For Czechoslovakia, *Statistická ročenka Československé Socialistické Republiky 1969* (Prague, 1969), p. 131.

Thus the workforce is performing at a much lower level of skill than the economy can afford.

No one can tell how much the lack of income incentive costs the Czech people, though it seems probable that the incomes, even at the low end of the scale, are lower than they would be if the income distribution were more like the American one. Still less can anyone say firmly that the high approximation to equality is not worth its cost in material goods and services. All one can say confidently is that the Czech experience shows that the inefficiency engendered by a high degree of egalitarianism is more than a theoretical specter; it happens.

PROBLEMS OF MEASUREMENT

The kind of data introduced in the last section contains the best information we have and are likely to have about the distribution of income. Yet they are only an inaccurate approximation to what we should like to know. We cannot interpret these distributions correctly unless we are alert to their shortcomings.

At the very foundation lie the concept and measurement of a family's income. We encountered a similar problem before, when we saw that the concept

233

of a firm's profits contained pitfalls for the unsuspecting. The concept of a family's income is even more vague and arbitrary. Families are not in the habit of keeping accurate financial accounts, and anyone who has filled out an income-tax form or tried to reconstruct his budget knows how rough and inaccurate his records and recollections are. Even in a highly monetized economy there are many and important nonmonetary forms of income that have to be treated arbitrarily.

One of the most important arises from homeownership. As long as a family lives in the house it owns, the rental value of the dwelling is not counted as part of its income in the personal income distribution,[1] but if it rents its home and lives elsewhere, then the excess of the rent it receives over real-estate taxes, interest, and other expenses of owning a house is counted. Such a move is likely to promote the family to a statistically higher income bracket, without improving its circumstances in any real sense. The omission of the rental value of owner-occupied dwellings distorts the personal income distribution. Since homeownership is more prevalent among well-off families than among poor ones, it reduces the apparent inequality of incomes. Since ownership is more prevalent among whites than among nonwhites, it reduces the apparent discrepancy between the average income levels of the two races.

There are many other nonmonetary forms of income, and they all distort the distribution. Low-income families are entitled to purchase food stamps and to live in subsidized housing projects. If equivalent benefits are given to them in cash, their recorded incomes would increase. As things stand, these benefits are not counted, and to this extent the inequality of income is overstated by the records. Everyone benefits from a variety of public services for which no charges are made—schooling, subsidized transportation facilities, parks, and recreational facilities are among the more important. Some of these benefit the rich primarily, and some the poor. No one knows how they affect the distribution of real income on balance. These uncharged-for services are important primarily in making international comparisons, since they vary greatly among nations. For example, if we included in Czech incomes the value of services that are free there but paid for in the United States—principally medical care, higher education, and housing [2]—their income level would be higher and even more egalitarian than is reported.

The personal income distribution shown in the statistics is the before-tax income, and not the after-tax income that is really all that the family has available. Since the income-tax schedule is progressive through most of its range, the use of before-tax income leads to an overstatement of the degree of income inequality.[3] But there are counteracting distortions. Capital gains, which are enjoyed primarily by high-income families, are not included in their incomes.

[1] The rental value of owned homes is counted, however, in the functional income distribution, which is based on different statistical sources.

[2] Rents are often nominal in Czechoslovakia.

[3] This source of distortion is moderate under current tax schedules. See Fig. 9–4.

One of the reasons for the recorded spread of incomes is that the receipts of young families tend to be smaller than those of middle-aged families with established wage earners and some accumulated savings. So even if everyone had the same lifetime cycle of incomes, the record for any year would show some income inequality. Nonwhite families are younger than whites, so this effect leads to some overstatement of the difference between their incomes on a lifetime basis. Another reason for the spread is that some people work harder and longer (for example, moonlighting) than others. The moonlighters are recorded as having higher incomes than those who elect to have more leisure. If the value of leisure were included as a form of nonmonetary income, the degree of inequality would be smaller than is recorded. On the other hand, factory medical care, recreational facilities, expense-account privileges, and nonmonetary fringe benefits of all kinds are omitted from the accounts. These omissions probably tend to make the recorded income distribution appear to be less unequal than it really is.

Finally, since the days of Marcus Aurelius people have been pointing out with more or less sincerity that money isn't everything and that income cannot be equated with welfare or happiness. Since it is welfare, and welfare over the long pull, that concerns us when we talk about the inequality of income, the recorded data for a single year provide only a crude reflection of the really pertinent facts. Most of the detailed difficulties mentioned above are aspects of this broad thesis. In a market economy, however, the comparative welfare of families is probably fairly well approximated by their money incomes or would be if the major adjustments indicated above could be made. At any rate, those are the best data we have, and one must infer from them as best he can how well-off families are, and how equal their incomes are in any real sense.

THE GENERATION OF INCOMES

We have remarked before that a man's income is determined by the quantities of productive factors that he contributes to the economy and by the prices, or wages, that he obtains for them. In this section we shall study the second of these influences, the prices commanded by factors of production. We shall not have much to say about the distribution of wealth.

The great books about economics divide the factors of production into three great classes: land, labor, and capital. Once upon a time these corresponded to three great social classes: the landed gentry, the laboring poor, and the merchants. But over the course of time the landed gentry has atrophied, the boundary between the other two classes has become smudged, and the classes have become much more diversified internally. Nowadays we have to distinguish among blue-collar and white-collar workers, skilled and unskilled, managers and professionals, proprietors and investors, and so on.

With some exceptions, however, the ancient trinity is still a useful framework for analysis. The exceptions are important. For example, the earnings of a fashion model are classified as wages, and the receipts of a scenically located apartment house are rents. But both are payments for the privilege of viewing a scarce and irreproducible natural resource with aesthetic value, and the amounts of both payments are determined by similar economic considerations. In fact, though the national income accountant records the model's earnings as wages, the technical economist regards them as rents.[4]

Furthermore, the ancient classification lumps together interest payments, dividends, businessmen's profits, and speculators' gains under the heading of "profits of stock." Once, when businessmen typically owned and operated their enterprises and corporations were scarcely invented, fine distinctions among these forms of income were irrelevant. But now, the earnings of a gas-station proprietor are more akin to wages than they are to the receipts of a large stockholder. So, again, the traditional classification ignores distinctions that have become important. Nevertheless, we shall use the old classification to organize our discussion, since the bulk of incomes do conform to it.

Marginal Productivity

One principle plays a role in the determination of all incomes: marginal productivity. That is why we dwelt on it so extensively in our discussion of the principles of production. Let us review the major conclusion of that discussion.

The businessman has two interrelated production decisions: how much to produce and how much of each factor to employ in producing it. This second decision establishes his demand for each factor and, when added up for all businessmen, the demand curve for each factor. That is half of the story of the determination of factor prices, the supply curve being the other half.

In deciding on the quantities of factors, the businessman simply hires additional units of each factor as long as it is worth his while. This is as long as one of two things is true: (1) The cost of a unit of the factor is less than the value of the output the unit would produce, which is the price of the product times the marginal productivity of the factor. Thus the businessman is satisfied when

$$p_x = p_o MP_x.$$

(The notation is the same as that used in Chapter 4.) (2) The cost of a unit of the factor is less than the cost of the amount of any alternative factor for which it can be substituted without affecting the volume of output. This leads to the formula for the relation between the prices of any two substitutable factors of production:

$$\frac{p_x}{p_y} = \frac{MP_x}{MP_y}.$$

[4] For an economist, a rent is any payment for the use of a resource whose supply is fixed and whose price is not related to the opportunity cost of the resource as measured by its value in other employments. Land rent is the most important form, but payments for irreproducible art objects, rare talents, and television channels are also rents. More of this below.

These formulas determine the amount of any factor that will be demanded, given its own price, the prices of competing factors, and the prices of products. If we imagine the price of the factor to vary, all other prices remaining constant, we can trace out the demand curve for the factor.

Since the marginal productivity of a factor normally falls as more of it is employed, given the quantities used of other factors, a decrease in the price of a factor will induce an increase in its usage, giving rise to a demand curve of the usual shape. Actually, a decrease in the price of a factor has a second important effect. It will induce a decrease in the production costs of the commodities made with its help, and thereby increase their outputs. So when the price of a factor falls, more of it is used per unit of product (substitution effect) and the output of the products for which it is used increases (expansion effect). These are the main ingredients of the demand curve for a factor, but there are complexities that we shall not pursue.

In principle, these conclusions apply as much to wages as to any other factor price. They do not determine the level of wages, of course, but merely the amount of a particular type of labor that employers will wish to hire at a given wage.

In practice, it is very hard to ascertain the marginal productivity of labor, and rough judgments combined with rules of thumb have to suffice. What is the marginal productivity of a foreman, or a floor-sweeper, or one man on the production line, or, for that matter, a professor? The employer "knows by experience" about how many of each he needs, and from time to time he experiments with the consequences of hiring more or fewer.[5] The higher the wage of any particular kind of labor, the more likely he is to discover that he can cut costs by hiring less of it. This is such an uncertain and sporadic process that in the short run the substitution effect is not very powerful. But, given time, machinery and processes become adapted to economizing on expensive forms of labor and other factors of production.

With the rare exceptions created by union work rules, a businessman will not employ factors of production (knowingly, at least) if their prices exceed the value of the products he can make with them. On the other hand, he cannot pay any factor less than its contribution to the value of his output. This is not because of fair-mindedness on his part. It is because if any factor were priced below the value of its marginal product, either he would hire more of it until the value of the marginal product fell to the factor's price, or some other employer would hire it away from him. So there are strong forces that impel businessmen to behave in accordance with the factor demand curves computed from the marginal-productivity formulas. These formulas apply to

[5] Unions generally do not approve of this kind of experimentation, or of the substitution effect in general. They inhibit them by imposing "work rules" that specify tasks and working conditions. In extreme forms these work rules include "featherbedding," that is, requiring the employer to engage workmen for whom he does not perceive any function, and ludditism, the prohibition or destruction of labor-saving machinery. These practices clearly shift the demand curve, so that the employer engages workers beyond the point where the value of their marginal product is equal to their wage.

all factors of production, though with diminished force when the productivity of the factor cannot be ascertained readily.

About 40 per cent of American families depend entirely on "earned" incomes—wages, salaries, professional income, and self-employment income. Another 50-odd percent receive some property income, government payments, or pensions in addition to earnings, and for the great bulk of them earnings are the major source of income. Less than 10 per cent live entirely on sources other than earnings.

It follows that when we talk about the distribution of wage income, or earned income, we are talking about the heart of the whole question of income distribution. For the great majority of people, income is virtually equivalent to earnings.

The earned income of any family depends primarily on the occupational classification of its principal wage earners. To cite the extremes, in 1968, physicians and surgeons earned, on the average, $23,300; less than 1 per cent of service workers earned that much. (Their average income was $4,000.) So the explanation of the distribution of earned incomes comes down to two things: explanation of the differences in earnings of different occupations, and explanation of the distribution of workers among occupations. Actually, the problem is even more unified. Since we already know the principles that determine the demand for different kinds of workers, we need only discuss the principles that determine the supplies in order to complete the determination of earnings. But the discussion of the supply curves of workers of different kinds is simultaneously a discussion of the distribution of workers among occupations. So that is the main task.

Before tackling the supply curves, a conceptual question has to be faced. Supply curves of what? A supply curve for all labor would not be very helpful or very meaningful. At the other extreme, a supply curve for a very narrowly defined kind of worker would not be very meaningful, either. For example, what would be the meaning of a supply curve for filing clerks? In any city there is a large pool of unspecialized office workers, any of whom can do filing after a little coaching. From the viewpoint of resource allocation, filing is just one form of utilization of a type of resource that we can call unspecialized office workers. In general terms, a meaningful category of workers for economic analysis must include all workers who can do the same kinds of work with the help of minor additional training. The definition of such categories of fungible workers is necessarily somewhat arbitrary. For example, the Census Bureau uses the classification shown in Table 9–3, plus a few subclasses. This listing illustrates the degree of refinement that is usual in analyzing the general labor market. It is a good deal less refined than one would like for theoretical analyses,[6] but it serves.

[6] For example, in the "craftsmen, foremen" category, carpenters cannot do the work of electricians because union rules forbid it, among other reasons. Some quite narrowly defined classes of workers,

Table 9-3   U.S. CENSUS CLASSIFICATION OF WORKERS

	Number Employed March, 1969 (thousands)	Average Earnings 1968
Professional, technical, and kindred workers	10,795	$ 9,150
Farmers and farm managers	1,784	4,739
Managers, officials, and proprietors, excluding farm	7,822	10,513
Clerical and kindred workers	12,464	4,659
Sales workers	4,509	5,779
Craftsmen, foremen and kindred workers	9,789	7,609
Private household workers	1,826	1,113
Service workers, except private household	7,702	3,475
Farm laborers and foremen	1,005	2,318
Laborers, except farm and mine	3,416	4,277
All classes	75,075	$ 6,241

Source: Bureau of the Census, Current Population Reports, Series P-60, No. 66 (December 23, 1969), Table 42.

The question then is: What determines the number of workers available in any category, conveniently defined, at different rates of pay for that kind of work? Tastes have something to do with it; not everyone likes professional and technical work well enough to enter such a career, even at very high rates of pay. The distribution of native ability plays a part; not everyone who would like to be an engineer can learn enough to become one. But there is much evidence to indicate that the range of opportunities that is part of every man's social environment plays a very significant, if not preponderant, part in his choice of career. Indeed, the social environment can be so constraining that there is not much real choice.

The strength of the influence of social opportunity is indicated by Table 9-4, which is based on a large sample survey that compared father's and son's occupations. In this table all occupations are divided into nine categories. The entries in each column show for all workers in that occupation the percentage whose fathers were in each occupation. Before interpreting it, it should be noted that it is an historical table, dated 1962. It shows a picture of an economy in transition, along with the effects of continuing social and economic forces. This can be seen most clearly by comparing the last column and last row. For example, 21 per cent of the workers were in the professional-managerial category, but only 9 per cent of all workers had fathers in that class. At the other extreme, 8 per cent of the work force were farmers or farm laborers, but 31 per cent were farm boys. (Not only were farmers more numerous in the preceding generation; they were also more prolific than other workers.) This accounts for the fact that such large percentages of workers in all occupations were the sons of farmers.

The general picture conveyed by the table is one of considerable, but not

such as carpenters, do have well-defined supply curves because of special conditions such as union restrictions, licensing regulations, or highly specialized training. Others, such as file clerks and custodians, do not.

Table 9–4 OCCUPATIONAL BACKGROUNDS OF WORKERS, BY OCCUPATIONAL CLASS, 1962

(Per cent of workers in each category whose fathers were in category shown in first column)

Father's Occupation	Son's Occupation, 1962									
	Professional, managerial	Salesmen, not retail	Proprietors	Clerical	Retail salesmen	Craftsmen	Operatives and service	Laborers	Farmers and farm labor	Percentage of fathers
Professional, managerial	21	17	7	10	8	5	4	3	1	9
Salesmen, not retail	5	8	3	2	5	1	1	*	*	2
Proprietors	14	14	18	8	17	5	4	2	2	8
Clerical	6	6	3	5	3	3	2	2	1	3
Retail salesmen	3	5	3	2	3	1	1	1	1	2
Craftsmen	19	17	18	22	16	26	17	14	3	19
Operatives and service	16	18	17	22	20	23	27	22	4	20
Laborers	3	4	3	8	6	7	10	14	2	6
Farmers and farm laborers	13	11	28	22	22	29	34	42	86	31
Percentage of work force	21	3	8	7	2	21	24	6	8	100

* Less than ½ per cent.

Source: Adapted from P. M. Blau and O. D. Duncan, The American Occupational Structure (New York: John Wiley & Sons, Inc.), 1967, Table J2.1.

unlimited, father–son occupational mobility. Seventy-nine per cent of professional and managerial workers had fathers in other occupations. On the other hand, the 9 per cent of professional-managerial fathers contributed 21 per cent of the current workers in that class. The occupation that attracted fewest recruits from the outside was farming, partly because it is a declining occupation, and partly because it is so specialized. Eighty-six per cent of farmers came from farm backgrounds.

The first five occupational categories are professional and white-collar occupations, the remainder are blue-collar trades and farming. Notice the sharp break: only a negligible proportion of blue-collar workers and farmers come from white-collar backgrounds, though the reverse is not true. Still, the proportion of white-collar workers whose fathers were laborers is very small.

These broad tendencies can be seen more sharply in the summary, Table 9–5. There it is seen that 24 per cent of families have white-collar backgrounds; they provided 42 per cent of the current generation of white-collar workers whereas the 45 per cent of families that had blue-collar backgrounds supplied only 41 per cent of white-collar workers. On the other hand, 54 per cent of blue-collar workers had blue-collar fathers; only 13 per cent had white-collar fathers. The general picture is one of impeded but not negligible mobility.

Table 9–5 OCCUPATIONAL BACKGROUNDS OF WHITE- AND BLUE-COLLAR WORKERS AND FARMERS, 1962

Father's Occupation	Son's Occupation, 1962			Percentage of fathers
	White-collar	Blue-collar	Farming	
White-collar	42	13	5	24
Blue-collar	41	54	9	45
Farming	18	33	86	31
Percentage of work force	41	51	8	100

Source: Adapted from Blau and Duncan, *The American Occupational Structure.*

This intergenerational, interoccupational viscosity accounts in large measure for the inequality of wage incomes. Sons of fathers in low-income, low-prestige occupations need exceptional ability and determination to overcome the obstacles standing between them and higher-prestige work. As a result, the supply curves of high-prestige workers are farther to the left than they would be if entrance to those occupations were open to all on equal terms. And therefore these supply curves intersect the demand curves for the same types of workers at points corresponding to relatively high levels of earnings. Inequality of opportunity clearly stands behind inequality of earnings. For example, in the Soviet Union, where entrance to the medical professions is much easier than here, doctors stand much lower on the scale of relative incomes than they do in this country.

One obvious implication of this analysis is that he who wishes to increase the earnings of any group of workers must somehow restrict the supply of that kind of worker. Such varied groups as professional associations and craft unions have known this since time immemorial, almost by instinct. The trouble is that it is not practical to restrict supply except for very narrow classes of workers, such as carpenters or physicians. When a large number of unions and professional associations attempt this tactic, they simultaneously increase the supply of labor seeking employment in the less well-organized trades. The result is a twisting of the wage structure: organized workers gain at the expense of the unorganized and, on balance, income inequality is more likely to be increased than reduced.

Industrial unions have followed the more open policy of pressing for increased wages without erecting barriers to employment in their industries. The success of this policy depends on the ability of the employers to pass along the wage increases to consumers in the form of price increases,[7] thus preserving the equality $p_x = p_o MP_x$. When widespread, the price increases virtually cancel the initial gains secured by the wage increases in an inflationary spiral.

The fact seems to be that because earned incomes are such a predominant proportion of the total, the gains secured by any group of workers must be largely at the expense of other groups. The union movement has improved the lot of workers in many respects, but it is still debatable whether it has been successful in increasing the share of income going to workers.

This discussion of the determination of wages, or earned incomes, has necessarily been incomplete. One important omission has been the supply of female workers, who comprise more than a third of the total. Another has been the role of part-time employment, which is very elastic. About a third of male workers and two-thirds of female are part-time workers. But the main considerations have been raised.

Interest and Profits

The second major category of factors of production is capital. People who provide capital for the use of the economy are paid for its use in various forms called dividends, interest, profits, and sometimes rent. The determination of these forms of income is one of the more confusing aspects of economics, and we shall not delve deeply into it.

Capital can be regarded, and has to be regarded, in two ways. The first is *real capital*. Real capital consists of all produced means of production separable from human persons. It is therefore a collection of diverse physical objects, called individually *capital goods*. Every machine, tractor, office building, article in inventory, or any other produced thing that assists in the work of the economy is a capital good. And each is also an ordinary commodity whose price is determined by principles already explained.

The second aspect of capital is *financial capital*. It consists of titles

[7] Remember that because of the slope of the demand curves for products an increase in a single wage will normally induce a smaller increase in price. Widespread wage increases are a different story.

and claims to real capital and to the income earned by real capital. Examples are stocks, bonds, mortgages, deeds, bank accounts, and so on in great profusion. Financial capital, as distinct from real capital, can be viewed conveniently as an amount of monetary value. The dividends, interest, and profits that concern us now are payments for the use of financial capital. But business firms are willing to pay for financial capital chiefly to gain access to real capital goods.[8] So the demand for financial capital arises from the demand for real capital. The relationship between the two is logical, but a little complicated.

The supply curve of a capital good is the marginal-cost curve of the industry that produces it. The demand curve depends on its marginal productivity, the amount that the annual profits of a firm would increase if an additional unit of it were acquired. Here is where the complication arises: the price of a capital good cannot be compared directly with its marginal productivity because a capital good is likely to last a long time. For example, a truck costing $5,000 might be expected to save a firm $1,400 a year. Would the truck be worth acquiring (that is, would the truck be demanded) at that price? The answer is not apparent from the two figures given. It depends on the life of the truck (seven years, let us assume) and on how much $5,000 can earn when invested in other ways.

A little compound-interest figuring will show that a loan of $5,000 repayable in seven annual installments of $1,400 each earns an interest rate, or rate of return, of 20 per cent per year. If the firm can borrow for less than 20 per cent interest, it would be wise to do so and buy the truck. This, of course, is true in general. Whatever the rate of interest may be, firms will be willing to borrow or to use their own funds (it is not essential which) to acquire all capital goods that can earn more than the going rate of interest.

From this, several things follow. The earning prospects of every capital good can be expressed as a rate of return on its price, just as we have done with the truck. Firms will acquire capital goods to the point where the rate of return on one more unit (the marginal rate of return) will be approximately the same for every type of capital good, and for all will be about equal to the rate of interest at which firms can borrow. The market rate of interest therefore determines the total amount of money that firms would like to invest: the lower the rate of interest, the greater the amount of investment that will appear profitable. Thus a decrease in the rate of interest at which firms borrow has three consequences: it increases the demands for the capital goods (shifts their demand curves upward), it increases the prices of capital goods in accordance with their supply curves, and it increases the amount that firms would like to invest in capital goods. The relationship between the rate of interest and the amount that firms want to invest is the *demand curve for capital*. (In this context, "capital" means financial capital.) This demand curve has the ordinary, downward sloping shape.

The *supply curve for capital* shows correspondingly the amount of finan- **243**

---

[8] Other uses, of course, are to pay wages and rents. But forget this complication.

cial capital that would be made available to firms at different market rates of interest. Interest earnings entice funds into investment uses. When interest rates are low, people prefer to keep their wealth in the form of safe and ready cash and to use their incomes for consumption. For these reasons, less money (that is, financial capital) is available for investment at low rates of interest than at high ones. The supply curve for capital slopes upward like the supply curve for an ordinary commodity.

The intersection of these two curves determines the market rate of interest, the total amount of investment or purchases of capital goods, and the rate of return earned by the marginal unit of every kind of capital good.[9]

But we have oversimplified, and badly. Our most serious misstatement was to say that firms will invest in any type of capital good as long as the rate of return on that form of investment is at least as great as the rate of interest at which it can borrow. If investment did not entail any risks or troubles, they might do so, but that is not the case. Our truck example was somewhat realistic: firms do expect returns of 20 per cent or more from the capital goods they invest in. At the same time businessmen are outraged if they have to pay half that much interest for the financial capital they borrow. The firm in our example would not, in fact, buy the truck if it had to pay 20 per cent interest on its loan, but only if it could borrow for substantially less. The difference between the rate of return on the investment and the rate of interest on the loan is the firm's margin of profit on the investment.

This circumstance raises a problem for us. An essential foundation of all our reasoning has been that businessmen, in their efforts to maximize profits, will seize every profitable opportunity. In particular, this entailed that they will undertake every investment that promises to yield revenues in excess of its costs, by however little. Now we find that this is not so—that businessmen require the incentive of an appreciable profit before investing. How can this conflict be resolved, and how much damage does it do to the structure of our whole analysis?

Up to this point we have been ignoring an important ingredient of economic life: uncertainty. When a businessman makes an investment, he really does not know what the return will be, if any. Business may fall off, and the new truck may just stand idle. In order to induce people to make investments in these conditions, there have come to be two forms of financial capital, riskfree capital and venture capital. Riskfree capital, for example, a well-secured bond. is guaranteed its return by the full faith and credit of the borrower. Venture capital, for example, a corporate stock, receives no guarantee, but in compensation for bearing the brunt of ill-fortune and bad judgment, it is entitled to share in the gains from good luck and good judgment. For anyone to advance venture capital he must judge that on balance he is likely to receive a greater

[9] For a more complete discussion of the determination and consequences of the rate of interest, see Charles L. Schultze, *National Income Analysis*, 3rd ed., in this series.

return than he could receive by putting up the same amount as riskfree capital. Furthermore, a business cannot be financed entirely by riskfree capital. There must be a certain proportion of venture capital, or equity, to make the guarantee effective.

Now this means that any investment made by a firm must promise to yield enough to cover two kinds of capital costs. It must pay for the ordinary interest and amortization on its cost; this component we have already discussed. And it must also pay for the risk premium required to attract the necessary venture capital or equity. This explains why businessmen do not undertake investments unless they expect that there will be something left over after ordinary interest charges have been met.

Previously, when we ignored the element of risk, it appeared to be rational for businessmen to undertake investments as if the only capital costs to them were the interest costs on borrowed funds and the forgone interest on their own funds that they committed. But risk introduces a new element of cost, since every investment increases the amount of capital at hazard. This new element is measured by the opportunity cost of venture capital. Just as the opportunity cost of riskfree capital is the market rate of interest—what those funds would earn if loaned to some other enterprise—so the opportunity cost of venture capital is what the funds would earn if invested as venture capital in some other firm. Because most people are reluctant to assume risks, the cost of venture capital is higher than the cost of riskfree capital.

We have now come across a new "factor of production," willingness to expose capital to risk. Like other factors, it is scarce and must be allocated. Therefore this new factor and the profits that correspond to it fit into our framework. Both riskfree and venture capital are allocated by the price system along with other factors of production in order to achieve an efficient structure of productive effort in the economy. The dynamic and innovative aspects of the economy rely heavily on the existence and allocation of venture capital.

The demand for venture capital obeys the principles of marginal productivity, like the demand for every other factor of production. There is a unique feature, however. In the nature of the case there is no contractual price for venture capital, but only some basis on which a prospective investor can form a judgment about how much he is likely to receive. The clearest indicator of the price of venture capital at any time is the earnings–price ratio of common stocks.[10] A firm's demand for venture capital is governed, as we said, by marginal-productivity considerations: a firm will demand venture capital to the extent that doing so promises to increase its profits enough to cover the costs, including the shares of the new stockholders, and leave something for the old shareholders. When the earnings–price ratio falls, so that the cost of venture

---

[10] For a number of technical reasons the ratio of dividends to common stock prices has been much lower than market interest rates in recent years. The ratio of corporate profits to share values (the earnings–price ratio) has been higher except during episodes of abnormally high interest rates.

capital declines, firms will demand more of it unless their profitable opportunities have also diminished.

There is also a supply curve for venture capital, and the interaction of the supply and demand curves determines the rate of return to it. But this determination is rough and shifting (as shown by stock-market fluctuations) because vague conjectures play such an important role on both the supply and demand sides.

Payment for the commitment of venture capital accounts for the existence of "normal profits," the profits in excess of ordinary interest on capital that are earned in an industry in long-run equilibrium. In addition, we have previously encountered two other sources of profits. There are the transitory profits that are earned in a growing industry not in long-run equilibrium, that serve to attract new capital to the industry and that are eventually competed away. And there are the monopolistic profits received by monopolies and oligopolies.

Rent

Our final distinguishable income share is rent. The genesis of rent was explained in our analysis of long-run supply curves, in Chapter 3,[11] and only a sketch is needed here.

Rent is a payment for the use of any nonproducible resource. Land rents are typical, and are the most important kind. Other examples are the high incomes earned by especially talented individuals, the value of television channels, and the values of artificially scarce resources, such as taxicab licenses in New York. By definition, the supply of a rentable resource cannot be changed. The supply curve is a vertical line. The price, or rent, is its value to the user in whose hands it is most productive, to whom it has the highest marginal productivity.

Rent is the purest of unearned incomes. One receives it simply by owning something unique, and one need do nothing about it except to drive a hard bargain. Nevertheless, it has an economic function: it allocates unique resources to be the uses in which their products are most beneficial according to the test of the market.[12] What has no particular economic function is the identification of rent for the resource—which is a genuine social opportunity cost—with income for the resource owner. Rental income could be entirely taxed away without any ill effects on the operation of the economy. Instead, we sometimes seem to go out of our way to donate rents to various individuals. Examples are giving away television licenses, charging nominal prices for taxicab medallions, and underpricing irrigation water in arid parts of the country. These giveaways are actually deleterious. They create artificial vested interests and generate struggles for gaining access to the rentable resources.

---

[11] See pp. 68–72.

[12] Rents do not always perform this function very well. Urban land rents are very high, but no one would claim that urban land typically is well utilized. The difficulty here is that urban land use entails significant externalities (positive and negative), and we have seen repeatedly that externalities are just what automatic market adjustments cannot contend with.

This completes our survey of the determination of wages, interest rates, profit rates, and rentals—the prices of the basic factors of production. These prices have a double significance for the economy. On the one hand they are the basic guides for the allocation of economic resources: they tell the businessman what a unit of each factor is worth to the economy because they correspond to the marginal productivities of the factors if used for other purposes or other opportunities. On the other hand they are the foundation of the distribution of personal incomes, since they determine how much each person or household will receive for the resources he contributes to the economy.

These two aspects of factor prices are closely related, but they are not identical and the connection is not rigid. There is in principle no reason for the reward received by the owner of a factor of production to be the same as the price charged to the business that employs that factor and, in fact, the two frequently differ. For example, when a business firm rents land, some of its rental payment is rental income for the landowner, part is payment for insurance and other expenses of land owning, and part is real-estate taxes, which drive a wedge between rental payment and rental income. The most obvious instance is income taxes: The income received by a salaried worker in a fairly high tax bracket is in the neighborhood of two-thirds of the salary that his employer pays for his services. Discrepancies in the other direction are less usual, but still occur. Through various farm programs the government assures owners of farmland returns that exceed the marginal products of their property. There are proposals that the earnings of unduly low-paid workers be increased by governmental wage supplements or by subsidies for the employment of disadvantaged workers.

This slippage between the market value of a productive factor and the income of its owner provides scope for rectifying the distribution of income generated by heartless and heedless market forces. No one is sure how great this scope is—how far income received can be forced away from income earned without giving seriously false signals to the owners of factors of production. We saw reason to suspect, in the case of Czechoslovakia, that underpricing trained and responsible forms of work may dry up their supply. In this country relatively little has been done to redress the income distribution generated by market forces. Figure 9–4 indicates the extent of conscious effort in this direction. It compares the Lorenz curves of family income before and after federal income taxes in 1960. The differences are visible but mild. The upper 1 per cent of families received 7.6 per cent of before-tax family income; 6.3 per cent of after-tax income. The lower 20 per cent received 4.6 per cent before taxes; 4.9 per cent after taxes. How much potential there is for revising the distribution by government taxes and transfer payments is a question that is very hard to answer without experimentation and even harder to experiment about. But the potentiality is there.

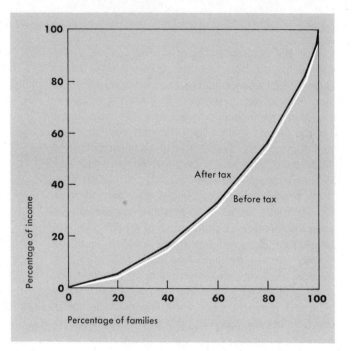

FIG. 9–4 Distribution of family personal income before and after federal income tax, 1960. Lorenz curve shows that after-tax income is somewhat more egalitarian. Source: Richard Goode, *The Individual Income Tax* (Washington, D.C.: The Brookings Institution, 1964), p. 263.

INEQUALITY AND POVERTY

Causes

It is banal to remark that different families have different incomes because they control different quantities of differently priced factors of production. Figure 9–5 may help us get a little behind that superficial observation. It contrasts three Lorenz curves. The middle one shows the inequality of family incomes in 1962. This is the curve we wish to explain. The other two curves reveal some of the underlying forces.

The most extreme curve shows the distribution of tangible wealth among families in 1962. It shows far more inequality than any income distribution. The lower 80 per cent of the families own less than a quarter of the wealth. At the other extreme, less than one-half of 1 per cent of families were worth $500,000 or more, but those families also owned about a quarter of the total wealth owned by families. Here we are interested in wealth chiefly as a source of income, property income, but its social importance goes far beyond that. Wealth confers position and influence, and even more important, security and independence and the potential for acquiring more wealth.

The distribution of property income—interest, rents, and profits—is even more unequal than the distribution of wealth because the wealthier families are too astute, experienced, and well-informed to keep their money in savings

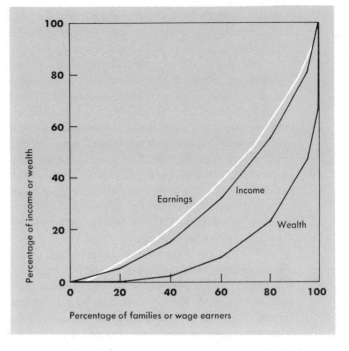

FIG. 9–5 Lorenz curves of distributions of earnings, money income, and wealth. Distribution of earnings is fairly egalitarian; distribution of wealth is extremely unequal. Sources: Earnings of fully employed male wage earners, 1968, from Bureau of the Census, *Current Population Reports,* Series P-60, No. 66, Table 43. Family personal incomes, 1962, from E. C. Budd, ed., *Inequality and Poverty* (New York: W. W. Norton & Company, Inc., 1967), p. xvi. Net worths of families, 1962, from *Federal Reserve Bulletin,* March, 1964, p. 291.

banks, which is what less-affluent families do with the bulk of their liquid assets. So the inequality in the distribution of wealth contributes to income inequality. But it is not the dominating cause—notice the wide gap between the distributions of income and wealth. This is because property income amounts to less than a quarter of total personal income. Transfer payments, which are about a third as great as property income, are skewed heavily in favor of low-income families and help offset this source of income inequality. But earnings are the major source of personal incomes, accounting for about 70 per cent of the total.

We have already devoted a good deal of attention to the sources of inequality of wage rates and salaries. Those are the major explanations of the curvature of the most egalitarian distribution in Fig. 9–5. That curve shows the distribution of earned incomes in 1968 of full-time male wage and salary earners who did not suffer unemployment.[13] In addition to the forces previously discussed, which emphasized the occupational distribution of workers, outright discrimination contributes to inequality. In almost every occupation, nonwhite and minority-group workers earn less than comparably qualified whites.

As far as this curve goes, inequality is only moderate. The lower half of the full-time male workers earned nearly a third of the earnings of this group.

[13] Unfortunately, data on all three of these distributions are not available for any single year. This is not serious; the curves do not change much over time.

Any judgments about degrees of inequity are arguable. Yet when it is recalled that apprentice hod carriers and veteran surgeons are all included here, this distribution appears to be at least tolerable.

But it is a long step from wage and salary rates to earned incomes received by families. Some of the more important sources of inequality of earnings not reflected in this curve are: the numbers of wage and salary earners in the family, whether they are full-time or part-time workers, whether they have suffered unemployment and how much, whether they are male or female (women suffer discrimination like members of minority groups). Put these all together and you can construct a curve for the distribution of earned incomes of all workers. I have spared you this additional Lorenz curve, but it is rather less egalitarian than the family-income curve, which is shown. The extra inequality is erased mostly by transfer payments (unemployment compensation, Social Security benefits) and partly by the tendency of low-income families to have supplementary wage earners.

The net resultant of this examination seems to be as follows. Wealth is extremely unequally distributed. This is socially undesirable on its own grounds but makes only a secondary contribution to the inequality of incomes, which can be explained virtually entirely by the unequal distribution of earned incomes. The earned incomes of full-time, fully employed males are tolerably equally distributed, and would be even more so if not for discrimination against nonwhites and other minority-group workers. The major source of inequality of family incomes is inequality of opportunity to work at all or to work regularly. Elderly families and families headed by women suffer especially acutely. But all families whose breadwinners are exposed to high rates of unemployment or are excluded from the labor force are likely to have unacceptably low incomes and to contribute to the observed degree of inequality. Here, perhaps unexpectedly, is where the major trouble lies.

We can confirm this diagnosis by turning from inequality to the twin problem of poverty. Poverty and inequality are not synonymous problems. A country could have great inequality and no poverty, and perhaps this would be the best of all possible worlds. (A great deal of the art, culture, variety, and amenity of life is the by-product of having a few very rich families.) A country could have no inequality and universal poverty, a rather sad prospect. But in practice the two conditions occur together, and in a certain sense poverty is the result of inequality. At any rate, poverty is what happens to people at the low end of the income distribution, so from their point of view their poverty and their unduly low share of total income are the same thing and arise from the same causes.

It is not so easy to define poverty. The official American definition is that a family is poor if its income is less than about $3,500 in terms of 1968 prices.[14] This particular figure was arrived at by estimating the cost of a

[14] That is the poverty line for a family of four living in a city or town. Add $500 for every family member above four. Further adjustments are needed for rural families and to allow for other family characteristics.

minimum adequate family budget. This rather arbitrary working definition is an application of a more general concept of poverty: that a family is poor if it cannot afford the levels of food consumption, housing, clothing, medical care, and education that are regarded as decent in its society. Poverty is therefore not an absolute concept. A family at the poverty line by American standards would not be poor by Indian standards. But it is not entirely relative. A larger proportion of Indians are poor, by their own standards, than Americans by ours. In the United States, the proportion of poor persons has been decreasing steadily, from 22 per cent in 1959 to 12–13 per cent in recent years. Quite conceivably absolute poverty could be eliminated entirely.

The causes of most poverty in the United States are indicated by Table 9–6, which is a sketchy selection from the mass of available data about the poor. Fifteen percent of American households [15] were poor in 1968. In more than two-thirds of them the head did not hold a full-time job at any time during the year. Here then is the most prevalent source of poverty, not low rates of wages but no wages at all. The other data help illuminate this one. In 39 per cent of poor households the head was beyond normal working age, in 53 per cent the head was female.[16] Eliminating duplication in these figures, 69 per cent of poor households lacked a male head of normal working age. To lack a male head of working age was not quite fatal: only 31 per cent of such households were poor, but this was more than four times the incidence of poverty among households with working-age fathers.

This seems to be the heart of the problem. The income allocation process that we have surveyed has its capricious and unfair aspects, but it does not generate nearly as much poverty as the social arrangements that exclude whole blocks of the population from participating in the economy. A well-planned war on poverty would have to concentrate its main attack on the problems of these people. To be sure, the other 31 per cent of poor households cannot be ignored, but the main problem is those who lack access to full-time gainful employment for reason of age or sex.

The lower half of the table shows comparable data for nonwhite households. Poverty is more than twice as prevalent among them, and they account for nearly a quarter of all poor households. If the head of the household had full-time work, a nonwhite household was no more likely to be poor than a white household, but all other circumstances were much more adverse for them. About three-sevenths of nonwhite households lacked a male head under sixty-five.

Objectives and Correctives

The social objectives with respect to poverty is clear enough: it should be eliminated. The only conceivable reservation is that the means taken should

[15] A household is a family or a single individual living apart from relatives.

[16] To some extent our current programs generate families without male heads. Sometimes a father with inadequate earnings will "leave" his family so that they may qualify for the Aid to Families of Dependent Children program, or similar programs. This is a particularly vicious quirk in our legislation.

Table 9–6 INCIDENCE OF POVERTY BY SELECTED HOUSEHOLD
CHARACTERISTICS, 1968

Type of Household	Percentage Who Are Poor	Percentage of Poor Households
All households	15	100
Employment of head		
Some full-time work	7	32
No full-time work	40	68
Age of head		
Sixty-five and over	31	39
Less than sixty-five	11	61
Sex of head		
Male	9	47
Female	36	53
Households with nonwhite head	33	24
Employment of head		
Some full-time work	7	10
No full-time work	64	14
Age of head		
Sixty-five and over	53	6
Less than sixty-five	29	18
Sex of head		
Male	22	11
Female	54	13

not generate still more poverty. But of this, considering the nature of the problem, there is little danger. The most direct method for combatting poverty among the elderly would be to supplement the Social Security system (Old-Age, Survivors, and Disability Insurance) by payments that would bring eligible households up to the poverty line, at least. It is not quite so easy to maintain the incomes of families headed by females because making the absence of a male head a condition for eligibility is likely to have perverse social consequences.

The Gordian knot can be cut at one stroke by any of various devices that guarantee adequate minimum incomes to all families. The negative income tax is administratively probably the simplest of these devices. All such plans, however, run afoul of the objection that they may encourage reliance on the public fisc instead of determined efforts at self-support. It cannot be denied that there are lazy people in the world, and that you do not have to be very lazy to prefer relying on an income guarantee to some unpleasant, low-paid jobs. Nevertheless, this fear may be chimerical. The few experiments that have been conducted have not shown any noticeable effect of income guarantees on employment behavior. None of these experiments have been decisive, but there is no good reason to assume the worst, and the problem is so acute that it seems worthwhile to run some risks to solve it.

Proper social objectives regarding income inequality are by no means so clear. We saw in earlier chapters that there is no economic question that is so divisive, so embittering, or so unresolvable as the question of the division of income. It must be so, because the issue at stake is no less than what every man deserves from his society.

For many years economists thought that they had an answer to the question of the proper distribution of income. We shall inspect this economic solution to the problem and see why it cannot be accepted. It rests on the premise that the purpose of economic activity is to maximize the total amount of satisfaction in the society, and that income should be distributed with this objective in mind. Furthermore, it presumes that the amount of happiness or satisfaction enjoyed by any individual (technically called his "utility") depends primarily upon his income and that income should be distributed with the fundamental objective in mind.

With that background consider any two individuals: Mr. A with an income of $2,500, well below the poverty line, and Mr. B with an income of $25,000, well above it. What would be the effect on the total of happiness if Mr. B were to lose $50 and Mr. A were to find it, or if Mr. B were to be taxed $50 so that it could be given to Mr. A? Clearly, the sum of happiness would be enhanced. After a momentary chagrin Mr. B would hardly notice his loss, whereas Mr. A would be able to buy something of great importance to him.

From this it is easy to see that so long as incomes are not equal, any transfer from richer to poorer will increase the total amount of happiness. Complete equality is the distribution that makes the total amount of happiness as great as possible. That is the economist's answer. This is precisely the argument that progressive income taxation accepts but does not follow to the logical conclusion. More sophisticated and subtle versions exist, but they all depend on the same premises and principles.

The catalog of objections to this argument is long and cogent. The argument rests on the notion of a "sum total of happiness" which is to be maximized, but this is a nonsense concept. It presumes that we can say meaningfully that an additional $50 will make more difference to Mr. A's happiness than to Mr. B's, a presumption that cannot be supported.[17] But the defect that seems most fundamental to me is that it misconstrues the issue. The egalitarian theorem is probably valid enough for all practical purposes as a guide for distributing a once-over gift or bonus. Any gift would be appreciated more by the poorer members of the population. But the real issue in the distribution of income is the adoption of a continuing social rule that determines how each member participates in whatever income the society collectively may produce. It is easy to see that the equal-distribution rule would not maximize total happiness (assuming that there is such a thing). You only have to modify it to permit members of society to transfer portions of their income voluntarily. Then the more avari-

[17] In our initial example, the poor Mr. A might be a drifter and the well-off Mr. B might be hard-pressed by medical and other problems.

cious members will perform services or sell things that the more relaxed members will buy. Each such transaction will increase the happiness of both parties, and incomes will no longer be equal. Thus total happiness would be increased by not insisting that all incomes be equal.

Strict equality of incomes, then, does not make the sum total of happiness as great as possible. This objective could be attained, however, if there were an all-wise economist who knew what combination of income and economic effort would make each man as happy as it is in his nature to be while still providing enough economic effort in toto to produce the required total of incomes. No economist or anyone else is that wise, but it is instructive to notice one thing that such an economist would have to do. He would have to arrange for each individual to be paid for his efforts in accordance with our old friend, his marginal productivity. To see this, suppose that Mr. A is paid initially at a rate equal to half his marginal productivity. Then Mr. A will desist from further exertion when he has reached a level where his reward for further work (half his marginal product) is just as important to him as the inconvenience and effort of working more. Now suppose that his rate of reward is increased to 70 per cent of his marginal product. Then he will work a bit more or harder, his income will be increased by 70 per cent of the result of this additional work, and he will be at least as well off as before. In addition, 30 per cent of his additional output will be available for increasing somebody else's income. On the whole, happiness will be increased, and such increases are possible so long as anybody is not rewarded in accordance with his marginal productivity.

This argument presumes that each individual can choose how much he wishes to work in response to any given reward or other incentive. We have already seen that such freedom is essential to maximizing happiness. It also exists to some extent in the real world, though the scope for choice is hard to measure. Workers exercise this freedom in practice through such devices as absenteeism, moonlighting, voluntary overtime, acquiring higher skills and accepting more demanding jobs, "rate-busting," and others.[18] Payment according to marginal productivity motivates workers to just that degree of exertion at which the social gain just justifies their additional exertion.

But this perception leads straight into a serious difficulty. Income taxes, and particularly progressive income taxes, are an essential device for financing the provision of public goods and for rectifying the distribution of income in accordance with notions of social justice. But they inherently violate the precept we have just discovered, by making the worker's after-tax reward for his efforts smaller than his marginal product. National product is necessarily reduced by such taxes. But national happiness (still staying with that superficial abstraction) is not. The reason is inequality of opportunity, which also prevents many workers from being paid in accordance with their marginal productivities. In

[18] "Rate-busting" occurs in industries where workers are paid by piece rates or other incentive systems. A rate-buster is a worker who turns out more product per hour than average, thus increasing his income but raising the possibility of a downward revision of the pay scale.

this circumstance the second wrong helps cancel the first by transferring income to deprived members of society who cannot increase their incomes by their own efforts. It would be more efficient to transfer income by imposing lump-sum levies on the members of society who are not disadvantaged, but there seems to be no practical way to do this.

These considerations argue for payment at least roughly in accordance with marginal productivity, but they do not throw much light on the basic question of the ideal distributions of income and economic effort. Economists have thoughts about these matters, like everyone else, but they have no resolution to offer and we need not study their musings here.

SUMMARY

The personal income distribution shows the proportions of individuals or households with incomes in given ranges, but it provides no insight into the underlying causes or forces. Some insight is provided by the functional distribution of income, which shows the proportion of a society's income that is earned by various broad categories of factors of production. Wages typically account for about two-thirds of all incomes. Other major categories are proprietors' incomes, dividends, interest, and rents. Transfer payments—such as Social Security benefits and welfare payments—are an increasingly important category.

The degree of inequality in the personal income distribution is best shown by the Lorenz curve, a graph that displays the proportion of total income that is received by the lowest x percent of income receivers.

The distribution of income in a free market economy is a by-product of its productive operations; each member receives as income the value of the services of the productive factors he happens to own. The values of these services are determined by the usual principles of supply and demand. The demand curve for any factor results from the fact that the price at which a given quantity will be demanded is the value of its marginal product when that quantity is employed, that value being the same in all industries using the factor. The supply curves for factors of production arise from other considerations. The amount of labor of any type offered in response to any wage is influenced by sociological and psychological factors, particularly by impediments to occupational mobility. The supplies of land and other irreproducible resources are fixed, by definition. The supply of financial capital is determined by the willingness of income receivers to retrench their consumption and to part with ready cash under the inducement of different rates of interest and different prospects for making profits.

Poverty, for practical purposes, is defined as depending on an income that is inadequate to support a healthful and decent standard of living, as judged by the standards of the society. The poverty line for a family of four is about

$3,900. There is nothing very obscure about the major cause of poverty in the United States. About seven poor families out of ten lack an employable adult male wage earner, a situation that is far more prevalent among nonwhite than among white households.

As a social problem, inequality is distinguishable from poverty, though the two are obviously connected. Granted that our current distribution of income is not "ideal," there does not seem to be any basis for agreement about what the ideal degree of inequality would be. The most common proposal is perfect equality but that can easily be seen to be fallacious as well as impracticable.

Postscript

If you have ever written anything, you will know that books have a way of growing by themselves and seldom end up exactly as they were intended. This book was intended to be a clear and dispassionate exposition of the way our economy works. But as it proceeded, particularly in the later chapters, evaluative comments became more and more insistent. They were prompted by fear—fear that through lack of understanding of our delicate economic machine we should lose much that is valuable by incompetent attempts to correct much that is wrong.

The main moral of this book must be that we have inherited a very delicate and subtle economic machine that has evolved slowly and painfully and without planning, and is still evolving. We can foster this evolution in desirable directions, or we can throw some sand into the works. The better we understand this machine, the less likely we are to damage it.

It is a special-purpose machine. It produces goods and services, and it does that very well. It does not produce happiness or social justice, nor is it intended to. For that we need other machines such as cultures, religions, educational systems, governments. What we can ask of the economy is that it produce the "material substratum" without impairing other social functions.

This book has tried to show how our economic system produces that material substratum and how difficult that task is. The heart of the problem is its very enormousness and complexity. No mind, still less computing machine or bureaucracy, can comprehend all the ins and outs of the economy. The billions of decisions are made by millions of people, and have to be. These decisions have to be well informed and well motivated, and the sheer problem of conveying that much information to that many people is stupendous. The prices that emerge from predominantly competitive markets serve this coordinating function, not perfectly but with remarkable subtlety, terseness, and economy. It appeared from our analyses that prices and responses to prices have to be the foundation of economic co-ordination. The results of fully automatic responses to fully automatic prices are not completely satisfactory and have to be modified in numerous detailed respects. But they remain the basis of economic decision making.

However, merely producing the material substratum of social life is not enough. If the economy cannot produce happiness and social justice, surely it must not be allowed to prevent them. The impact of economic activity on higher ends is a very difficult subject, and if anyone speaks about it with assurance he is in danger of fooling both you and himself. A few things can be said confidently. Marx was surely right when he emphasized the importance of economic relationships for the "ideological superstructure." It is important, but no one knows, other than dimly, how it works.

One thing is clear: the market-oriented economy has grown hand in hand with democratic institutions, meaning habits of thought that emphasize the worth and independence of every individual. It is not clear why this has been so, but there may be a causal relationship. I shall not take the space to speculate about that. At least the market-oriented economy has not stifled democratic attitudes.

One other thing is clear: the market-oriented economy diffuses economic power and separates it from political and other forms of power.[1] The diffusion is not egalitarian; we noted how concentrated the control over wealth is. The separation is not complete. Wealth in the hands of individuals or corporations obviously confers undue political and social influence. But the diffusion is greater and the separation is greater than any other known economic system achieves. To this extent it defends the individual against the power structure.

If democratic institutions are precious, so is the economic system that seems to have fostered them. This is not ground for complacency in the face of manifest injustice. It is reason for caution, though. And ground for looking for correctives *within* the framework of the system that has worked that well.

---

[1] Galbraith denies this, though. See J. K. Galbraith, *The New Industrial State* (Boston: Houghton Mifflin Company, 1967).

Selected Readings

The classic work on the price system is Alfred Marshall, *Principles of Economics,* 8th ed. (London: Macmillan, 1920). It is long and often dull but full of insight and always understandable. The most famous brief exposition, though somewhat old-fashioned by now, is Sir Hubert Henderson, *Supply and Demand* (Cambridge: Cambridge University Press, 1921 and later).* *The Theory of Price,* by George J. Stigler (New York: Macmillan, 1952), is a succinct, intermediate level treatment of the material covered in this monograph. So is Joe S. Bain, *Price Theory* (New York: Holt, 1952). Edwin Mansfield, *Microeconomics, Theory and Applications* (New York: Norton, 1970) is a thoroughly up-to-date intermediate text that includes more complete and rigorous treatments of most of the topics in this book. It is clear and authoritative. Richard Leftwich, *The Price System and Resource Allocation* (New York: Holt, 1960) is somewhat easier and very popular. It covers the same material as the first six chapters of this text.

Chapters 3 and 4, on the theory of production and the behavior of firms, are influenced by Joel Dean, *Managerial Economics* (Englewood Cliffs, N.J.: Prentice-Hall, 1951). Richard M. Cyert and James J. March, *A Behavioral Theory of the Firm* (Englewood Cliffs, N.J.: Prentice-Hall, 1963) explores the anatomy of decision making in the firm and contains some instructive case studies. James R. Nelson, ed., *Marginal Cost Pricing in Practice* (Englewood Cliffs, N.J.: Prentice-Hall, 1964) presents some very sophisticated applications of the principles of these chapters. William J. Baumol, *Economic Theory and Operations Analysis,* 2nd ed. (Englewood Cliffs, N.J.: Prentice-Hall, 1965) contains an exposition of maximization within the firm with emphasis on modern techniques such as linear programming.

For Chapter 5, Ruby Turner Norris, *The Theory of Consumer's Demand* (New Haven: Yale University Press, 1941) is a brief and detailed exposition of the theory of consumption. A modern and rigorous treatment is presented in Peter Newman, *The Theory of Exchange* (Englewood Cliffs, N.J.: Prentice-Hall, 1965). The literary classic on this subject—and very enjoyable reading—is Thorstein Veblen, *The Theory of the Leisure Class* (New York: Macmillan, 1899, and many other editions).*

* Indicates material available in paperback.

The most accessible additional reading about market behavior, Chapter 6, is Richard Caves, *American Industry: Structure, Conduct, Performance*, 3rd ed., in this Series. Two classics in the field are E. A. G. Robinson, *The Structure of Competitive Industry* (Cambridge: Cambridge University Press, 1931)*, from an applied point of view, and E. H. Chamberlin, *The Theory of Monopolistic Competition* (Cambridge, Mass.: Harvard University Press, 1933), from a theoretical viewpoint. *The Structure of American Industry*, edited by Walter Adams (New York: Macmillan, 1961)* presents a number of interesting case studies. Joe S. Bain, *Industrial Organization* (New York: Wiley, 1959) is a particularly well-informed and thorough text. The best empirical analysis of American industrial structure is probably Bain's *Barriers to New Competition* (Cambridge, Mass.: Harvard University Press, 1956).

There are many important works on the purposes and achievements of the competitive price system. Adam Smith's *Wealth of Nations* (1776 and many later printings) is the greatest statement, but by no means the first. It is still very impressive reading. Most of the concepts discussed in Chapters 7 and 8 are covered in Baumol's *Economic Theory and Operations Analysis*, cited above. Some of the interesting conceptual issues are analyzed in Lionel Robbins, *An Essay on the Nature and Significance of Economic Science*, 2nd ed. (London: Macmillan, 1935), and the entire theory is expounded beautifully in Tjalling C. Koopmans, *Three Essays on the State of Economic Science* (New York: McGraw-Hill, 1957). Koopman's presentation is mathematical in spirit, but accessible. E. H. Phelps Brown, *The Framework of the Pricing System* (London: Chapman and Hall, 1936) presents the whole theory of price with emphasis on the general equilibrium system.

The towering classic on welfare economics is A. C. Pigou, *The Economics of Welfare* (London: Macmillan, 1920). Reading it is a formidable task, but there is no real substitute. The best text is probably Tibor Scitovsky, *Welfare and Competition* (Chicago: Irwin, 1951). Abba P. Lerner, *The Economics of Control* (New York: Macmillan, 1946) is a more modern and terser treatment of the same theory. Charles J. Hitch and Roland N. McKean, *The Economics of Defense in the Nuclear Age* (Cambridge, Mass.: Harvard University Press, 1960) is a fascinating application of the principles of economic allocation. Friedrich A. von Hayek (ed.), *Collectivist Economic Planning* (London: Routledge, 1935) contains thoughtful, though hostile, assessments of the possibilities of applying those principles in a socialist state.

The questions of inequality and poverty are, of course, the subjects of an enormous literature of widely varying quality. Probably the best place to begin is the readings in Edward C. Budd, ed., *Inequality and Poverty* (New York: Norton,1967). * James E. Meade, *Efficiency, Equality and the Ownership of Property* (London: George Allen & Unwin, 1964) is a brief and stimulating essay on some of the causes of inequality and on its relationship to economic efficiency. But it would be impossible to even try to list the highlights of the vast outpouring, historical and current, on these topics.

263